MILITARY INTELLIGENCE, 1870–1991

Recent Titles in
Research Guides in Military Studies

The Peacetime Army, 1900-1941: A Research Guide
Marvin Fletcher

Special Operations and Elite Units, 1939-1988: A Research Guide
Roger Beaumont

The Late 19th Century U.S. Army, 1865-1898: A Research Guide
Joseph G. Dawson III

U.S. Military Logistics, 1607-1991: A Research Guide
Charles R. Shrader

Celluloid Wars: A Guide to Film and the American Experience of War
Frank J. Wetta and Stephen J. Curley

MILITARY INTELLIGENCE, 1870-1991

A Research Guide

Jonathan M. House

Research Guides in Military Studies, Number 6
Roger J. Spiller, Series Adviser

GREENWOOD PRESS
Westport, Connecticut • London

Library of Congress Cataloging-in-Publication Data

House, Jonathan M. (Jonathan Mallory)
    Military intelligence, 1870-1991 : a research guide / Jonathan M.
House.
      p. cm.—(Research guides in military studies, ISSN
0899-0166 ; no. 6)
    Includes bibliographical references and indexes.
    ISBN 0-313-27403-7 (alk. paper)
    1. Military intelligence. I. Title. II. Series.
UB250.H68   1993
355.3'432—dc20   93-226

British Library Cataloguing in Publication Data is available.

Library of Congress Catalog Card Number: 93-226
ISBN: 0-313-27403-7
ISSN: 0899-0166

First published in 1993

Greenwood Press, 88 Post Road West, Westport, CT 06881
An imprint of Greenwood Publishing Group, Inc.

Printed in the United States of America

The paper used in this book complies with the
Permanent Paper Standard issued by the National
Information Standards Organization (Z39.48-1984).

10 9 8 7 6 5 4 3 2 1

For two intelligence officers, my parents:

Laura M. Griffin [House], Lt, j.g., U.S.N.R., OP-20G,
Department of the Navy, 1943-45

and

Albert V. House, Jr., Major, A.C., A-2, Headquarters,
U.S. Army Air Forces, 1943-44

Contents

Series Foreword

In 1974 a former officer in British military intelligence, Frederick Winterbotham, published a book that he called *The Ultra Secret*. The book was part memoir, part historical melodrama. It told of a highly-classified, hitherto unknown Allied intelligence program that had managed to spy upon the most intimate military secrets of the Axis powers from 1942 to 1945. Winterbotham claimed that this was *the* Allied secret of the Second World War, and that all involved at the time realized it, hence its designation as "Ultra" secret.

At the heart of the Ultra secret was the "Enigma" encoding machine, an electro-mechanical typewriter with revolving drums that rotated texts in combinations then believed by its German masters to be virtually impenetrable. Given the state of the art of encryption and codebreaking at the time, their expectations were not unrealistic. In an affair worthy of any espionage potboiler, Polish intelligence agents retrieved an Enigma machine from a luggage storeroom in a Warsaw train station one night in 1939 on the eve of the German invasion. They dismantled it, examined and recorded its design, reassembled it, and returned it to the storeroom before its disappearance could be discovered. From there, the secret of the Enigma was handed, often a step ahead of advancing German armies, first to the French, and then finally to British intelligence. Once in England, codebreakers at an ugly country house called Bletchley Park managed to turn the Enigma's secrets on its original owners, producing military intelligence of the most valuable sort. Those who conducted this operation were sworn to absolute secrecy, on pain of imprisonment and hints of worse fates, then and forevermore. The few high-ranking Allied commanders privy to the Ultra Secret, as the intelligence take from the operation was sometimes called, were not permitted to place themselves in any situation that might expose them to capture and interrogation by the enemy. The Ultra Secret, if it had not won the war, certainly contributed to its victory, and sooner than otherwise would have been the case. That, at least, was the story Winterbotham had to tell.

Winterbotham's revelations, if in any way true, seemed to have certain implications for history's account of the Second World War. If this feat was as successful, and therefore as important as claimed, how were history's explanations of the major events of the war to be regarded?

I read Winterbotham's book as soon as it came out and was impressed as much by what was not said as what was. Mostly, I was intrigued not by the book but by the fact that military history seemed to have passed by entirely the effect of intelligence operations upon the course of that war. At the time, neither the British nor the American official military histories made any but the most passing references to either intelligence or "special" operations such as those conducted by the Office of Strategic Services or the British Special Intelligence Services. Since then, of course, the British have attempted to rectify this oversight with several volumes under the general editorship of F. A. Hinsley, but the Americans have shown no interest whatever in completing what, if Winterbotham was to be believed, was certainly an incomplete record. Furthermore, academic military historians seemed even less interested than the official historians.

Eventually I wrote two highly speculative essays addressing the potential implications of Winterbotham's revelations. After the first of these, I was invited to a conference in which the Winterbotham book was to be discussed-- a smallish conference, I thought. Instead, several hundred people attended, and, still a graduate student, I was far the least distinguished member of the panel. The panel discussion was uneventful, mostly going over ground that had by then been discussed in public (but not academic) articles as well as a segment of *60 Minutes*.

It was when the discussion was thrown open to the audience that the conference became interesting. At one point, someone asked how upwards of 35,000 people (the number then estimated to have been involved in the codebreaking operations) could have managed to keep such a secret for so long. A man rose to speak, obviously surprising his wife who sat next to him. "I'll tell you how," he said, "We gave our word." Until that moment, this man's wife had no idea he'd been involved in the Ultra operations. He had kept his cover for forty years.

That was when I decided that the real history of the war, if "real history" is to imply any honest attempt at a compre- hensive view of an event, had no chance of ever being written. If the comparatively lax culture of secrecy and conspiracy known in the Second World War could exact such a hold on sources so long overtaken by events, how much more difficult could any approach to this secret world be when the culture of secrecy had been strengthened by years of Cold War hostility and outright paranoia?

It is true enough that the habits of mind and behavior I have noted here may have their origins in practical reasons: the protection of sources long after the data they have produced have been overtaken by events, or concealment for diplomatic purposes that may have become so in the time since the secrets were created, or any number of other causes. But it is also true that these are the very reasons traditional, non-official history has little chance of making a reasonable approach to the history of intelligence.

Gradually, the Winterbotham revelations did create a small wave of articles and books, some sensational, some sober, that addressed various aspects of World War II intelligence, and in the process some very interesting history has been produced. Under ordinary circumstances, one would think that, as with most historical subjects, this process would continue until--at some time in the distant future--a fairly clear view of this part of the war would have been made available to students of the war. But as of this writing, I confess I do not see much evidence that this will happen. What has happened is that several very good books have been produced which treat intelligence intelligently; that is, their authors set intelligence operations within their military context. This, rather than a complete uncovering of intelligence operations in and of themselves, is the best way at the moment of getting at the influence of intelligence upon the Second World War.

Under these circumstances, any attempt to bring order to a branch of historiography which is distinctly without order is welcome, and that is why the student of military history should welcome Jon House's professional approach in his *Military Intelligence, 1870-1991,* the most recent Greenwood Research Guide in Military History. House is himself a professional historian and a professional military intelligence officer, a combination not at all rare since many of the working methods of one translate well into the other. The student of history is unlikely to find as systematic a discussion of the forms and functions of military intelligence in "open" sources as in House's own introduction, and his bibliography continues this systematic and informed approach in the cataloguing and evaluating of sources--which, in the end, is the craft of both the historian and the intelligencer.

Roger J. Spiller

U. S. Army Command &
General Staff College

Preface

This guide is concerned with military intelligence, including the organizations, means of collection, problems of analysis, and historical results of armed forces attempting to learn about the enemy forces, terrain, and weather they face in wartime. For ease of reference, I have limited the bibliography essentially to published, English-language sources concerning military intelligence since 1870. Of necessity, this bibliography embraces two related subjects:

Electronic warfare, in the broadest sense of manipulating the electronic spectrum to protect friendly communications and other electronic systems while interfering with or misleading those of the enemy, directly impinges on one of the most lucrative sources of intelligence information, signals intercept. In practice, it is impossible to separate the pure intelligence function of signals intercept from the broader, operational role of electronic warfare. At its most basic, for example, the decision as to whether to exploit an intercepted signal for its intelligence value, or to jam or mislead it as part of military operations, can have a significant impact on a battle. Chapter Six is devoted to the burgeoning literature on this subject.

Military deception, by which one army or nation attempts to mislead its opponents and thereby achieve some measure of surprise in battle, is equally significant, because it represents one of the principal obstacles to accurate military intelligence. Many of the historical issues of intelligence failure, such as the strategic surprise achieved in the German invasion of the Soviet Union or the Japanese attack upon the United States in 1941, are in part questions of the ability of intelligence agencies to overcome deception, whether deliberate action by the attacker or self-delusion on the part of the defender. Indeed, intelligence warning and surprise is one of the few areas where significant theories and procedures have been developed in response to historical experience. Chapter Seven includes a variety of studies of deception and military surprise.

Given this scope, the careful reader will note a number of gaps in the following bibliography. Some of these gaps are unavoidable, and represent fruitful fields for future historical research. Because of the classified nature of many intelligence operations in the twentieth century, the history of those operations, and of the organizations and procedures that made them possible, lags far behind the history of actual military operations. For decades after 1945, historians were unaware of, or not allowed to describe, the allied success in reading German military messages sent using the ENIGMA encryption device. Once the secret of ENIGMA was declassified, some writers swerved to the opposite extreme, assuming that such high-level signals intelligence was responsible for all allied successes. This simplistic approach neglects the mundane but equally important areas of imagery interpretation, prisoner interrogation, and order of battle analysis. Such subjects remain largely unexplored, as attested to by the gaps in this bibliography.

Other omissions have been deliberate, intended to limit this bibliography to sources on military intelligence only. Insofar as those sources permit, I have excluded works on political, economic, and diplomatic intelligence, accompanied by the vast literature on non-military espionage, except where the results seemed clearly to impact on military decisions. Similarly, covert or special operations, especially those that went beyond intelligence collection to include assassination, sabotage, or small unit attacks upon enemy installations, are beyond my intended scope.[1] For example, I have included some accounts of the U.S. Office of Strategic Services (OSS) in World War II, but generally excluded OSS covert operations such as the Jedburgh teams or their British cousins, the Special Operations Executive (SOE.) In practice, of course, it has not always been possible to make a clear distinction between accounts of human intelligence and those concerned with special operations.

As with other authors, I am indebted to the staffs of a number of research facilities, including

> Library of Congress, Washington, D.C.,
> U.S. Army Center of Military History, Washington, D.C.,
> Combined Arms Research Library, Ft. Leavenworth, Ks.,
> U.S. Army Military History Institute, Carlisle Barracks, Pa., and
> Naval Historical Center, Washington, D.C.

It is customary and appropriate for an author to accept responsibility for any errors of fact or interpretation. As a serving intelligence officer, however, an additional disclaimer is necessary. I developed this guide, outside of my normal duties, at a time when I was serving as a military historian and did not have access to intelligence sources or methods. No classified or restricted information was used. Although I entered the service after completing graduate school in

---

[1]   See Roger Beaumont's excellent study in this same series, *Special Operations and Elite Units, 1939–1988.* (New York and Westport, Ct.:   Greenwood Press, 1988.)

history, my own military training and experiences have inevitably influenced my views of intelligence. However, *nothing in this book is intended to represent the official position of the Department of Defense, the Department of the Army, or any other official body.* The opinions, like the errors, remain solely those of the author.

Introduction

Judging by the crowded shelves of any popular bookstore, historians and the general public alike are fascinated with the history of intelligence. Quite apart from the intrinsic historical importance of this subject, it appeals to the cynic in all of us. Popular accounts of intelligence organizations and operations fuel the suspicion that many historical events can be explained simplistically in terms of a conspiracy by a few influential individuals, rather than as the product of the great intangible forces of ideology, nationalism, and economics. In the minds of credulous readers and critical journalists, the intelligence agencies of the major powers appear as shadowy, all-powerful secret governments. Supposedly, these agencies can photograph any location, however remote, and listen to any conversation or radio message, however well encrypted. Their spies are to be found in every major city and enemy camp. Armed with this vast knowledge, heads of state and of intelligence agencies send forward individual agents or entire secret armies to interfere in the sovereign affairs of foreign powers. Thus observers of a variety of political hues find it convenient to ascribe foreign diplomatic and military events to the nefarious machinations of the U.S. Central Intelligence Agency (CIA), the British Secret Service, or the Soviet Committee of State Security (KGB.) The great problems of history are reduced to the plotting of a few evil men.

A moment's reflection will demonstrate the fallacy of this conspiracy approach to intelligence. If, in fact, intelligence agencies were as omniscient as this theory alleges, then how explain the great instances of strategic surprise, such as the Japanese attack on Pearl Harbor in 1941 or the Chinese intervention in Korea in 1950? How and why would nations continue to blunder into conflict, misjudging their opponents' vital interests and reactions as Argentina did when it occupied the Falkland/Malvinas Islands in 1982? If the CIA can see and control political events throughout Latin America, how did Fidel Castro obtain and for over thirty years hold power in Cuba, on America's doorstep? If the KGB and its satellite intelligence agencies ruthlessly monitored and controlled all

political events in the Warsaw Pact, how explain the
disintegration of the communist bloc in 1989?

In short, the murky world of international espionage and
covert political action looms much larger in books than it does
in reality. Whatever the true extent of espionage or high-
technology surveillance systems, the craft of intelligence
remains primarily a matter of methodically assembling and
analyzing small, readily-available pieces of information in
order to discern an opponent's organization, disposition,
capabilities, and (if possible) intentions. This is especially
true with regard to military intelligence, the focus of this
bibliography.

This introduction is intended to provide a brief review of
the realities of modern military intelligence. It begins with
a simple description of the subdivisions of that field, and
then identifies some major threads in the growth of
intelligence as a branch of the military profession. Finally,
this section will sketch a few of the recurring issues and
potential research areas in the history of intelligence.

Categories of Intelligence[1]

*To bring structure to the amorphous field of military
intelligence, a number of terms and concepts are necessary. As
in so many other professions, this unavoidably includes more
than a few acronyms and artificial words. These acronyms are
compiled in a single list in Appendix A, beginning on page 151.*

First and foremost, **Intelligence** is the product of
systematic efforts to collect, confirm, evaluate, and correlate
information from a variety of sources. The resulting conclusions are often subjective and tentative, representing the
best informed estimate of the analysts involved. By contrast,
information is just that, unevaluated reports of every description. Rarely if ever does a single source or single piece of
information provide perfect intelligence about an opponent, and
the analyst must constantly question both his sources and their
reports to avoid a premature conclusion based on inadequate
data.

Obviously, in any government many agencies develop intelligence that is essentially non-military in nature. In the
United States, for example, a host of executive departments or
agencies, ranging from the Department of State to the Department of Commerce, may assembly and analyze information in the
normal performance of their functions, gathering it from the

---

[1] This discussion of terminology is based generally on
the following sources: U.S. Department of the Army, Field
Manual 30-5, **Combat Intelligence** (Washington, D.C., October
1973); Field Manual 34-1, **Intelligence and Electronic
Warfare Operations** (Washington, D.C., August 1984); and
Jorge H. Felix Mena, **Intelligence: The Challenge of the
Century** (By the author, 1984).

routine, legal activities and reports of their representatives at home and abroad. Examples of such intelligence could include the political and diplomatic activities of a foreign government, the purely theoretical research of foreign scientists, and the economic capabilities and interests of foreign governments and multinational businesses. Ultimately, of course, such political/diplomatic, scientific, and economic developments may lead to the use or threat of force, but defense intelligence agencies normally focus on the specifically military aspects of foreign events.

Military Intelligence, therefore, is concerned primarily with the armed forces of enemy or potential enemy powers, but also includes analysis of the terrain, weather, industrial production, weapons development, local diseases, and many other factors that affect military operations quite as much as the enemy force in the field. Beyond this basic scope, military intelligence may be categorized in a variety of ways, including the level of focus or structural level at which such intelligence is generated, the specific objective or purpose for which it is collected, and the functional methods used to collect and evaluate such intelligence.

First, different levels of military organization naturally gather and analyze information in different degrees of detail for different purposes. A head of state or commanding general is interested in a broad picture of the situation, while junior commanders need to know in detail the immediate threat in their own area. The different levels of focus have changed throughout history, along with the rest of warfare. Today, however, these levels may be divided into four, in descending level of organization and detail, corresponding to the levels of military command and planning--strategic intelligence, operational intelligence, tactical intelligence, and combat information.

Strategic Intelligence, as the name implies, is the highest level, concerned with the basic capacity of a nation to produce military forces, the overall dispositions and missions of such forces, and the possible effects of any opponent's military forces upon the national or strategic military objectives of the analyst's own nation. An important subset of strategic intelligence is strategic indications and warning, the systematic effort of national- and theater-level military intelligence agencies to identify and warn against a possible attack by an adversary nation. Indications and warning is, however, not a separate discipline or category of intelligence but simply a critical responsibility of all military intelligence analysts.

Operational Intelligence is an intermediate level, in which a theater, field army, air force, or corps/naval battlegroup commander seeks intelligence that will affect the campaign plan or contingency plan intended to accomplish strategic or national objectives. Examples of operational intelligence include the location, capabilities, missions and movements of major enemy units--divisions or corps, air wings, or naval task forces.

Tactical Intelligence, often called *Combat Intelligence*, is the traditional focus of military intelligence, seeking to understand the composition, disposition, doctrine, and if possible intentions of enemy units that immediately threaten friendly tactical units. Commanders of a few hundred or a few thousand men need to know about the enemy units, weather, and terrain that define the situation in which those commanders will fight. The tactical intelligence requirements of a naval or air commander may differ from those of a ground commander, but are normally concerned with the same if not greater levels of detailed information about opposing forces and weather. Thus, while a ground intelligence officer may track enemy battalions or regiments, his counterparts in the Air Force or Navy may have to maintain records down to the level of individual enemy aircraft or installations. Indeed, these levels of detail constitute one of the unavoidable differences in outlook and procedures between analysts of the three armed services. Such differences in perspective, which are often mistakenly ascribed to "service parochialism," may complicate intelligence cooperation between the services.

Combat Information may be considered a subset of tactical intelligence. In this case, the term "information," rather than "intelligence," implies that little if any effort is expended on verifying or analyzing that information; it is composed of raw reports rather than evaluated intelligence. Combat information may be as basic as a report from a company commander that indicates a possible target for artillery or air support--the next higher commander and his staff act on such a report immediately, with only the most rudimentary effort to determine the validity or the possible wider significance of that information.

Regardless of the organizational level or focus, certain aspects of military intelligence are best described in terms of their specialized objectives or functions. In addition to the weather and terrain aspects mentioned above, counter intelligence is best considered as a separate field of this type.

Weather Intelligence is obviously significant, yet its history is largely neglected. Examples of weather's effects on war abound, beginning as early as the great storms that destroyed navies such as the Spanish Armada of 1588. The most famous case of weather *intelligence* may well be General Dwight Eisenhower's decision, on June 5, 1944, to launch the invasion of Normandy the next day, based on his meteorologists' forecast of a brief lull in a major storm system. Eisenhower's German opponents, who had no weather observation stations in the North Atlantic, were unable to predict this lull. More generally, senior commanders must consider climate--the historical record of typical and extreme weather in a theater of war--when choosing the timing, organization, and equipment of major military operations. At the tactical level, commanders of all three services must constantly be aware of the actual and predicted weather as it affects a host of factors. Wind, temperature, and humidity can dramatically alter the effective-ness of smokescreens and chemical agent attacks; air density directly determines the capacity of aircraft to carry military payloads; and storms can cause more damage to ships, aircraft, and troops than any military action.

Indeed, many would argue that, at least for land operations, weather is really a subset of *Terrain Intelligence.* The trafficability of soil, that is the ability of men and equipment to move across a given area of land, can only be predicted by examining the interaction of the basic soil characteristics with the weather. Waterlogged ground is less trafficable than the same ground after a prolonged period of dry weather. Similarly, the degree of concealment provided by foliage varies with the season of the year and even with the extent of rainfall in a given year. Considerations such as this have made terrain intelligence an enormously complex, if historically neglected, field. Long before the development of specialized terrain intelligence analysts, commanders had to rely on amateur cartographers to map the land and on military engineers to evaluate such factors as potential sites for crossing a river or the number and strength of bridges in an area.

Regardless of the historical time period, any ground commander, intelligence analyst, or historian seeking to understand an area of operations must at least consider the five basic terrain factors known the U.S. Army as OCOKA. This acronym includes (1) *O*bservation and fields of fire, that is, the ability of one side to see and fire at the other; (2) *C*over and concealment, which is the converse question of how well the terrain protects or conceals soldiers from enemy observation and fire; (3) *O*bstacles, the natural and manmade impediments to movement; (4) *K*ey terrain, those points whose possession or control provide a marked tactical advantage to one side or the other; and (5) *A*venues of approach, the routes of most rapid movement into and out of the battlefield.

Counter Intelligence is, as the name implies, the defensive arm of intelligence, the effort to defeat the intelligence collection means of an opponent. Counter intelligence is traditionally, but not exclusively, concerned with preventing or identifying enemy espionage efforts. As such, it has received a prominent, glamorous spot in the fictional and historical accounts of intelligence, especially during the Cold War. The reader must recognize, however, that counter intelligence is not simply "spy catching" in an atmosphere of false passports and cloak and dagger. Counter intelligence officers are just as important to troop operations in the field, performing mundane if necessary functions such as monitoring friendly units to prevent accidental disclosure of information useful to the enemy.

Finally, military intelligence may be categorized by the sources and methods used to collect and develop that intelligence. The oldest such category is undoubtedly *reconnaissance*, the process of collecting intelligence information by visual or other observation of the area of operations. Whether using individual scouts or entire light cavalry formations, effective commanders have always sought to learn everything they could about the enemy and the terrain before the main bodies of the opposing forces came into contact. Even when those forces did collide, the observations of front line units were normally collected and forwarded to the intelligence officer, who attempted to synthesize a more complete view of the opposing force.

The importance of the reconnaissance function is underlined by the fact that, when new weapons of warfare such as airplanes or submarines were introduced, commanders tended to see those new devices as means of reconnaissance long before they considered them as striking forces in their own right. Conversely, the same reconnaissance elements might be used as *counter-reconnaissance* to prevent the enemy's scouts from learning important information, intercepting or driving off opposing reconnaissance elements as far as possible away from the main armed force.

Under the general rubric of reconnaissance, two important sub-sets should be noted. *Surveillance* differs from reconnaissance in that it involves continuous, stationary observation of a single selected point such as a critical road junction or rail hub, whereas reconnaissance implies that the observer is moving, searching through an area. *Target Acquisition* is really a form of combat information, seeking to identify potential targets for friendly artillery or other fire power by using observers' reports, radar, signals intercept, and various esoteric techniques such as sound ranging and crater analysis to estimate the direction from which an enemy artillery unit fired at friendly positions.

In the twentieth century, the airborne camera has supplemented and in some instances supplanted the human eye as a means of gathering intelligence. The resulting images must be carefully analyzed, using overlapping photographs to gain a stereoscopic, three-dimensional view of the objects captured on film, with elaborate calculations of scale to identify the size and type of equipment involved. This process is often described as *Photographic Intelligence* or *PHOTINT*, but in recent years that term has been supplanted by *Imagery Intelligence* or *IMINT*. This is not a mere different of semantics, but reflects the fact that the images involved are often derived from methods far removed from conventional photography. To cite but one such method, the use of infrared photography identifies personnel and equipment even at night because of the different rate at which different objects absorb and release heat energy.

Human Intelligence or *HUMINT* often appears as the antithesis of the "high-tech" world of imagery intelligence. Human intelligence does indeed include espionage, at least insofar as such espionage is directed against the military rather than political activities of the adversary nation. Yet the term HUMINT is used deliberately, because it includes extensive information obtained from human sources that could hardly be considered spies. For example, interrogation of enemy prisoners of war, deserters, refugees, and a host of other unintentional witnesses can often provide indications of enemy morale, training, maintenance, and intentions that could never be obtained from imagery interpretation. Unfortunately, interrogation is often despised and neglected because of the horrible tortures perpetrated by, for example, the French in Algeria or the North Vietnamese throughout Indochina. Yet sophisticated interrogators can obtain significant intelligence information without torturing or physically depriving their prisoners. The psychological shock of capture disorients any prisoner, and skillful questioning can often elicit far more information than the prisoner intended to provide or even consciously knew he possessed. The World War II career of the German Luftwaffe interrogator Hans Scharff provides a fascinating glimpse of how such non-coercive questioning can succeed.[2]

Another aspect of HUMINT that is rarely explored is the role of military attaches and observers. It is far too simple to regard these dedicated, professional officers as legalized spies with a license to steal. Indeed, few attaches today would recruit or even associate with spies per se. Instead, they provide a useful network for the exchange of military information and opinion between friendly and even adversary powers, while viewing events in the country to which they are accredited with an educated military eye.

Technical Intelligence, the study of enemy equipment design and development, is of ever-increasing importance in modern warfare. At the simplest level, the analysis of captured documents and equipment is often performed by the same interrogators who question prisoners and refugees. However, every major army has profited from capturing and "reverse-engineering" enemy equipment to determine how that equipment was designed and produced. For example, in 1942 the Germans captured an American-supplied 2.36 inch antitank rocket launcher, popularly called a "bazooka," from the Soviets and used the basic design of this weapon to develop the larger and more effective *Panzershrek* antitank weapon.[3] Yet few of these developments have been studied even by historical enthusiasts fascinated with weapons development. Two exceptions that have been chronicled both came from World War II: the German system and the British countermeasures against radio navigation for bomber aircraft, and the American-British ALSOS effort, a technical intelligence mission concerned primarily with determining German and Japanese progress in the development of the atomic bomb.

In recent years, the term Measurement and Signature Intelligence, or MASINT, has come into vogue to describe a miscellaneous group of esoteric scientific techniques, such as chemical analysis of the residue produced by military manufacturing or nuclear storage facilities. As such, MASINT

---

[2] Raymond F. Toliver, *The Interrogator: The Story of Hans Scharff, Luftwaffe's Master Interrogator*. (Fallbrooke, Ca.: Aero Publishers, 1978).

[3] John Weeks, *Men Against Tanks: A History of Anti-Tank Warfare*. (New York: Mason/Charter, 1975), p. 67-102.

is both more specialized and less inclusive than the older term "Technical Intelligence." The few historical accounts of such matters generally use the older label, which is therefore retained in Chapter Three of this study.

Signals Intelligence or SIGINT, the intercept and analysis of enemy electronic signals, bulks largest in existing historical studies, as reflected in Chapter Six of this study. This is especially true since the 1974 revelation of the Allied use of ULTRA intelligence to defeat the Germans in World War II.[4] The actual capabilities and limitations of SIGINT will be discussed below as a major issue in the historiography of military intelligence. As a minimum, however, the researcher or general reader needs to be aware of two of the principal subdivisions of SIGINT, known as communications intelligence and electronic intelligence. Communications Intelligence or COMINT involves the intercept, decryption, and interpretation of signals that carry word messages, whether voice radio, morse code ("continuous wave"), or teletype. By contrast, Electronic Intelligence or ELINT, sometimes called Non-Communications SIGINT, is concerned with electronic signals that do not convey words. For example, the identification and location of a radar normally associated with a specific type of air defense weapon is a significant indication of the presence of that weapon, which can be critical not only as targeting information, but also to locate the enemy headquarters or other important installations protected by those air defenses.

in fact, both COMINT and ELINT are so critical to a commander's view of the battlefield that it is in practice impossible to separate the purely-intelligence aspects of these electronic signals from the operational problems of identifying, deceiving, destroying, or otherwise defeating enemy electronic emitters. This broader field is known as Electronic Warfare or EW, which may be loosely defined as the manipulation of the electronic spectrum to maximize friendly use of communications and non-communications emitters while interfering with enemy use of the same spectrum.

Electronic Warfare, in turn, may be subdivided into three principal efforts, normally known by their acronyms as ESM, ECM, and ECCM. Electronic Support Measures (ESM) is that portion of EW involving actions that seek to intercept, locate, and identify enemy command, control, and other systems that emit electromagnetic signals. If this sounds like another definition for SIGINT, that is because the two involve essentially the same practical activities of signals intercept and analysis. The difference lies in how the resulting information is used--SIGINT attempts to analyze information for its intelligence value, while ESM uses the same information to provide locations, frequencies, call signs, and other information necessary to target enemy emitters for destruction or jamming.

---

[4]   Frederick W. Winterbotham, The Ultra Secret. (New York: Harper and Row, 1974).

Electronic Counter-Measures or *ECM* is the offensive arm of EW, using ESM data to jam or deceive selected enemy emitters. Most casual readers are familiar with the basic idea of jamming, using a strong radio signal to interfere with an enemy radio, radar, or other emitter. By contrast, electronic deception may take several different guises. For example, the ECM unit may provide false friendly communications, designed to give the enemy an inaccurate picture of friendly force activities, or may attempt to imitate the enemy's own electronic signals. Moreover, false radar reflectors may be used to confuse the picture presented to enemy radars, and false navigational signals may cause enemy aircraft or vessels to stray off course.

Finally, *Electronic Counter-Countermeasures (ECCM)* is the defensive arm of electronic warfare, involving efforts to prevent the enemy from identifying or interfering with the functions of friendly electronic emitters.

It should be evident from the foregoing discussion that the intelligence analyst's concerns about signals intelligence and deception are inextricably linked with the military planner's or commander's use of electronic warfare as an aspect of military operations. This is especially true for naval and air operations, where the interception, jamming, and deception of enemy radar signals are crucial to success in battle. To further complicate matters conceptually, in recent years the U.S. Department of Defense, at least, has argued that EW is but one component of an overall strategy known as Command, Control, and Communications Countermeasures (C3CM). C3CM seeks to combine electronic warfare, operations security, deception, and firepower focused on enemy headquarters and electronic emitters in order to deny effective command and control to the enemy while protecting friendly command and control from enemy action. The result of such concepts is that, as reflected in Chapter Six below, signals intelligence must be defined very broadly in order to keep it in the expanded context of electronic warfare.

There remains one final category of military intelligence, a category that to some extent brings the results of all other functional areas together for analysis. This category may be termed *Basic Intelligence*, but is more commonly called *Order of Battle Intelligence* or *OB.* Order of Battle involves comparing a host of intelligence reports against the known organization, equipment, strength, leadership, training, doctrine, and past performance of an enemy force, in order to develop a fuller picture of enemy dispositions and possible actions. OB is the basis for intelligence analysis in almost any unit or agency, and is often a simple matter of common sense. Consider, for example, the location of enemy artillery units. Moving artillery from one location to another is a time-consuming process, a process that any soldier seeks to avoid at times when the support of that artillery is most needed. Thus, when a military organization is planning to defend a particular locale, the natural tendency is to locate supporting artillery relatively far behind the front lines, so that those guns will not have to move suddenly to avoid capture if the attacker should succeed in penetrating the defender's forward positions. By contrast, in preparation for an attack the artillery would be positioned much closer to the front lines, so that it will be able to provide supporting fire to the maximum possible range as the attacking friendly forces advance into enemy positions, moving farther and farther away. The knowledge of the battlefield position and maximum effective range of a particular artillery unit may be an important indication to the order of battle analyst that the enemy is expecting to attack or to defend. By itself, such an indication is not conclusive, but it can be used in conjunction with other information to develop a fuller picture of the enemy. If, in addition, a certain number and caliber of weapons are normally associated with a particular size of enemy unit (brigade, division, or other unit), then locating that type of artillery unit may help the analyst determine the size and disposition of the force arrayed against him. The knowledge that this artillery unit is located at a particular place may come from reconnaissance, imagery, signals intercept, or human intelligence, but that knowledge must be confirmed by other sources and compared to the enemy's known organization and habits of operation.

This discussion is also a simple illustration of the process known as the *intelligence cycle.* If a commander wishes to know certain information about the enemy, his intelligence officers decide what indications they must look for, then direct different functional organizations to seek those indications. Once the raw information is collected, it must be processed by comparing, evaluating, and interpreting different reports to develop the best available picture of the enemy. The absence of an expected indication may be useful as negative information, suggesting what the enemy is not planning to do. The analytical picture arising from this process is then provided to the commander and to other levels of the military chair. The cycle of directing collection, collecting information, processing the data, and disseminating the results of such analysis, is continuous.[5] This appears easy in theory, but in fact the effort may be quite complicated, and the results both subjective and ambivalent at best.

Historical Trends

In spite of, or perhaps because of, this complex typology of military intelligence, the history of that discipline remains largely unwritten. Whereas military organization and operations are the subjects of thousands of memoirs and studies, equivalent scholarly works on military intelligence are almost unknown.[6] What follows is therefore a highly

---

[5] FM 30-5, *Combat Intelligence*, p. 2-15.

[6] Three exceptions to this generalization are: Bruce W. Bidwell, *History of the Military Intelligence Division, Department of the Army General Staff, 1775-1941.* (Frederick, Md.: University Publications, 1986); Thomas G. Fergusson, *British Military Intelligence, 1870-1914: The Development of*

impressionistic attempt to outline the development of military intelligence as a discipline and as an organization.

If money has always been the first essential for successful military operations, knowledge of the terrain and enemy was undoubtedly the second. As European standing armies evolved between the 15th and 18th Centuries, rudimentary procedures for gathering and analyzing intelligence also developed. Alongside the paymaster or muster-master who counted and paid hired troops, and the quartermaster-general and sergeant-major-general who supplied and maneuvered those troops, early modern commanders often had a "scoutmaster-general" or "spymaster" for intelligence.[7] The functions of such persons were quite broad, providing not only information about enemy movements, but also guides to lead troops in unfamiliar territory. Whether a general had a designated scoutmaster or controlled his own intelligence network, the number of personnel involved was usually quite small.

The more general roles of reconnaissance and counter-reconnaissance naturally fell to an army's horse cavalry, especially lightly armed and armored units such as hussar regiments. Great light cavalry leaders, such as Napoleon's General Charles Lassalle, were as much concerned with reconnaissance and intelligence as they were with the battlefield shock action of heavier cavalry forces. Even when European cavalrymen tended to focus on the shock action role during the later 19th Century, the various colonial light horse formations that helped conquer and control the British and French empires remained true to the concept of cavalry as a reconnaissance as well as a combat force.

Unfortunately, in more conventional wars the two functions of collecting information and fighting enemy forces were often difficult for cavalrymen to reconcile. A recurring complaint against cavalry commanders was that they separated themselves from the main army to conduct raids or even pitched battles in the enemy rear, thereby depriving the army not only of their strength but also of their vital information about the enemy. Whether justified or not, such criticism has been leveled at Marshal Emmanuel de Grouchy, Napoleon's cavalry chief in the Waterloo campaign of 1815, and at General J. E. B. Stuart, the Confederate cavalry commander who was so conspicuously absent at Gettysburg in 1863.

Quite apart from spies, scouts, and cavalry screens,

---

a *Modern Intelligence Organization.* (Frederick, Md.: University Publications, 1984); and Marc B. Powe and E. E. Wilson, *The Evolution of American Military Intelligence.* (Ft. Huachuca, Az.: Department of the Army, 1973). This section owes much to these works.

[7] See, for example, the command and staff organization during the English Civil War, as described in Chapter 3 of Charles H. Firth's classic *Cromwell's Army.* (London: Methuen, 1962; original edition 1902.)

generals had a pressing need for terrain and cartographic information. Until surveyed and standardized military maps were developed during World War I, commanders had to make do with maps that varied widely in accuracy and detail. Even in the 1500s, the Spanish Army employed specialized maps and map makers to help move its troops, while in 1803 the early Prussian General Staff of 21 officers was supplemented by six "officer-geographers" and several engravers to produce maps.[8] In Great Britain, the first permanent organization devoted to military intelligence was in fact concerned with map-making and related geographical information. After the suppression of the 1745 rebellion in Scotland, Lt. W. Roy was assigned to develop accurate military maps of the Scottish Highlands. From this beginning came the Ordnance Survey maps of the entire British Isles. In 1803, the Duke of York widened this task to form the Depot of Military Knowledge, whose functions in peace and war were to accumulate topographic and general order-of-battle information about Britain's continental adversaries and overseas colonies.[9] A similar organization existed in the War Depot of 19th Century France.

Yet even such rudimentary organizations often atrophied in peacetime, leaving military intelligence to the individual initiative and experience of field commanders. Only in the later 1800s did military intelligence, like the rest of the officer corps, emerge as something approximating a modern profession. The models for this transformation were the American Civil War (1861-65) and the German Wars of Unification, including the Danish War (1864), the Austro-Prussian War (1866), and the Franco-Prussian War (1870-71.)

What made these wars unprecedented was not simply the vast size of the armies involved--the French Revolutionary government and even Louis XIV had developed systems to mobilize and equip hundreds of thousands of troops. Rather, the wars of the 1860s were characterized by the more rapid concentration and central control of such armies, made possible by the railroad and the telegraph. The American Civil War exceeded the Prussian example in this regard, since the Union employed this technology not only to move troops over long distances, but also to supply them in the field, building new railroad lines in a matter of days.

The Prussian/German model did, however, set the standard for other armies by using a reservist army, with vast numbers of soldiers being trained, released to civilian life, and then recalled to active duty and employed in battle with little or no time for refresher instruction.

Much the same technology and personnel structure also

---

[8] Geoffrey Parker, *The Army of Flanders and the Spanish Road, 1567-1659.* (Cambridge: Cambridge University Press, 1975), p. 86-105; Walter Goerlitz, *History of the German General Staff.* (New York: Praeger, 1965), p. 21-22.

[9] Fergusson, *British Military Intelligence,* p. 17-18.

encouraged the continued development of the naval profession. Steam-powered vessels were no longer at the mercy of contrary winds, and could maneuver more quickly than sailing vessels. Major powers developed a network of naval bases, often connected by undersea telegraph cables, to provide coal to fuel their fleets. Thus at the outbreak of war with Spain in 1898, the U.S. Secretary of the Navy, John D. Long, telegraphed orders to Admiral George Dewey, commander of the Asiatic Squadron, half a world away in Hong Kong. Within four days, Dewey's complex warships had steamed 600 miles to the Philippines, reconnoitered the situation, and destroyed the Spanish squadron at Manila Bay.[10] By 1914, the British Royal Navy had developed a vast reserve structure that rapidly manned its older ships even before the outbreak of war.

Training such reservists, planning their mobilization and movement by railroad and steamship, and controlling vast armies in the field and fleets at sea by the use of telegraphs and later primitive radios, all required a new group of uniformly-trained staff officers and commanders. In addition to training, operations, movements, and logistics, intelligence seemed a natural function for such officers. In the 1880s, if not before, virtually every major nation established small central staffs for naval and military intelligence.

At the same time, to share their ideas on the complex intellectual challenges posed by all these new functions, officers began to read and write for professional journals and other publications. This same interest in the developments of modern warfare led to a great expansion in military observers sent to foreign armies and wars. Every major army had always had a small body of restless souls and soldiers of fortune who were eager to travel in order to observe or even participate in wars that did not involve their own nation. With the wars of the 1860s, however, military observers became a standard, official representation of neutral armies seeking to learn the lessons of foreign wars. Such observers, together with a greatly-expanded system of military attaches, provided vital human intelligence for their parent services.

This trend towards a more educated, intellectually-challenged officer corps was encouraged by the fact that many other professions--attorneys, educators, physicians, and the like--were also developing standards of education, ethics, and performance, as well as professional organizations and journals, during the later 1800s. Whether or not the general public considered military and naval officers to be professionals, the officer corps themselves consciously developed the attitudes and institutions of a profession.

World War I put that professionalism to a profound test, and also provided vast new sources for intelligence collection. The airplane provided reconnaissance, aerial photography, and (by 1918) aerial adjustment for artillery fire. Indeed,

---

[10] Walter Millis, *The Martial Spirit.* (New York, 1931,) p. 149-150, 185-194.

accounts of the great fighter battles of the war often overlook the fact that fighter pilots were struggling for an air superiority that would allow the more vulnerable reconnaissance aircraft and tethered balloons to perform their mundane but vital intelligence and target-acquisition functions.

The same war also saw the birth of signals intelligence. Fleets and armies maneuvered in response to signals intercepts, which at first were not even encrypted. The Royal Navy was able to intercept the German High Seas Fleet at the climactic Battle of Jutland in 1916 only because of British SIGINT. On land, even the field telephones that tied the trenches together proved vulnerable to intercept; the Germans were able to monitor British conversations because the British field telephones used the soil, rather than a separate wire, as a ground to complete the telephone circuit.

The vital importance of industrial production made sabotage a significant threat, while the psychological mobilization of entire populations made those populations hyper-sensitive to any possibility of subversion and espionage. These factors led to the rapid expansion of counter intelligence, often called "negative intelligence" to differentiate it from the "positive intelligence" collected against the enemy. In the U.S. Army, this produced the first individuals and organization dedicated exclusively to intelligence. Whereas intelligence staff positions in troop units were largely filled by combat arms officers detailed on a temporary basis, the counter intelligence agents known as intelligence police formed a permanent body, composed primarily of enlisted soldiers.

With the gradual return of peace after 1918, however, most armies underwent drastic demobilizations and reductions in force, and the promising intelligence efforts of the war were often lost. Major nations still sent a small number of officers to study the language, culture, and armed forces of potential adversaries, but many bright soldiers regarded such assignments as a dead end that would take them away from the normal career progressions of command and operations. In the United States, the joint War Department-State Department Cipher Bureau provided invaluable intelligence not only during the war, but also at the time of the 1922 Washington Conference on naval armaments. However, in 1929 the newly-appointed Secretary of State, Henry Stimson, was horrified to learn about this organization, and ordered it dissolved on the grounds that gentlemen did not read each other's mail![11] Not until the rearmament and warfare of the later 1930s did military intelligence functions begin to revive.

World War II again brought a major expansion in military intelligence functions and organizations, with increasing specialization in terms of personnel and equipment. Aerial

---

[11] Bidwell, *History of the Military Intelligence Division*, p. 327-330; see also Herbert O. Yardley, *The American Black Chamber*, (Indianapolis, 1931.)

photography, prisoner of war interrogation, and partisan and guerrilla forces all became standard sources of information. Long range reconnaissance units and special operations forces used parachutes, landing craft, and simple infiltration to range through enemy rear areas, creating a significant threat for enemy security and counter intelligence elements. This again raised the problem of prioritizing the intelligence and operational capabilities of such forces. After all, small detachments of soldiers were sometimes able to catalyze vast guerrilla armies behind enemy lines in France, the Balkans, and elsewhere, tying down much larger German forces to control those areas. The special operations and guerrilla potential of such units seemed so great that decision makers were often tempted to use both those units, and the local populace that aided them, for combat operations rather than simple HUMINT collection. Indeed, Bradley F. Smith has argued convincingly that this temptation has consistently prompted the American OSS and its successor, the CIA, to exaggerate the possibilities of covert action and neglect basic HUMINT.[12]

Yet it was signals intelligence, with its corollary of electronic warfare, that received the greater attention both at the time and in historical accounts of World War II. Different services developed different relationships with SIGINT and EW. For the British and American air forces, radar became an essential element of air combat, and thus procedures to identify and thwart enemy radars became a commonplace by the end of the war. As a result, airborne "electronic warfare" often meant only ELINT and related jamming procedures, rather than COMINT. Such ELINT and airborne countermeasures were integral to air offensives, and were never restricted solely to intelligence channels.

By contrast strategic SIGINT, especially the Allied ability to decrypt portions of high-level German and Japanese communications, was a closely guarded secret both during and after the war. Possession of this information was an invaluable, if dangerous, tool for senior Allied commanders, as will be described in the intelligence issues section below. However, the extreme security precautions taken to protect this so-called "ULTRA" intelligence often produced ludicrous situations, in which some commanders and intelligence officers had access to the information while that access was denied to others who were equally responsible for combat operations. Transmitting ULTRA to field commanders required the creation of a separate special security system of intelligence officers and highly-encrypted communications, a system that often rivaled the normal intelligence staff officer as a commander's principal advisor on intelligence matters.

Yet, if the Allies had an enormous advantage in strategic SIGINT, both sides also gained much from small units that intercepted enemy short range communications. In fact, German Field Marshal Erwin Rommel owed a significant measure of his

---

[12] Bradley F. Smith, *The Shadow Warriors: O.S.S. and the Origins of the C.I.A.* (New York, 1983.)

North African successes to the activities of a single German intercept company, which was able to exploit the woefully inadequate and unencrypted British system of tactical radios to give Rommel a clear picture of his enemy's dispositions and actions.[13]

World War II produced a vast new spectrum of intelligence collection methods, but it was the Cold War that made military intelligence a permanent, major subset of the military profession. When the western democracies demobilized in 1945-46, most of the brilliant amateurs who had provided wartime intelligence collection and analysis returned to civilian life. Once the Cold War became an acknowledged fact in the later 1940s, however, large military intelligence organizations also became a permanent part of life. In many instances, intelligence collectors or advisors were among the first American troops committed to the many counter-insurgency campaigns of the era.

Effective organizations to provide strategic indications and warning intelligence are in fact essential for economies in defense spending, on the premise that such organizations can provide time to mobilize and deploy smaller armed forces, rather than maintaining overwhelming force in every area of potential conflict. To accomplish this, however, U.S. and other defense intelligence organizations have had to operate at a quasi-wartime level on a continuous basis, constantly collecting and analyzing information in many portions of the world. The end of the Cold War has if anything increased the need for such worldwide oversight and early warning of regional threats.

Issues in the Historiography of Intelligence

Of all the major questions in the history of intelligence, that of *Intentions versus Capabilities* is surely the most crucial. In its simplest form, this is an endless debate between those who believe that intelligence analysts should and must predict enemy intentions, and those who argue that such prediction is not only difficult but often dangerously misleading. Instead, so the argument goes, intelligence officers should simply present their commanders with a catalog of the enemy's military capabilities, together with those indications that tend to confirm or deny each such capability. Of course, at some point the enemy's commitment of resources to a particular capability becomes so great that the capability itself is an indication of that enemy's intentions, but the opportunities to misunderstand or miss-estimate such a commitment are immense.

Rare indeed is the radio intercept operator or the spy who

---

[13] The best discussion of this extraordinary situation is by John Ferris, "The British Army, Signals, and Signal Security in the Desert Campaign, 1940-42." *Intelligence and National Security,* (5:2), April 1990, p. 255-291.

can provide creditable, accurate, and timely warning of what an enemy head of state or commander actually intends to do. Even when such an apparent gem appears, the intelligence analyst must be alert to a host of questions about the knowledge-ability, access, and personal biases or hidden agenda of the source providing this statement. The consequences of accepting a particular interpretation of enemy intentions, however logical that interpretation may seem, can be disastrous. History is strewn with instances in which, for example, one nation assumed that an adversary would not initiate hostilities, or at least could not do so without providing ample advance warning. Such assumptions about enemy intentions can blind analyst and commander alike to signs that, in retrospect, appear to provide unambiguous warning of enemy attack. Similar assumptions and errors also abound at the operational and tactical level. Thus, although professional intelligence analysts develop subjective opinions about the likely future course of enemy operations, such analysts are often reluctant to state such opinions, at least without so many caveats and qualifiers that the decision maker will place little credence on these predictions.

The problems of intelligence analysts seeking to establish and maintain credibility may appear to the outside observer to be a parochial side issue in the history of intelligence. In fact, however, these problems are *central* to that history, because the finest intelligence analysis in the world is useless if the commander or decision maker does not believe and act upon that analysis. Although intelligence analysts are by no means infallible about enemy intentions, the credibility gap, the organizational tendency to stifle or ignore analysts, is often at the heart of intelligence failure.

Commanders and decision makers at all levels seek unambiguous projections of enemy intentions. No matter how sophisticated the intelligence consumers may become, they naturally seek clear-cut predictions about enemy intentions to provide a basis for their own decisions. Combat arms officers simply cannot allow uncertainty and ambiguity in their situations. From the moment of entering service, such officers learn that making a prompt decision, taking some action however hastily conceived, is always preferable to hesitation and indecision. Hesitation in a combat situation will almost certainly produce unnecessary friendly casualties. Hence commanders must evaluate situations rapidly and arrive at rapid, almost instinctive decisions. Civilian policy makers are equally prone to seek immediate solutions and decisions about any issue that is presented to them.

This approach to problem solving contrasts strongly with the intellectual framework necessary to be an effective intelligence analyst. Instead of reducing issues to simple, black or white alternatives, the analyst must be alert to an infinite variety of grays, of different possible interpreta-tions of the same set of facts. Although recognizing the operational necessity to make timely predictions about the enemy, the analyst knows that such predictions must be reviewed constantly to ensure that he or she has not been deceived, either by deliberate enemy actions or by his own assumptions. From this intellectual background, the intelligence staff officer often finds himself forced to describe "worst case" interpretations of the available facts. This pessimistic view of the enemy is an important check in the staff planning process, ensuring that staff officers and commanders do not unconsciously overlook or even assume away dangerous enemy capabilities. However, in the process an unwary intelligence analyst may come to sound like a Cassandra, a defeatist whose warnings soon lose credibility in the eyes of commanders and operational planners. In short, even if the analyst feels qualified to attempt prediction of enemy intentions rather than just capabilities, he or she may well fail in the crucial test of convincing the commander of the validity of those predictions.

This difference in mental outlook leads to a second recurring historical issue, the low status and consequent lack of credibility enjoyed by many professional intelligence officers. Again, such seemingly-parochial issues are often essential to understanding the use and misuse of intelligence.

As described above, although great commanders have always been their own best intelligence analysts, the increasing complexity of intelligence methods and of warfare in general compels modern leaders to rely on dedicated intelligence staff officers. During the two world wars, a disproportionate number of such officers were civilian academics and other intellectuals commissioned for the duration, bringing with them (at least in the most successful cases) the detached, analytical approach so necessary for effective analysis. Unfortunately, such people rarely remained in uniform in peacetime, and in any event lacked the military training and experience necessary for effective staff officers. Nevertheless, even in peacetime the requirements of intelligence analysis have tended to attract officers with a more analytical approach than those who enter the combat arms. Such intelligence officers are neither better nor worse than their peers who rise to command maneuver units, but the difference is real even if difficult to quantify.

A unique pattern of career development often exacerbates the differences between commanders and intelligence officers. While the former traditionally spend extensive time as troop leaders and operations or plans officers, the intelligence specialists often undergo a very different program of training. Language training, civilian education in history or political science, service in foreign nations as attaches or simply to learn about potential adversaries, specialized courses in the esoteric skills of counter intelligence and electronic warfare--all these take the budding intelligence analyst away from the "mainstream" of command and staff assignments. As his career progresses, the intelligence specialist may be denied the opportunities he needs to develop as commander and operations officer in battalion or larger units precisely because he did not serve the necessary apprenticeship in such positions at a lower level. Ambitious officers must therefore think carefully before accepting the limited prospects for command and promotion provided by a career in intelligence. Such limited prospects rob intelligence agencies of many potential analysts.

The resulting lack of experience, status, and credibility in intelligence is subconsciously emphasized by the fact that, in tactical unit staffs, the intelligence officer has little visible impact on unit operations and produces few tangible products. Staff officers concerned with personnel, operations, plans, logistics, maintenance, and communications generate reams of reports and take actions that clearly affect the unit's day-to-day performance. By contrast, the intelligence officer, at least in peacetime, produces few reports or staff actions. Even when intelligence estimates are issued, their security classification makes them inconvenient to handle, so that only a minority in the headquarters ever read or hear such reports. Subconsciously, the rest of the staff may come to regard the intelligence officer as a person with fewer responsibilities and a smaller workload than his peers.

The net result is that intelligence officers have to struggle to achieve the status and credibility necessary to advise their commanders effectively. Commanders looking to "solve a problem" are tempted to be their own intelligence analysts, rejecting the best efforts of their intelligence experts. This situation was not confined to the Cold War U.S. Army, but in fact has arisen repeatedly during the evolution of many professional military intelligence corps. To cite but one example, Horst Borg has documented a similar situation in the staffs of the German *Luftwaffe*. German air intelligence officers were consistently junior in rank to, and subordinated to, the operations officers in the same headquarters; the operations officers regularly wrote their own intelligence appreciations and dismissed any views provided by the intelligence officers. Of course, the intelligence analyst has no monopoly on predictive accuracy. Indeed, Borg argues that the air intelligence officers in question often allowed their political biases to cloud their view of the enemy threat.[14]

One alternative to this depressing spiral of poor status and credibility is to have combat arms officers serve as intelligence analysts, with few if any individuals pursuing a pure intelligence career in uniform. Unfortunately, this may leave the commander with inadequately-trained intelligence advisors, and tempts that commander to reassign his intelligence officer to fill any command vacancies that develop. Moreover, the most qualified combat officers often avoid intelligence duty precisely because it reduces the opportunities for command and promotion.

Turning from the intelligence profession to the sources of intelligence, another significant issue is the use and significance of signals intelligence in general, and especially of ULTRA information during World War II. As indicated above,

---

[14]   Horst Borg, "German Air Intelligence in World War II" in *Aerospace Historian* (33:2), Summer 1986, p. 121-129, and "German Air Intelligence in the Second World War" in *Intelligence and National Security* (5:2), April 1990, p. 350-424.

the 1974 disclosure that the Allies had access to the most highly encrypted communications of the Axis caused some commentators to conclude that SIGINT alone could explain Allied successes during the war. Such commentators therefore argued that the existing histories of the war were completely obsolete because they failed to address SIGINT. In fact, however, the effectiveness of SIGINT is subject to a number of important restrictions. What follows is focused on the specific question of ULTRA intelligence in World War II, but many of the same restrictions apply to other SIGINT operations.[15]

First, the enemy had to make the information available by broadcasting it over a medium that can be intercepted. Although the French resistance forces did provide the Allies with encrypted German communications sent on telephone lines, in many instances the high-level communications of German ground forces could not be monitored because they were sent by landline and not broadcast by radio. By contrast, the *Luftwaffe,* the U-Boat commanders, and overseas German commanders such as Erwin Rommel in North Africa had to transmit detailed plans by radio, allowing at least a theoretical possibility that the messages could be intercepted.

Second, the Allies must in fact have intercepted the message in question. Even if the intelligence service was monitoring the correct frequency at the correct time, the vagaries of radio propagation are such that not all messages were actually "copied" in complete and comprehensible form.

Moreover, the interceptors needed to receive not just one critical message, but rather a group of such messages over a period of time, for two reasons. Such a volume of messages provided more opportunity for cryptanalysis to decipher the code; a code used for only one short message might well prove completely indecipherable. Even if it were deciphered, that single message might be meaningless if taken out of context. Rare indeed was the message that laid out a complete enemy course of action; instead, the analyst had to learn the enemy's patterns of behavior and assemble the facts from a group of messages.

Fourth, these intercepted messages had to be deciphered in a timely manner. Contrary to popular impression, even at its height the British and American cryptanalysis effort was never able to decipher every message immediately. The German Enigma encryption system had different codes for different headquarters, and changed those codes to some degree every twenty-four hours. Periodically, the Germans made major changes in both

---

[15] This discussion is based on a variety of sources on ULTRA, including Patrick Beesly, *Very Special Intelligence: The Story of the Admiralty's Operational Intelligence Centre, 1939-1945.* (New York, 1981); Anthony Cave Brown, *Bodyguard of Lies.* (New York and Evanston, 1975;) Harold C. Deutsch, "The Influence of ULTRA on World War II," *Parameters* (8:4), December 1978, p. 2-15; and Roger J. Spiller, "Assessing Ultra," *Military Review* (59:8), August 1979, p. 13-23.

the code keys and the hardware of the Enigma machine. After such changes, the Allies might take weeks or even months to "break" the new code. Thus, for example, Germany changed virtually all its code keys on May 1, 1940, blinding the British SIGINT effort for three weeks. In the interim, the German offensive through the Ardennes had doomed France. On February 1, 1942, the German Navy adopted a new code known as "Triton" for its Atlantic submarine operations; the British ULTRA effort was unable to break this code until December of that year. Some analysis of training operations and of the external characteristics of Triton messages was still possible during this period, but the Royal Navy was certainly not privy to German operations for a crucial ten month period.[16]

Fifth, the analyst had to integrate decrypted messages with other sources of intelligence to arrive at an accurate assessment of enemy intentions. Reliance on one intelligence source, however lucrative, could be fatal. In February 1943, the Allied forces in Tunisia were surprised by the German offensive of Sidi-bou-Zid-Kasserine Pass because available SIGINT indicated that higher German headquarters had disapproved the plan for such an operation. Unknown to the analysts, Rommel and other German commanders met face to face on February 9 and developed the plan for Sidi-bou-Zid. The result was a sharp defeat for American arms, retrieved only by desperate fighting.[17]

Finally and perhaps most difficult, the analyst with the correctly decrypted and interpreted message traffic still had to convince his commander of the value of this intelligence. Even if the commander were willing, as Allied leaders increasingly were, to believe ULTRA intelligence, they were not necessarily as skilled as the analyst at using that intelligence without reading too much into it.

All of this is not meant to deny the enormous value of ULTRA intelligence. However, such intelligence was by no means an omniscient wonder weapon that by itself ensured Allied victory in World War II. No intelligence, however timely, accurate and sophisticated, can replace the efforts of the combat forces that exploit such intelligence in battle.

The very fact that the ULTRA secret was kept for three decades after the war illustrates one of the lesser issues of intelligence historiography, the conflicting need for military secrecy and public knowledge in a democratic society. As the guardians of information security, military intelligence officers will always be involved in this debate, which has at least two aspects. First, when intelligence and operational

---

[16] F.H. Hinsley, E.E. Thomas, C.F.G. Ransom, and R.C. Knight, *British Intelligence in the Second World War: Its Influence on Strategy and Operations*, Vol. I (London, 1979,) p. 144; Beesly, *Very Special Intelligence*, p. 110-113.

[17] Hinsley et al, *British Intelligence in the Second World War*, Vol. II, p. 581-587, 739-746, and 757-763.

information is first produced, military and political leaders have a real requirement to protect that information in order to deny it to the enemy. By contrast, the press feels an equal need to ferret out and publish such information, often regardless of the possibility that such disclosures may endanger intelligence agents and other friendly troops. While responsible journalists may recognize the requirement for such secrecy, the constant media competition to be the first to publish a story seems to make self-censorship of this kind unlikely and ineffective.

In the longer run, after the battle, politicians, historians, and others naturally seek access to the classified documents to determine what happened. Again, the conspiracy approach to intelligence historiography assumes that such documents remain classified because the government in question wishes to avoid criticism and embarrassment about its past actions. In fact, of course, the classified information may no longer have any operational value itself, but might allow a hostile power to deduce information about the current capabilities and limitations of a nation's intelligence collection system. Classification is often intended not to safeguard the information itself, but rather to protect the intelligence sources and methods used to obtain that information. Thus, in the case of ULTRA, one reason for its secrecy was that the German ENIGMA system remained in use by many nations after 1945, and British and American analysts did not wish to expose their capability to decrypt such communications. In any event, the rise of automated information systems during the Cold War has produced literally billions of classified documents, making review and declassification of such documents a time-consuming and expensive task. Like the U.S. Army's chemical weapons inventory, more money may have to be expended on the safe storage and disposal of obsolete chemicals and old intelligence reports than can be spent producing new weapons and intelligence!

The basic issue of protecting classified information in a democracy may never be resolved. In Great Britain, the government retains strong powers to suppress news reports or other publication of such information, while in the United States the federal government has far less control over the press. Both solutions have difficulties, of course, and neither can completely eliminate the deliberate "leaking" of classified information for political purposes.

The legitimate needs of national security can also clash with civil liberties in the area of counter intelligence. During the 1960s, U.S. Army counter intelligence organizations were drawn into the controversial area of surveillance of American citizens who opposed government policies. Initially, this effort was a relatively-legitimate attempt to develop information that might be necessary if the military were again charged with controlling civil disorders such as the Newark and Detroit riots of 1967. By 1969, however, Army counter intelligence agents were providing so much manpower for surveillance of various opposition groups that the Justice Department and other agencies refused to allow the Army to halt such activities. When this surveillance was publicized, the outcry concerning violated civil liberties resulted in severe legal prohibitions against even necessary military counter-intelligence activities within the U.S.[18]

Deception--the attempt to suppress actual indications of a force's military operations while portraying spurious indications to mislead an enemy--is one of the best documented aspects of intelligence historiography, but the issue is so significant that further work is always valuable. After the fact, the great surprises of modern military history appear incomprehensible, as if the intelligence organizations and government leaders were criminally negligent. To some extent, this is the reverse side of the issue of intentions versus capabilities--it is always risky for an analyst or policy maker to assume such a knowledge of an adversary's intentions that indications of that adversary's military capabilities and preparations are ignored. In the case of strategic warning prior to the initiation of hostilities, it is difficult to avoid the two extremes of complacently assuming that no adversary will attack, and seeing a threat around every corner. The possibility of enemy deception makes the problem of strategic warning infinitely more complicated.

The German surprise attack on the Soviet Union in June, 1941, remains the textbook example of both intelligence failure and deception success. At its simplest level, one must conclude that Joseph Stalin had deluded himself that Adolf Hitler would not attack that year, if at all. Only such a delusion can explain why Stalin ignored literally dozens of specific indications and warnings, forbidding his armed forces to take necessary precautions against surprise attack for fear of provoking the Germans. Of equal importance, however, is Barton Whaley's thesis that, up to the day of the attack, the impact of such indications and warnings was completely dissipated by the German deception story that Hitler would demand further concessions but had no immediate intention to attack.[19] One should note, however, that German intelligence was in its own way quite as faulty as that of its new opponent. While the Soviet Union failed to perceive German intentions to attack, the Germans completely underestimated the size and mobilization capacity of the Red Army. Whether this under-estimation was a deliberate self-deception or a matter of faulty order of battle analysis, the German armed forces began their offensive with a totally inadequate estimate of the number of divisions and weapons the Soviets controlled. Again, human intelligence about Japanese intentions *not* to attack in Siberia allowed the Soviet government to use the total resources of the Red Army against the Germans.

---

[18]   See Emil L. Havich. The Watchdog Barks at Snooping: American Political Spying From 1967 to 1970 and the Media That Opposed It. University of Arizona M.A. thesis, Journalism, 1974, p. 35-42.

[19]   Barton Whaley. *Codeword Barbarossa.* (Cambridge, Ma.: M.I.T. Press, 21973), p. 242-244.

Gaps in the History of Military Intelligence

Despite such extensive analysis, much work remains to be done in the history of strategic warning and surprise. Scholars have naturally focused on Pearl Harbor and other famous cases in which strategic warning was ignored or never given. Yet, to put such intelligence failures in context, we need to develop a more complete picture of the history of such warning, of its successes as well as its failures. Intelligence analysts and agencies find it expensive, institutionally, to "cry wolf" about threats that may not arise. Even if the warning proves to be accurate and timely, the paradox of strategic warning is that such warning may allow a leader or commander to *take actions that deter or reduce the very threat identified by the analyst.* In such circumstances, a success of strategic warning intelligence may well go unrecorded, and the intelligence officer may appear to have "cried wolf" yet again. The same paradox may well exist at the tactical and operational levels.

Strategic warning is also a fertile field for comparative studies of intelligence organization. For example, the strategic surprise of Israel (and the United States) in the 1973 Yom Kippur War is often attributed to excessively unified intelligence organizations, in which all analysts were pressured to support a single, generally derogatory, view of Arab intentions and capabilities. Thus, it has been argued, intelligence structures at the strategic and national levels need competition, with multiple analytical agencies and alternative means of reaching key decision makers. Yet earlier historians of Nazi Germany have frequently criticized such competition and decentralization among intelligence agencies as excessive and debilitating. The explanation of this apparent contradiction may be significant not only for historians but also for national leaders.

Apart from these recurring issues, there are vast areas of military intelligence that are as yet largely unexplored:

First, all aspects of tactical intelligence have been neglected. Despite hundreds of monographs and articles on the use of strategic-level ULTRA signals intelligence, we still know very little about the interception and exploitation of military communications at corps level and below—How were SIGINT and EW units recruited and trained? Who controlled and logistically supported those units? How effective were they against the various armies of the 20th Century? When and how was jamming first used on a large scale in land warfare?

Similarly, how did the different major powers use photographic intelligence in the field? At what level of command could intelligence officers obtain and interpret aerial photographs in a timely manner? What was the organization, training, and functions of intelligence staffs at different levels and in different armies? Beyond the generalization that such staffs became larger and more specialized along with the intelligence sources they employed, how and why did such staffs develop?

Second, with the partial exception of submarine warfare, the entire field of naval intelligence appears sadly neglected. Throughout the two World Wars, many procedures that today would be regarded as naval intelligence were in fact considered to be integral parts of naval operations. Of necessity, naval commanders had to depend heavily on signals intelligence from the first introduction of wireless communications. Yet, even the most complete signals intelligence still required systematic plans for aerial and submarine reconnaissance, as the U.S. Navy employed to locate the Japanese at the start of the Battle of Midway in 1942. At what level were these collection plans developed, implemented, and evaluated? How did the presence or absence of radar and sonar affect different World War II naval battles? In modern warfare, where opponents engaged at ranges of 15 miles or even (using carrier aircraft) 200 miles, how was the damage to the enemy assessed, and how were changes in enemy weapons and tactics identified?

The problems of assessing battle damage applies equally to questions of air intelligence. The novelist Derek Robinson has used Royal Air Force documents to cast serious doubt on the conventional casualty estimates for the Battle of Britain.[20] During one two-week period in August 1940, for example, Robinson asserts that the RAF claimed to have shot down 636 German aircraft, but found only 113 wrecks on British soil. Even allowing for the possibility that many Germans crashed at sea, this suggests that the British estimates were unintentionally exaggerated by as much as 200 per cent, apparently because of the difficulty of reconstructing events that occurred in the frantic melee of air combat. Two pilots shooting at the same target might claim two separate "kills." Using such faulty intelligence, Britain might well have lost the campaign while believing that it was winning.

Similarly, assessing the effects of aerial bombardment is notoriously difficult. The initial devastation of even non-nuclear bombing encourages both the air commander and his imagery interpreter to conclude that an enemy target has been totally destroyed. In the case of World War II German factories, however, it often proved possible to restore production within a few hours or days while allowing those factories to appear superficially destroyed. Only frequent reexamination of past targets, coupled with repeated air attacks on those sites, could ensure that a "destroyed" target actually stayed out of action.

This issue of "Bomb Damage or Assessment" or BDA received enormous publicity during and after the 1991 Gulf Conflict. Journalistic accounts falsely claimed that U.S. intelligence agencies in Washington and in Riyadh were bitterly divided in assessing the success of Coalition bombing attacks. In fact, the analysts in both locations were dealing with the type of ambiguity that is common to military intelligence. When looking at photographs of bombed Iraqi units, imagery analysts

---

[20] Derek Robinson, *Piece of Cake.* (New York: Knopf, 1986), p. 656-657.

found it difficult to determine if enemy equipment had been destroyed unless, for example, those attacks had blown the turrets of tanks or produced other catastrophic damage. All participants in the Department of Defense recognized the ambiguities inherent in imagery interpretation and in pilot reports, and attempted to reconcile such ambiguities and reach a concerted estimate of remaining Iraqi capabilities. Still, BDA remains one of the least developed and most often ignored aspects of intelligence.

Turning to other recent military history, much basic work remains to be done on the organizational and functional history of American military intelligence. Since the end of the Vietnamese conflict, the U.S. Army has greatly expanded both the size of tactical-level intelligence organizations and the number of people allowed access to the intelligence products of such organizations. The "Green Door syndrome," the frequent accusation that intelligence was too closely guarded for it to reach the junior commander who needed that intelligence, has almost disappeared. Tactical electronic warfare planning has become almost as familiar to the American ground commander as it has long been for his naval and air counterparts. Yet the story of why and how this fundamental transformation happened remains to be told, at least in a format available to the general public. After the Gulf conflict, it should also be possible to critically evaluate this expensive new organization, to compare the costs and benefits of combat intelligence and electronic warfare (CEWI) units.

The intimate relationship of intelligence officers with the civilian population is almost unique to military forces, and includes multiple areas for further research. During World War II, for example, the intelligence provided to Allied armies by occupied populations was at least as important as the guerrilla and resistance operations of those populations. In the battles to retake France and the Philippines, the U.S. Army relied heavily on reports by the local populace, while their German and Japanese opponents fought almost blindly by comparison. In the many insurgencies of the post-war era, the ability of intelligence officers to elicit such support from local populations was often decisive. The most effective such officers often acquired a broad base of knowledge about the local economy and government that gave them unique qualifications to advise policy makers.

Virtually every modern army has produced a few such experts, but they were often eccentrics or academics put into uniform for the duration of a particular conflict. Since 1945, however, this phenomenon of the soldier-statesman, the trained expert on a particular area of the world, has been institutionalized, at least in the United States. Civilians--both cabinet officials and career intelligence professionals--remain in control, but the evolution and effects of this broader role for military intelligence officers remain largely unexamined. Such officers are on the thin edge that separates the military profession from governmental policy and diplomacy, and defining their proper role may pose a significant change to the concept of a professional officer corps.

In short, the history of military intelligence remains in its infancy. While civilian students may be fascinated by espionage and the "war-winning" potential of strategic signals intelligence, the most important research needs lie in more mundane fields. The relationships of intelligence analysts to military commanders and civilian policy-makers, the development and actual functions of tactical intelligence staffs, and the institutional history of various intelligence corps all demand further study if future historians are to place military intelligence in its proper context.

1

General and Strategic Intelligence

General and Introductory Works

1.   Clausewitz, Karl von.   *On War.*   Michael Howard and Peter Paret, eds. and trans. Princeton: Princeton University Press, 1976.
     See Book 1, Chapter 6 (Intelligence in War,) and Book 3, Chapter 9 (Surprise.)

2.   Colby, William E.   "Intelligence Secrecy and Security in a Free Society." *International Security* (1:2), Fall 1976, p. 3-14.
     Written immediately after the author's retirement from the Central Intelligence Agency, this is a philosophical discussion of the issues of public access and the need to know intelligence information.

3.   Deacon, Richard. *The Silent War: A History of Western Naval Intelligence.*   Newton Abbot and London: David and Charles; New York: Hippocrene Books, 1978.   288 p.
     A history of British, German, and American naval intelligence from the revolutionary war, with special emphasis on submarine intelligence.

4.   Deutsch, Harold C.   "Commanding Generals and the Uses of Intelligence." *Intelligence and National Security* (3:3), July 1988, pp. 194-260.   A variant appeared in Handel, Michael I. (ed.) *Leaders and Intelligence.*   London: Frank Cass, 1989.
     A review of major decisions made by British and American World War II commanders, as well as by Rommel, in the light of their use of signals intercept and other intelligence. Deutsch attempts to evaluate the degree to which these commanders, none of whom was trained in intelligence, were successful in using intelligence organizations and sources.   He concludes that intelligence officers were rarely able to correct commanders' errors of perception about the situation.

5.   Dulles, Allen.   *The Craft of Intelligence.*   New York: Harper and Row, 1963.   277 p.
     Although primarily concerned with the CIA and national-level intelligence, this is a classic introduction to the problems of the profession.

6.   Evans, Allen. "Intelligence and Policy Formation." *World Politics* (12:1), October 1959, p. 84-91.
A review article of Roger Hilsman, Washington Platt, and other works on national-level intelligence.

7.   Grisham, Austin E. Intelligence Support to Arms Control: an Individual Study Project. Carlisle Barracks, Pa: U.S. Army War College, typescript 1990. iii + 41 p.
Considers issues of policy and organization for arms control verification, rather than procedures of collection and analysis.

8.   Haldane, R. A. *The Hidden War*. New York: St. Martin's Press; London: Robert Hale Ltd., 1978.
Discusses a wide variety of intelligence activities in World War II, including ULTRA and MAGIC signals intelligence and various famous spy rings. Primarily at the national and strategic intelligence level.

9.   Handel, Michael I. (ed.) *Leaders and Intelligence.* London: Frank Cass, 1989. 300 p.
This set of conference papers includes essays on Hitler, Westmoreland, Churchill, etc.

10.   Hastedt, Glenn P. (ed.) *Controlling Intelligence.* Studies in Intelligence Series. London: Frank Cass, 1991. 190 p.
Places the development of intelligence in a political context, focusing on the CIA and examining national-level intelligence estimates, covert action, and counter intelligence. The book also contains a case study in how Canada placed governmental controls on intelligence organizations.

11.   Hinsley, Francis H. "The Intelligence Revolution: A [sic] Historical Perspective." *Harmon Memorial Lectures in Military History, No. 31.* Colorado Springs, Co: U.S. Air Force Academy, 1988. 12 p.
The great practitioner and historian of British intelligence considers the four sources of intelligence information in World War II - physical contact (documents, censorship, and interrogation), espionage, aerial reconnaissance, and signals intelligence.

12.   Hinsley, Francis H., E.E. Thomas, C.F.G. Ransom, and R.C. Knight. *British Intelligence in the Second World War: Its Influence on Strategy and Operations.* 5 vols. New York: Cambridge University Press, 1979, 1981, 1984, and 1990.
The monumental British official history of intelligence, especially signals intelligence. Prof. Hinsley combines superb academic credentials with his own experience as a senior official in British intelligence. See also Hinsley et al, Vol. 4: *Security and Counter-Intelligence* in Chapter 4, Human Intelligence and Counter Intelligence, and Michael Howard, Vol. 5: *Strategic Deception* in Chapter 6, Deception and Strategic Surprise.

13.   Hughes, Thomas L. *The Fate of Facts in a World of Men* -

Foreign Policy and Intelligence Making. Headline Series No. 233. New York: Foreign Policy Association, 1976. 62 p.
A provocative, well-considered analysis of the relationship between national decision makers and their intelligence advisors.

14.   Jackson, B. "The Service of Military Intelligence." Washington, D.C.: War College Division, General Staff, 1913. 63 p. (MHI)
An early effort by the U.S. War Department's General Staff to trace the organizational history of military intelligence, as well as the sources of strategic and tactical intelligence. This lecture addresses everything from instructions for military attaches to press censorship and air reconnaissance.

15.   Johnson, Lock K. "Decision Costs in the Intelligence Cycle." *Journal of Strategic Studies* (7:3), Sept 1984, p. 318-335.
Johnson discusses the bureaucratic costs and risks associated with production of intelligence estimates at the national level in the US. For example, repeated false alarms in prediction will dull the consumer/decision maker's attention to future threats.

16.   Kendall, Willmoore. "The Function of Intelligence." *World Politics* (1:4), July 1949, p. 542-552.
A slightly cynical, provocative insider's view of national-level intelligence in the U.S. This is an early expression of criticisms that have frequently been leveled at the U.S. intelligence community.

17.   Kennedy, William V. (ed.) *Intelligence Warfare: Today's Advanced Technology Conflict.* New York: Crescent Books, 1983. Originally published as *The Intelligence War: Penetrating the Secret World of Today's Advanced Technology Conflict.* London: Salamander Books, 1983. 208 p.
A "coffee table book" with chapters on electronic warfare, intelligence of all services, and espionage.

18.   Konecny, Anthony D. Net Assessment: An Examination of the Process. M.A. Thesis (National Security Affairs), Naval Postgraduate School, 1988. vi + 66 p.
This is a discussion of the evolving analytical procedures for comparing capabilities of opposing forces, using the nuclear balance of submarine-launched ballistic missiles as an example. The author advocates separating net assessment from intelligence analysis per se.

19.   Mathams, Robert H. *The Intelligence Analyst's Notebook.* Strategic and Defence Studies Center Working Paper No. 151. Canberra: Australian National University, 1988. 36 p.
An introductory texts, which describes the components and issues of strategic and national-level intelligence.

20.   "Military Intelligence Critical Attributes." London: Aviation Studies Atlantic, c.1983. unnumbered pages.
An effort to analyze the U.S. (and to a lesser extent the

Soviet) intelligence system in terms of functions and budgets, including cryptology, counterintelligence, general intelligence, tactical intelligence, etc. A useful introduction to the acronyms and collection systems of all services.

21.   O'Toole, G. J. A. *The Encyclopedia of American Intelligence and Espionage: From the Revolutionary War to the Present*. New York, Oxford: Facts on File, 1988. xvi + 539 p.
    The reference provides good brief accounts of intelligence institutions and events, but little about purely military intelligence.

22.   Pettee, George S. *The Future of American Secret Intelligence*. Washington, D.C.: Infantry Journal Press, 1946. 118 p.
    A World War II analyst/academic who foresaw the revolution in intelligence collection capabilities.

23.   Platt, Washington. "The Nine Principles of Intelligence." *Military Review* (36:11), February 1957, p. 42-49.

24.   Robinett, Paul M. "Reflections on the Role of Intelligence Officers." in *Military Review* (32:8), November 1952, p. 28-32.
    An experienced combat commander discusses the need for special training and development of military intelligence officers. Among his suggestions are that a prospective operations officer should first serve as intelligence officer on the same staff.

25.   Spector, Ronald H. *Eagle Against The Sun: The American War With Japan*. THE MACMILLAN WARS OF THE UNITED STATES. New York: Free Press/Macmillan, 1985. xvi + 589 p.
    Chapter 20, "Behind the Lines" (pp. 445-477) describes the various means used for allied intelligence against the Japanese: communications intelligence, coastwatchers, the Allied Translator and Interpreter Section, the Allied Geographic Section, the Office of Strategic Services, etc.

26.   Woodward, Bob. *The Commanders*. New York and London: Simon & Schuster, 1991. 399 p.
    Woodward attempts to portray the interaction of key decision makers, civilian and military, in the decisions to intervene in Panama (1989) and in the Arabian Gulf (1990-91.) Despite technical errors, this is an interesting portrayal of the use and misuse of intelligence at the highest levels of government. However, Woodward's strength is also his greatest weakness--by focusing on a few key decision makers, he ignores the influence upon those decision makers exercised by hundreds of staff officers and analysts.

Bibliographic Surveys

27.   "Bibliography of Cryptography." *American Mathematical Monthly* (50), May 1943, p. 345-346.

28.   Bjorge, Gary J. *Deception Operations*. Combat Studies Institute Historical Bibliography No. 5. Ft. Leavenworth, KS:

U.S. Army Command and General Staff College, 1986). 32 p.
    An excellent annotated list, including translations of
Soviet publications and U.S. government studies.

29. Blackstock, Paul W. and Schaf, Frank L., Jr.
*Intelligence, Espionage, Counterespionage, and Covert
Operations: A Guide to Information Sources.* Vol. 2 of the
International Relations Information Guide Series. (Detroit,
MI: Gale Research Co., 1978) xvi + 255 p.
    As its title implies, this is primarily concerned with
espionage and covert operations, but it includes useful
sections on Military Intelligence (Ch. 6), Scientific and
Technical Intelligence (Ch. 10), and Communications and
Electronic Intelligence (Ch. 11.)

30. Bolin, Robert L. "Technical Intelligence Bibliography."
Athens, Ga: University of Georgia, [1985.] Typescript, 24 p.

31. Bryant, Melrose M. *Deception in Warfare: Selected
References from the Air University Library Collection.* Maxwell
Air Force Base, Ala: Air University Library, 1986. 114 p.

32. Cline, Marjorie W. et al. (eds.) *Scholar's Guide to
Intelligence Literature: Bibliography of the Russell J. Bowen
Collection in the Joseph Mark Lauinger Memorial Library,
Georgetown University.* Frederick, Md: University Publications
of America, 1983. 236 p.
    Col. Bowen assembled a vast collection on national-level
intelligence, security, and covert activities.

33. Cochran, Alexander S. "'Magic,' 'Ultra,' and the Second
World War: Literature, Sources, and Outlook." *Military Affairs*
(46:2), April 1982, pp. 88–92.
    This is a superior bibliographic essay on recent
publications in strategic signals intelligence.

34. Constantinides, George C. *Intelligence and Espionage:
An Analytical Bibliography.* Boulder, Co: Westview Press,
1983. 559 p.
    A superbly-annotated bibliography of human intelligence
and special intelligence, with occasional entries on the other
aspects of intelligence. Constantinides is an experienced
intelligence officer whose knowledge of organizations and
procedures provides a refreshing change from works by outsiders
who tend to romanticize and misinterpret intelligence. This is
an essential research tool for anyone interested in this
subject.

35. Cruickshank, Douglas N. (ed.) *Foreign Denial & Deception
(D&D): Soviet Maskirovka: A Bibliography.* U.S. Air Force
Intelligence publication 500-5. Washington, D.C.: U.S.Air
Force Intelligence Service, 1986. 114 p.
    This is a bibliography, coded by key words, of 337 Soviet
articles on the subject, with citations for the translated
versions of those articles.

36. Devore, Ronald M. *Spies and All That . . . Intelligence
Agencies and Operations: A Bibliography. Political Issues*

Series, Vol. 4, No. 3.   Los Angeles: California State
University, 1977.   71 p.
    This bibliography includes some SIGINT as well as
espionage, but has few annotations.

37.   Galland, Joseph S. *An Historical and Analytical
Bibliography of the Literature of Cryptology.* Evanston, Ill:
Northwestern University Press, 1945.   209 p.

38.   Harris, William R. (ed.) *Intelligence and National
Security: A   Bibliography   With   Selected   Annotations.*
Cambridge, Mass: Center for International Affairs, Harvard
University, 1966-68.   2 vols.
    The author produced this study in various drafts.   Vol. 1
is a bibliographic essay, while Vol. 2 is the actual
bibliography.   This includes Electronic Intelligence (Chapter
7, pp. 57-60), Strategic Intelligence (Chapter 24, pp. 277-
292), and Tactical Intelligence (Chapter 26, pp. 295-300).

39.   Library of Congress. Congressional Research Service.
*Soviet Intelligence and Security Services, 1964-1970:   A
Selected Bibliography of Soviet Publications, With Some
Additional Titles From Other Sources.*   Washington, D.C.:
Government Printing Office, 1972.   vi + 289 p.
    Primarily concerned with espionage.   Chapter II (Soviet
Military Intelligence, pp. 95-124) is an extensive list of
periodical literature, largely Russian language.   Chapter VI
(Soviet Intelligence Activities: A View From Other Sources, p.
269-273) includes western sources.

40.   McDonald, Robert A. *A Selected Bibliography on Imagery
Reconnaissance and Related Matters.* 2d ed. Washington, D.C:
Defense Intelligence College, 1986.   vii + 55 p.
    Primarily concerned with the technology and procedures of
imagery.

41.   Pforzheimer, Walter (ed.) *Bibliography of Intelligence
Literature.* 8th Ed. Washington, D.C.: Defense Intelligence
College, 1985.   90 p.
    Although primarily concerned with national level
intelligence and espionage, this annotated bibliography is
still an excellent source for strategic military intelligence.

42.   Powe, Marc B. "The History of American Military
Intelligence - A Review of Selected Literature." *Military
Affairs* (39:3), Oct 1975, p. 142-145.
    An excellent bibliographic essay by the acknowledged
expert on the subject.

43.   Ransom, Harry H. "Strategic Intelligence and Foreign
Policy." *World Politics* (27:1), October 1974, p. 131-146.
    A good review essay on much of the literature of national-
level intelligence.   His pessimistic conclusions may be
summarized as follows: intelligence agencies tend to report
what they believe leaders wish to hear, and decision-makers
hear what they wish to, regardless of what is actually
reported!

44.   Rocca, Raymond G. and John J. Dziak. *Bibliography on Soviet Intelligence and Security Services.*   Boulder,   Co: Westview Press, 1985.   xi + 203 p.
     US, Soviet, and other sources, concerned almost entirely with political, national-level human intelligence.   However, this   volume   includes   appendices   on   the   heads   of   Soviet intelligence, both KGB and GRU, and a good chart showing the development of all Soviet intelligence agencies over time.

45.   Shulman, David. *An Annotated Bibliography of Cryptography.* New York: Garland, 1976.   approx. 300 p.

46.   Smith, Myron J. Jr. *The Secret Wars: A Guide to Sources in English.* Volume I: *Intelligence, Propaganda and Psychological Warfare, Resistance Movements and Secret Operations, 1939-1945.* Santa Barbara, Ca and Oxford: American Bibliographical Center - Clio Press, 1980.   250 p.
     Sections   IV   (Military   Intelligence)   and   V   (Selected Military   Campaigns   and   Battles   Influenced   by   Intelligence Operations) are useful for purposes of this research guide.

47.   U.S. Department of State.   Division of Library and Reference Services.   *Intelligence: A Bibliography of Its Functions, Methods, and Techniques.* Bibliography No.   33. Washington, D.C.:   Department of State, 1948.   mimeographed. (MHI)
     This bibliography, in multiple languages, is not topically organized.   It   is   primarily   concerned   with   espionage   and political intelligence, but includes some military as well.

48.   Wilt, Alan F.   "The Intelligence Wave." *Air University Review* (31), May-June 1980, pp. 114-118.
     A prominent historian of intelligence critically reviews three recent works on World War II, including Patrick Beesly's *Very Special Intelligence.*

49.   Wing, Mark; Karen Wing; and Robin Higham (eds.) *Subject and Author Index to Military Review, 1922-1965.* Ft. Leavenworth, Ks: U.S. Army Command and General Staff College, 1967.
     This   index   of   the   premier   American   military   journal includes not only *Military Review* itself, which began in May 1945, but also its various predecessors.

Guides to Primary Sources

50.   Cochran, Alexander S.   *The MAGIC Diplomatic Summaries: A Chronological Finding Aid.* New York and London: Garland Publishing, Inc., 1982. xiv + 139 p.
     Despite its title, this is actually a brief summary of the subjects covered in each MAGIC periodic report derived from Japanese   communications,   including   extensive   military intelligence data.

51.   Drea, Edward J. "Ultra and the American War Against Japan: A Note on Sources." *Intelligence and National Security* (3:1), Jan 1988, pp. 195-204.

Strategic Intelligence

52.   Ambrose, Stephen and Immerman, Richard A.   *Ike's Spies:*
Eisenhower and the Espionage Establishment.   Garden City, NY:
Doubleday, 1981.
This study traces the relationship of Dwight Eisenhower to
intelligence agencies from World War II through the U-2
incident of 1960.   Although the focus is on the CIA, there are
many useful sections on strategic and operational intelligence.

53.   Armstrong, Peter F.C.   "Capabilities and Intentions."
Marine Corps Gazette (70) Sep, 1986, pp. 38-47.
In 1970-73, Colonel Armstrong was the chief of current
intelligence for Southeast Asia within the Defense Intelligence
Agency.   As such, he provides a superb example of the dangers
of confusing an analyst's beliefs about enemy intentions with
his knowledge of enemy capabilities.   Armstrong accurately
forecast the North Vietnamese 1973 spring offensive, but
civilian leaders did not wish to accept this estimate for
political reasons.   Armstrong is sufficiently honest to admit
that he himself made a similar error, believing that the North
would not attack into the I Corps area of South Vietnam for
fear of renewed U.S. bombing.

54.   Berkowitz, Bruce D. and Goodman, Allan E.   *Strategic*
Intelligence for American National Security.   Princeton, NJ:
Princeton University Press, 1989.   232 p.
An explanation of how strategic intelligence is produced
in the United States.   Pages 4-14 include a brief history of
such production since 1945.

55.   Betts, Richard K.   "Strategic Intelligence Estimates:
Let's Make Them Useful."   *Parameters* (10:4), December 1980, p.
20-26.
Betts, a long-time theorist about warning intelligence,
criticizes the bureaucratic structure used to produce National
Intelligence Estimates in the U.S.   He argues for more
creative, speculative estimates that might be more useful to
decision makers.

56.   Coakley, Thomas P. (ed.)   *C3I: Issues of Command and*
Control.   Washington, D.C.: National Defense University Press,
1991.   xxiii + 408 p.
This discussion of Command, Control, Communications, and
Intelligence (C3I) includes general concerns of U.S.
intelligence.

57.   Dyer, George B. and Dyer, Charlotte L.   An Introduction
to Strategic Intelligence With a Classification System for
Strategic Intelligence Source Materials.   University of
Pennsylvania Ph.D. dissertation, political science, 1950.   459
p.   LC No. AAC0008949.

58.   Ford, Harold P.   *Estimative Intelligence: The Purposes*
and Problems of National Intelligence Estimating.   Washington,
DC: Defense Intelligence College, 1989.   291 p.
This study guide was developed for the Defense

Intelligence College, and focuses on the process and procedures of national intelligence estimating. Section II is a history of strategic intelligence at the national level, with emphasis on the watershed experience of the Korean War.

59.   Freedman, Lawrence. *U.S. Intelligence and the Soviet Strategic Threat.* Boulder, Co: Westview Press, 1977. xv + 235 p.

60.   Gazit, Schlomo. "Estimates and Fortune-Telling in Intelligence Work." *International Security* (4:4), Spring 1980, p. 36-56.
    A former director of Israeli Military Intelligence discusses the relationship between decision-makers and strategic intelligence analysts, including the difficulties of collecting on enemy intentions and the problems of becoming captive to particular assumptions.

61.   Gelber, Harry G. "Technical Innovation and Arms Control." *World Politics* (26:4), July 1974, p. 509-541.
    The author considers the problems of research and development as they may invalidate arms control agreements, including a discussion of technical advantage as one of the areas that national-level intelligence must attempt to assess.

62.   Greenwood, Ted. "Reconnaissance and Arms Control." *Scientific American* (228), February 1973, p. 14-19.
    A summary of his earlier paper (see below), accompanied by illustrations.

63.   _____. "Reconnaissance, Surveillance, and Arms Control." Adelphi Papers No. 88. London: The International Institute for Strategic Studies, 1972. 28 p.
    The author includes technical descriptions of how photographic and electronic reconnaissance systems might be used to verify strategic arms control agreements.

64.   Heymont, Irving. "What Is the Threat?" *Military Review* (47:4), April 1967, p. 47-55.
    The need for threat analysis in all longterm military studies, weapons development, and cost effectiveness analyses. This includes considering politics, possible changes in opponents, developments in technology, etc.

65.   Hilsman, Roger. *Strategic Intelligence and National Decisions.* Glencoe, Ill.: The Free Press, 1955. 187 p.
    Although focuses on political and economic intelligence, this book does describe the evolution of military intelligence through the two world wars, leading to the OSS and CIA.

66.   Johnson, Ralph W. Phoenix/Phung Hoang: A Study of Wartime Intelligence Management. American University Ph.D. dissertation, Political Science, 1985.   510 p.   LC No. AAC8514487.
    A longtime CIA official discusses the controversial Phoenix program in Viet Nam, which included abduction and assassination of selected leaders.

67.   Kellis, James G. The Development of U.S. National
Intelligence,   1941-1961.   Georgetown   University   Ph.D.
dissertation, 1963, Political Science. LC No. AAC0204301.

68.   Laqueur, Walter. *A World of Secrets: The Uses and
Limits of Intelligence.* New York: Basic Books, 1985. 404 p.
   This survey of national and strategic intelligence in the
United States assesses intelligence aspects of the Missile Gap,
the Cuban Missile Crisis, and Vietnam.

69.   Lee, William T. *The Estimate of Soviet Defense Expendi-
tures, 1955-75.* New York: Praeger, 1977. xxiv + 358 p.

70.   May, Ernest R. (ed.) *Knowing One's Enemies: Intelligence Assessment Before the Two World Wars.* Princeton, NJ:
Princeton University Press, 1984. xiii + 561 p.
   A series of essays on intelligence and assessment
conducted by the major European powers prior to 1914 and to
1939.   The focus is on national-level prediction of enemy
military doctrine and capabilities. The editor contends that
general staffs normally overestimated enemy capabilities (p.
511).

71.   McRory, George W. Strategic Intelligence in Modern
European History. Georgetown University M.A. thesis, 1957. 74
p.

72.   McCune, Shannon B. *Intelligence on the Economic Collapse
of Japan in 1945.* Lanham, Md.: University Press of America,
1989.
   An attempt to examine Allied perceptions of the economic
state of Japan, perceptions which bore directly on decisions
such as invasion or employment of nuclear weapons against the
Japanese.

73.   McGovern, William M. *Strategic Intelligence and the
Shape of Tomorrow.* Westport, Ct: Greenwood Press, 1974.
First published Chicago: Regnery, 1961. vi + 191 p.

74.   Oseth, John M. The Regulation of American Intelligence
Operations, 1974-1982: A Study in Definition of the National
Interest.   Columbia University Ph.D. dissertation, Political
Science, 1983. 532 p. LC No. AAC8523215. A revised version
was published as *Regulating U.S. Intelligence Operations: A
Study in Definition of the National Interest.* Lexington, Ky:
University Press of Kentucky, 1985. xvii + 236 p.
   A discussion of various governmental restrictions placed
on intelligence operations, either for national self-
preservation or self-denial of some types of such operations.
The focus is upon how to supervise the U.S. executive branch in
intelligence.

75.   Ostholm, Hakon. The First Year of the Korean War: The
Road Towards Armistice.   Kent State University Ph.D.
Dissertation, 1982. 267 p. LC No. AAC0227965.
   Much of this study is concerned with national-level
estimates of Chinese and Soviet strategic goals.

76.   Platt, Washington.   "Forecasting in Strategic Intelligence." *Military Review* (37:2), May 1957, p. 42-49.
The former G2 of XIX US Corps in World War II describes the principles and difficulties of intelligence prediction.

77. _____. *Strategic Intelligence Production.* New York: Frederick A. Praeger, 1957.   302 p.
Urges intelligence officers to study the social sciences in preparation for strategic intelligence work.

78.   Prados, John F.   Analysis, Organizations and Politics: The Case of National Intelligence Estimates on Soviet Strategic Force 1945-1975. Columbia University Ph.D. dissertation, 1982. University Microfilms No. 8406536.   xx + 595 p.   A revised version appeared as *The Soviet Estimate: U.S. Intelligence Analysis and Russian Military Strength.* New York: Dial Press, 1982. xv + 367 p.
Prados examines American estimates of Soviet strategic nuclear capability from the first Soviet A-bomb onward, providing an excellent explanation of extremely technical subjects.

79.   Rosenberg, David A.   Toward Armageddon: The Foundation of United States' Nuclear Strategy, 1945-1961.   University of Chicago Ph.D. Dissertation, 1988. LC No. AAC0552688.
The dynamics of strategic targeting of the Soviet Union.

80.   Ruggles, Richard and Henry Brodie.   "An Empirical Approach to Economic Intelligence in World War II. *Journal of the American Statistical Association* (42) March 1947, p. 72-91.
The American use of markings on captured German equipment to estimate German production, estimates which were compared to actual production after the fall of Germany.

81.   Schaf, Frank L. Jr.   "The Evolution of Modern Strategic Intelligence." U.S. Army War College Student paper. Carlisle Barracks, Pa.:   1965   698 p.
Includes information on technical intelligence, the of Office of Strategic Services, and the Allied Combined Intelligence Objectives Subcommittee (CIOS).

82.   Schmidt, C. T.   "The Need for Economic Intelligence." *Military Review* (27:6), September 1947, pp. 36-40.
This essay, like that by Lt. Col. Sperry listed below, is useful not only as a basic introduction to the subject, but also as an indication of the broadening perspective required of Cold War military intelligence officers.

83.   Snyder, Jack L.   Defending the Offensive: Biases in French, German, and Russian War Planning, 1870-1914.   Columbia University Ph.D. dissertation, 1981.   442 p.   LC No.: AAC8406554.
In the process of reviewing the preconceptions of war planners, the author provides interest insight into the strategic intelligence problems of those planners.

84.   Sperry, F.M. "Strategic Intelligence - An Introduction."

Military Review (27:7), October 1947, p. 16-22.

85.   Strong, Sir Kenneth. *Men of Intelligence: A Study of the Roles and Decisions of Chiefs of Intelligence from World War I to the Present Day.* London: Cassell and Co., 1970. 183 p.
     Maj. Gen. Strong, himself a former senior officer of British military intelligence, has chosen to write about military intelligence chiefs in Britain, France, and Germany. In the case of the United States, however, his focus shifts to the national level, with Directors of Central Intelligence such as Allen Dulles and John McCone.

86.   U.S. Armed Forces Staff College. *Intelligence for Joint Forces.* AFSC Publication No. 5. Norfolk, Va: AFSC, 1965. 128 p. Revised ed. 1967. 96 p.
     Doctrine and organization for unified command/theater and higher   level   intelligence   organizations   within   the   U.S. Department of Defense.

87.   U.S. Department of the Army. Assistant Chief of Staff, G2.   Strategic Intelligence School.   *The Principles of Strategic Intelligence.* Washington, D.C.:   Office of the Assistant Chief of Staff, G2, 1950. 121 p.

88.   U.S. Department of Defense. Studies, Concepts, and Analysis Division, J4 Directorate, Organization of the Joint Chiefs of Staff.   "Logistical Intelligence for Low Intensity Conflict." Washington, D.C.: Joint Chiefs of Staff, February 1988. iv + 18 numbered p, plus 42 p. of appendices.
     The results of a study group seeking to define the information required by logisticians to develop and execute a logistical support plan.   This is a significant example of intelligence concerned with the terrain and environment, rather than the enemy forces.

89.   Wark, Wesley K. *The Ultimate Enemy: British Intelligence and Nazi Germany, 1933-1939.* Ithaca, NY: Cornell University Press, 1985. 304 p.
     Examines the evolving British interpretation of Germany's power, in terms of economic as well as military intelligence.

90.   Young, Douglas P. Jr.   The Mayaguez Episode: A Case Study in American Foreign Policy-Making in the Wake of the War Powers Resolution of 1973.   University of Georgia M.A. dissertation, Political Science, 1987. 100 pp.   LC Number AAC1331503.
     An examination of the May, 1975 seizure of the *Mayaguez,* including the performance of U.S. national-level intelligence.

91.   Zaloga, Steven J.   "The Tank Gap Data Flap." *International Security* (13:4), Spring 1989, p. 180-187.
     The difficulties of strategic estimates in comparing arms inventories of different nations. An informative critique of Malcolm Chambers and Lutz Underseher's "Is There a Tank Gap? Comparing NATO and Warsaw Pact Tank Fleets." *International Security* (13:1), Summer 1988, p. 5-49.

92.   Zlotnick, Jack. *National Intelligence.* Washington,
D.C.: Industrial College of the Armed Forces, 1964. vii + 75 p.
   Textbook terms and concepts.

93.   Zweig, Ronald. "The Political Uses of Intelligence:
Evaluating the Threat of a Jewish Revolt Against Britain During
the Second World War," in Richard Langhorne (ed.) *Diplomacy
and Intelligence during the Second World War: Essays in honour
of F.H. Hinsley.* Cambridge, England: Cambridge University
Press, 1985. pp. 109-125.
   Zweig argues that Churchill used exaggerated estimates of
the possibility of such a rebellion to support his efforts on
Jewish immigration to Palestine.

2

Institutional Studies

General Studies

94.   Godson, Roy (ed.) *Comparing Foreign Intelligence: The U.S., the U.S.S.R., the U.K., and the Third World.* Washington and New York: Pergamon-Brassey's 1988.   157 p.
       A collection of efforts by the consortium on intelligence, describing the state of study of intelligence organizations and procedures in these nations.

95.   Richelson, Jeffrey T., and Desmond Ball. *The Ties That Bind: Intelligence Cooperation Between the UKUSA Countries: The United Kingdom, the United States of America, Canada, Australia and New Zealand.* London and Boston: Allen and Unwin, 1985.   xvi + 402 p.
       This is a monumental effort to describe the intelligence communities of all five nations, with emphasis on signals intelligence and ocean surveillance. Appendix 1 contains a lengthy list of alleged signals intelligence facilities of the five countries.

Naval Intelligence Organizations

GERMANY

96.   Rogers, Charles C. "Naval Intelligence," in *Proceedings of the U.S. Naval Institute*, (27) 1883, pp. 659-692.
       After reviewing European military intelligence staffs, the author describes the German naval staff in some detail, with other nations covered more briefly.

97.   United States. Department of the Navy. Office of Naval Intelligence, OP 32-E. "German Naval Intelligence: A Report Based on German Documents." Washington, D.C.: 1946.   84 p.

GREAT BRITAIN/UNITED KINGDOM

98.   Aston, George. *Secret Service.* London: Faber and Faber; New York: Cosmopolitan Book Corp., 1930.   308 p.
       As a Royal Marine officer, the author was a pioneer member of British naval intelligence. The focus of these memoirs is

on counter intelligence and security during World War I.

99.   Wark, Wesley K.   "Naval Intelligence in Peacetime: Britain's Problems in Assessing the German Threat, 1933-39." p. 191-205 in Daniel M. Masterson (ed.) *Naval History: The Sixth Symposium of the U.S. Naval Academy.* Wilmington, De: Scholarly Resources, 1987.
    The Royal Navy's Intelligence Directorate "was the least well integrated service intelligence department in Whitehall in the 1930s." British ignorance of German naval construction was so complete that they embraced the 1935 Anglo-German Naval Agreement as a means of predicting the size of the German Navy. In fact this treaty, which limited Germany to 35% of the tonnage of the Royal Navy, was ample for the Germans to build as rapidly as they were capable of.

ITALY

100.   Maugeri, Franco.   *From the Ashes of Disgrace.*   Ed. Victor Rosen.   New York: Reynal and Hitchcock, 1948.   vii + 376 p.
    Memoirs of the unconventional admiral who headed Italian naval   intelligence   1941-43,   then   led   an   anti-German intelligence net until the fall of Rome. The books's focus is naturally on the latter period, although Maugeri describes some Italian SIGINT and deception operations prior to 1943.

JAPAN

101.   "Japanese Naval Intelligence." *ONI Review* (1), July 1946, p. 36-40.

UNITED STATES

102.   Dorwart, Jeffrey M.   *Conflict of Duty: The U.S. Navy's Intelligence Dilemma, 1919-1945.* Annapolis: Naval Institute Press, 1983.   263 p.
    Dorwart's thesis is that the Office of Naval Intelligence (ONI) was effective at collecting and analyzing information on foreign navies, but its officers became too involved in domestic counterespionage operations.

103.   _____.   "Naval Attaches, Intelligence Officers, and the Rise of the 'New American Navy,' 1882-1914." p. 260-269 in Robert W. Love, Jr. (ed.)   *Changing Interpretations and New Sources in Naval History: Papers from the Third United States Naval Academy History Symposium.* New York and London: Garland Publishing Inc., 1980.
    Contrary to Frederic Karsten, the Office of Naval Intelligence was *not* a bunch of young Turks during this period. In fact, the office provided rather poor intelligence during the Spanish-American War, and pedestrian publications in peacetime.

104.   _____.   *The Office of Naval Intelligence: The Birth of America's First Intelligence Agency, 1865-1918.* Annapolis: Naval Institute Press, 1979.   xiii + 173 p.
    ONI was influential in naval policy in the late 1800s and

again during World War I, but at other times was "insulated
from the public, the government, and the rest of the navy"
(141.)

105.   Green, James R.   The First Sixty Years of the Office of
Naval Intelligence.   American University M.A. thesis, History,
1963.   IV + 138 p. LC No. AAC1300534. (Navy Dept.)

106.   Leary, William M.   "Assessing the Japanese Threat: Air
Intelligence prior to Pearl Harbor." *Aerospace Historian*
(34:4), Winter/December 1987, pp. 272-277.
     Leary argues that, contrary to general belief, American
naval intelligence officers were acutely aware of the technical superiority of Japanese aircraft and crews in 1941;
unfortunately, they defined their job narrowly, passing
technical data along to intelligence consumers without any
serious assessment.

107.   Niblack, A. P.   *The History and Aims of the Office of
Naval Intelligence.*   Washington, D.C.:   Goverment Printing
Office, 1920.

108.   Reilly, John C.   "U.S. Naval Intelligence and the
Ordnance Revolution, 1900-1930." p. 325-339 in Robert W. Love,
Jr. (ed.)   *Changing Interpretations and New Sources in Naval
History: Papers from the Third United States Naval Academy
History Symposium.* New York and London: Garland Publishing,
Inc., 1980.
     The difficulties of untrained naval attaches attempting to
keep pace with the development of naval gunnery during a
crucial period.

109.   United States. Department of the Navy. Office of Naval
Intelligence.   *The Office of Naval Intelligence.*   4 vols,
unpublished.   Operational Archives, U.S. Naval Historical
Center, n.d.

Military and Air Intelligence Organizations

AUSTRALIA

110.   Andrew, Christopher.   "The Growth of the Australian
Intelligence Community and the Anglo-American Connection."
Intelligence and National Security (4:2), Apr 1989, pp. 213-
256.
     The prominent historian of intelligence outlines the
development of the Australian intelligence organization and its
relationships with Britain and the U.S.

111.   Ball, Desmond J.   "Allied Intelligence Cooperation
Involving Australia During World War II." *Australian Outlook*
(32), December 1978, passim.

112.   _____.   *Australia's Secret Space Programs.*
Canberra: Australian National University, 1988.   86 p.

113.   Mathams, Robert H.   *Sub Rosa: Memoirs of an Australian*

Intelligence Analyst. Sydney, Australia and London: George Allen & Unwin, 1982.   127 p.
Memoirs of a distinguished technical intelligence analyst who makes valuable comments on the history of Australian intelligence and its relationship with U.S. organizations.

CANADA

114.   Elliott, Stuart R. *Scarlet to Green: A History of Intelligence in the Canadian Army, 1903-1963.* Toronto: Canadian Intelligence and Security Association, 1981. 769 p.
This massive semi-official history not only traces the organization of Canadian military intelligence, but provides immense detail on the tactical functioning of that organization at all levels.   It is heavily anecdotal, but still a useful source.

115.   Hahn, J.E. *The Intelligence Service Within the Canadian Corps, 1914-1918.* Toronto: Macmillan, 1930. 263 p.

116.   Russell, W. Neil. "EW Canada--Looking Back, Looking Ahead." *Journal of Electronic Defense* (9:7), Jul 1986, pp. 49-51.
Brief but useful remarks on Canadian electronic warfare organizations from 1944.

117.   Wark, Wesley K. "The Evolution of Military Intelligence in Canada," *Armed Forces and Society* (16:1), Fall, 1989, pp. 77-98.
Primarily a survey of the organizational history of the intelligence corps, including signals intelligence.   The footnotes of this article are a fertile ground for further sources.

CHINA

118.   Deacon, Richard. *The Chinese Secret Service.* New York: Taplinger Publishing Co., 1974. 523 p.
The tireless author of popular histories produces his usual workmanlike effort, tracing Chinese intelligence from the late imperial period through the Kuomingdang republic to the Chinese Communists. Chapter 27 discusses Chinese espionage to obtain nuclear weapons information.

CUBA

119.   Castro Hidalgo, Orlando. *Spy For Fidel.* Miami: E.A. Seemann, 1971. 110 p.
These memoirs of a former agent of the Cuban General Directorate of Intelligence (DGI) are one of the few sources on that organization.

CZECHOSLOVAKIA

120.   Bittman, Ladislav. *The Deception Game: Czechoslovak Intelligence in Soviet Political Warfare.* Syracuse, NY: Syracuse University Research Corporation, 1972. xxv + 246 p.
The author was in Czech intelligence from 1954 until the

Soviet invasion of 1968; as such, he became deputy chief of Czech special operations in 1964. Although somewhat influenced by the 1968 disaster, this memoir provides a measured, reasoned discussion of Czech and Soviet tactical intelligence in peacetime.

121.   Moravec, Frantisek. *Master of Spies: The Memoirs of General Frantisek Moravec.* London: The Bodley Head; Garden City, NY: Doubleday, 1975. 240 p.
     Written from the notes of the head of Czech military intelligence 1937-45. This naturally includes Czech warnings of German invasions of Czechoslovakia, Poland, Western Europe, and the USSR, as well as Czech counterintelligence against the Germans and Hungarians.

DENMARK

122.   Borberg, Preben. *Military Intelligence Service as Part of Crisis Management.* Copenhagen: Information and Welfare Services of the Danish Defense Ministry, 1980. 23 p.
     An examination of Danish intelligence in the context of North Atlantic Treaty Organization (NATO) crisis actions.

FRANCE

123.   Faligot, Roger and Pascal Krop. *La Piscine: The French Secret Service Since 1944.* Oxford: Basil Blackwell, 1989. 344 p.
     Two journalists chronicle the "swimming pool," the nickname of the Service de Documentation Exterieure et de Contre-Espionnage (SDECE), and its successor, the Direction Generale de la Securite Exterieure (DGSE). The focus is on moles, feuds, corruption, and personalities, rather than on actual intelligence functions.

124.   Paquet, Charles. *Etude Sur Le Fontionnement Interne d'Un Bureau en Campagne.* Paris: Berger-Levrault, 1923. 330 p. Typescript translation (1937) by Col. O.L. Spaulding, U.S. Army War College. (MHI)
     The intelligence collection methods, with historical examples, used by the 6th French Army during World War I. This covers interrogation, radio intercepts, artillery observation, etc.

125.   Porch, Douglas. "French Intelligence and the Fall of France, 1930-1941." *Intelligence and National Security* (4:1), January 1989, pp. 28-58.
     An excellent analysis of the organizational problems of French military intelligence, which so admired Germany and was so convinced of French moral decline that it exaggerated German strength. Once war broke out, the Deuxieme Bureau was fragmented along with the French command structure, and lost many of its most reliable sources. The nature of French planning and the attitudes of senior commanders down-played the use of intelligence, but the available intelligence was insufficient in any case.

126.   Possony, Stefan T.   "Organized Intelligence: The

Problem of the French General Staff." *Social Research* (7), May 1941, p. 213-237.

127.   Stead, Philip J.   *Second Bureau.*   London: Evans Brothers, 1959.   vii + 212 p.
    A sympathetic British account of the experiences of French military intelligence before and during World War II, including the difficult task of serving the Vichy government.

128.   de Vosjoli, P.L. Thyraud.   *LAMIA.*   Boston;   Little, Brown, 1970.   334 p.
    The author was liaison officer of the French intelligence service in Washington during the 1960s, and claims extensive French involvement in intelligence aspects of the Cuban Missile Crisis.

GERMANY

129.   Boog, Horst.   "German Air Intelligence in World War II." *Aerospace Historian* (33:2), Summer/June 1986, pp. 121-129.
    A brilliant case study in how NOT to operate a military intelligence service.   The author describes the German Luftwaffe as placing very low priority on intelligence and subordinating the intelligence officer to the operations officer.   What analysis did occur was biased by a short-war mentality, political stereotypes about Britain and the Soviet Union, and a complete ignorance of economics and production procedures which prevented accurate production estimates and target selection.

130.   _____.   "German Air Intelligence in the Second World War."   *Intelligence and National Security* (5:2), April 1990, p. 350-424.
    A similar but far more detailed discussion of the Luftwaffe's intelligence weaknesses, including detailed examples of analysis failures and of electronic warfare successes.

131.   Brissaud, Andre.   *Canaris: The Biography of Admiral Canaris, Chief of German Military Intelligence in the Second World War.*   Trans. and ed. Ian Colvin.   London: Weidenfeld and Nicolson, 1973;   New York: Grosset and Dunlap, 1974.   (French original Paris: Librairie Academique Perrin, 1970.) xvii + 347 p.
    This biography of the tragic head of German intelligence includes how Canaris backed into intelligence work during World War I, when he infiltrated back to Europe after his ship was sunk off Chile, then hired resupply ships to supply German commerce raiders.   Chapters 5-7 provide considerable information about the organization of German intelligence prior to World War II.   See also Heinz Hohne's biography (below).

132.   Coumbe, Arthur T.   "German Intelligence and Security in the Franco-Prussian War."   *Military Intelligence* (14:1), Jan 1988, p. 9-12.
    Emphasizes the German superiority over the French in the use of patrols and screens, both mounted and dismounted.

133.   Gehlen, Reinhard. *The Service: The Memoirs of General Reinhard Gehlen.* Trans. by David Irving. New York: World Publishing, 1972; original Mainz: Hase and Koehler Verlag, 1971. xxx + 386 p.
Gehlen is most famous for his role in cold war espionage, but he was also head of German Foreign Armies East after April 1942. As such, he describes German intelligence operations on the eastern front.

134.   Hohne, Heinz. *Canaris.* Trans. J. Maxwell Brownjoh. Garden City, NY: Doubleday, 1979. (Original *Canaris: Patriot in Zwielicht.* Munich: C. Bertelsmann Verlag, 1976) xv + 703 p.
A thoroughly-researched study that focuses on Canaris's blind allegiance to an older code of military honor, bringing him into conflict with the Nazi regime.

135.   Kahn, David. "The Forschungsampt: Nazi Germany's Most Secret Intelligence Agency." *Cryptologia* (2:1), January 1978, p. 12-19.

136.   _____. *Hitler's Spies: German Military Intelligence in World War II.* New York: Collier, 1978. 670 p.
This popular study is primarily concerned with national-level intelligence, plus a few examples (such as Normandy) of German intelligence failures. However, Chapter 23 (Foreign Armies East and West) describes the organizational history of German military intelligence from 1919.

137.   Leverkuehn, Paul. *German Military Intelligence.* London: Weidenfeld and Nicholson, 1954. viii + 209 p.
The author was the chief of the Istanbul station of the Abwehr (1941-44). His description of German intelligence organization and functions includes the Brandenburg Regiment, designed for tactical intelligence and reconnaissance.

138.   Paine, Lauran. *German Military Intelligence in World War II: The Abwehr.* New York: Stein and Day, 1984. vii + 199 p.
Primarily the story of Admiral Wilhelm Canaris and the organization of the Abwehr, the highest military intelligence service in Germany.

139.   U.S. War Department, Military Intelligence Division. German Military Intelligence, 1939-1945. Frederick, Md: University Publications of America, 1984. 321 p.
This is a reprint of two studies done by the allies at the end of World War II: "The German G2 service in the Russian Campaign (Ic-Dienst Ost)" and "German Operational Intelligence." Although heavily concerned with the mechanics of organization and function, these studies include more general conclusions concerning the German intelligence corps. In particular, the German army suffered from the frequent problem that intelligence officers lacked rank and credibility with their commanders, who tended to ignore intelligence estimates.

GREAT BRITAIN/UNITED KINGDOM

140.   Andrew, Christopher.   "The Mobilization of British Intelligence for the Two World Wars," in N.F. Dreisziger (ed.) *Mobilization for Total War: The Canadian, American, and British Experience 1914-1918, 1939-1945.* Waterloo, Ontario: Wilfrid Laurier University Press, 1981, pp. 87-110.   Also published separately, under the same title, in Washington, D.C., by the Wilson Center's International Security Studies Program (n.d.)   28 p.
   Both wartime intelligence organizations were the work of brilliant amateurs.

141.   Butler, Ewan.   *Mason-Mac: The Life of Lt. General Sir Noel Mason-MacFarland.*   London: Macmillan, 1972.   230 p.
   Mason-MacFarland was a career British intelligence officer, including service as attache to Berlin in the 1930s, and as head of intelligence for the British Expeditionary Force in France in 1939-40.

142.   Clayton, Anthony.   *Forearmed: The History of the Intelligence Corps.*   London: Brassey's, 1990.   approx. 270 p.
   An attempt to describe British intelligence actions in every conflict from the Boer War to Northern Ireland, including signals intelligence, prisoner interrogation, imagery, etc.

143.   Deacon, Richard.   *A History of the British Secret Service.*   New York: Taplinger Publishing Co., 1970. x + 440 p.
   As its title implies, the main focus of this book is on national-level espionage and counter intelligence, from Nicholas Throgmorton (1559) through the British spy scandals of the 1960s.   It is well written in a popular style, with sections on some aspects of naval and military intelligence.

144.   East, C.J.   "Short Account of the Formation and Present Organization of the Intelligence Branch, Horse Guards, London." in Wheeler, George M.   "Notes on Military Intelligence Departments and General Staff, with Brief Account of the Intelligence Branch of the British War Office."   No publisher, 1891.   22 p. (MHI)
   Col. East's 1882 account is an appendix to an otherwise superficial account of European intelligence organizations, compiled by a retired U.S. Army officer.

145.   Fergusson, Thomas G.   *British Military Intelligence, 1870-1914:   The Development of a Modern Intelligence Organization.*   Frederick, Md: University Publications of America, 1984).   280 p.
   An excellent survey of the development of British intelligence, from a rudimentary reference library during the Napoleonic wars to a full range of intelligence collection procedures during World War I.

146.   Foot, M.R.D.   *S.O.E.:   An Outline History of the Special Operations Executive 1940-46.*   London: British Broadcasting Corporation, 1984.   280 p.
   A good popular account that clearly identifies SOE as an organization for covert and guerrilla operations, not

intelligence collection.

147.   Gudgin, Peter. *Military Intelligence: The British Story.* London; Arms and Armour Press, 1989. 156 p.
    Traces British intelligence organization to 1945, and then surveys various functions and types of intelligence, including SIGINT, HUMINT, imagery, counterintelligence, etc.

148.   Haswell, Jock. *British Military Intelligence.* London: Weidenfeld and Nicolson, 1973. 262 p.
    This history of British intelligence extends from the Napoleonic Wars to Borneo in the 1960s.

149.   Heather, Randall W.   "Intelligence and Counter-Insurgency in Kenya, 1952-56." *Intelligence and National Security* (5:3), July 1990, p. 57-83.
    Heather argues that a major impediment to British suppression of the Mau Mau insurrection was the failure to develop an adequate intelligence structure prior to 1956.

150.   Hunt, David. *A Don at War.* Savage, Md., and London: Frank Cass, 1990.
    Memoirs of British military intelligence in World War II.

151.   Jeffery, Keith. "British Military Intelligence Following World War I." in Robertson, Ken G. (ed.) *British and American Approaches to Intelligence.* New York: St. Martin's Press, 1987. pp. 55-84.

152.   Lewis, Norman. *Naples '44.* New York: Pantheon, 1979. 224 p.
    British intelligence officer's memoirs.

153.   Lord, John. *Duty, Honor, Empire: The Life and Times of Colonel Richard Meinertzhagen.* New York: Random House, 1970. 395 p.
    Meinertzhagen was one of a handful of gifted, self-taught officers who pioneered intelligence in the British Empire. He served in Africa and the Middle East both before and during World War I, and is most famous for the Meinertzhagen sachel, which he deliberately allowed to fall into Turkish hands as part of the deceptions of the Palestinian campaign.

154.   Medlicott, William N. *The Economic Blockade.* Vol. II. London: Her Majesty's Stationary Office and Longmans, Green, and Co., 1969. 727 p.
    Appendix IV, "MEW: the Study of Enemy Intelligence," describes the organizational history of intelligence within the British Ministry of Economic Warfare. This ministry included responsibility for some targeting as well as assessing the impact of economic measures against Germany.

155.   Occleshaw, Michael. *Armour Against Fate: British Military Intelligence in the First World War.* London: Columbus Books, 1989. xvi + 423 p.
    This book is a model of the kind of tactical intelligence history that remains to be written for other eras and nations. In addition to a discussion of intelligence organizational

structure, Occleshaw considers all different intelligence sources, including trench raids, reconnaissance, interrogation of prisoners and deserters, espionage, counterintelligence, etc. He also discuses the notable failures of British intelligence, including the defeat at Kut in Turkish Iraq, and the seemingly-over optimistic assessments of German morale in 1916 and 1917. Readers may quarrel with his conclusion that British intelligence was more effective than its general reputation, but this volume is well worth study.

156.   Parritt, Brian A. H. *The Intelligencers: The Story of British Military Intelligence Up to 1914.* Templar Barracks, Ashford, Kent: [British Army] Intelligence Corps, 1971, 1972.

157.   Pereira, Joclyn. *A Distant Drum: War Memories of the Intelligence Officer of the 5th Bn. Coldstream Guards, 1944-45.* Aldershot: Gale and Polden, Ltd., 1948, 1950;   reprinted Wakefield, Yorkshire: S.R. Publishers, Ltd., 1972.   213 p.
     Primarily the unit history of a tank battalion, but some details on tactical intelligence.

158.   Read, Anthony and David Fisher. *Colonel Z: The Secret Life of a Master of Spies.* New York: Viking, 1985.   361 p.
     A biography of Claude Dansey (1876-1947), who eventually headed the British MI6. It begins with Dansey's adventures in Borneo, South Africa, and other colonial outposts, and then traces his career and through that the organizational history of British intelligence during and between the two world wars. This book is more favorable to the US Office of Strategic Studies than are many British accounts.

159.   Streetly, Martin. *Confound and Destroy: 100 Group and the Bomber Support Campaign.* London: Macdonald and Jane's, 1978.   279 p.
     A history of 100 Group Royal Air Force, which provided spoofing, diversionary raids, jamming, and other electronic warfare support for the RAF bomber campaign. A good effort despite limited access to official records.

160.   Strong, Sir Kenneth. *Intelligence at the Top: The Recollections of an Intelligence Officer.* Garden City, NY: Doubleday and Co., 1969.   xvi + 366 p.
     The author was a British intelligence officer from the Irish revolution through World War II, culminating his career as Eisenhower's chief of intelligence and postwar head of the Political Intelligence department in the British Foreign Office.

161.   Wark, Wesley K. "British Intelligence and Small Wars in the 1930s." *Intelligence and National Security* (2:4), October 1987, pp. 67-87.
     An institutional examination of British intelligence reporting on the Spanish Civil War and related conflicts. The author argues that British military attitudes, which regarded Italy and Japan as not "efficient" militarily, prevented the British from learning the same lessons that the Germans derived from Spain.

162.   West, Nigel. (pseud.) *The Circus: MI5 Operations 1944-1972.* New York: Stein and Day, 1983. 196 p.

Because of the current time period and sensitivity of the subject, this volume is somewhat less detailed than the author's volume on the earlier history of the British security services (see below). However, this book includes a systematic review of moles in British intelligence, as well as tables of organization and known officials of MI-5 from 1945 through 1965.

163.   _____. *MI5, British Security Service Operations 1909-1945.* London, Sydney, and Toronto: The Bodley Head, 1981. 365 p.

West has made a serious effort to trace both the organization and major counter-intelligence cases in Britain. To a considerble extent, this is the story of Vernon Kell, the dominant figure in MI5 for most of this time period.   West contends that MI5 deliberately fostered the myth that it was peopled by bumbling colonial policemen, to hide its actual efficiency.

164.   _____. *MI6: British Secret Intelligence Service Operations, 1909-45.* New York: Random House, 1984. xvi + 266 p.

Like its companion volumes, this work attempts to trace both the organization and its key personnel despite official secrecy.   It is focused on World War II operations under Col. Stewart Menzies, including MI6's rocky relations with the Office of Strategic Services when both were placing agents in Europe, and an MI6 error that misled early interpretations of ULTRA signals intelligence.

INDIA

165.   Hoffmann, Steven A.   "Anticipation, Disaster, and Victory: India, 1962-71." *Asian Survey* (12:11), November 1972, p. 960-979.

According to Hoffmann, the 1962 Chinese border war took New Delhi by surprise because of excessive reliance on the assessments of its civilian intelligence bureau, and by an Indian tendency to pretend that defense problems had been solved.   As a result of this disaster, the Indian Army's Military Intelligence Directorate was expanded and improved, providing more effective support for the 1971 Bangladesh War.

ISRAEL

166.   Bar-Zohar, Michael. *Spies in the Promised Land: Iser Harel and the Israeli Secret Service.*   Boston: Houghton Mifflin, 1972. 292 p.

A biography that incidentally traces the development of the Israeli intelligence structure.

167.   Black, Ian, and Benny Morris. *Israel's Secret Wars: A History of Israel's Intelligence Services.* New York: Grove Weidenfeld, 1991. xvii + 603 p.

A solid effort to trace Israeli intelligence from 1947 to 1989, including the Mossad, the military intelligence service

(Aman), and the internal security agency (Shin Bet). The emphasis is upon human intelligence, but also describes the 1973 Yom Kippur surprise, the *Achille Largo* affair, and other issues. The authors also discuss alleged Israeli intelligence cooperation with the United States and with France.

168.   Cohen, Raymond. "Israeli Military Intelligence Before the 1956 Sinai Campaign." *Intelligence and National Security* (3:1), Jan 1988, pp. 100-140.
    This is a study of the Israeli military intelligence organization *Aman*, in terms of its sources and methods. The author concludes that *aman* was very effective at assembling facts, but less so at interpretation, especially in ascribing a high state of readiness to the Egyptian Army.

169.   Gazit, Schlomo. "Intelligence Estimates and the Decision-Maker." *Intelligence and National Security* (3:3), July 1988, pp. 261-287.
    This article is useful both because it describes the difficulty of establishing a reciprocal relationship between commander and intelligence officer, and because it provides valuable intelligence detail about major Israeli military operations such as the 1982 invasion of Lebanon.

170.   Heiman, Leo. "Israeli Military Intelligence." *Military Review* (43:1), January 1963, p. 79-84.
    Israeli intelligence since World War I, concentrating on organizations and functions. The examples used are more concerned with covert action and sabotage than with intelligence collection.

171.   Herzog, Chaim. *The War of Atonement: October 1973.* Boston: Little, Brown and Company, 1975. 300 p.
    Although primarily an operational history, this book is valuable because its author, as Director of Israeli Military Intelligence, analyzes the intelligence failures of his organization.

172.   Stevenson, William. *Zanek: A Chronicle of the Israeli Air Force.* New York: Viking Press, 1971. vi + 344 p. paperback New York and Toronto: Bantam Books, 1971. 338 p.
    This account includes such Israeli intelligence actions as the 1969 capture of a Russian-built search radar from Egypt.

JAPAN

173.   Coox, Alvin D. "Flawed Perception and Its Effect Upon Operational Thinking: The Case of the Japanese Army, 1937-41." *Intelligence and National Security* (5:2), April 1990, p. 239-254.
    Coox describes how the Imperial Japanese Army, like the German Luftwaffe, deliberately ignored intelligence specialists, and were biased by their stereotypes of American weakness.

174.   Deacon, Richard. *Kempei Tai: A History of the Japanese Secret Service.* New York & Toronto: Beaufort Books, Inc., 1983. 306 p.

Deacon concentrates on Japanese human intelligence from the 16th century to the present. However, Chapters 12 and 21 address cryptology, and chapter 16 describes naval intelligence against the U.S.

175.   Sanger, David E.   "Tired of Relying on U.S., Japan Seeks to Expand Its Own Intelligence Efforts." *New York Times* January 2, 1992, p. 6.
In the wake of the 1991 Gulf conflict, the Japan Self-Defense Agency began to build a version of the U.S. Defense Intelligence Agency, oriented on North Korea, the former Soviet Union, and the Arabian Gulf. The Japanese Foreign Ministry followed suit, reportedly frustrated by a lack of analytical capacity.

176.   United States. Strategic Bombing Survey. *Japanese Military and Naval Intelligence (Japanese Intelligence Section G-2.)* Washington, D.C.:   Strategic Bombing Survey, 1946.

KOREA

177.   Bermudez, Joseph S. Jr.   "North Korea's Intelligence Agencies and Infiltration Operations." *Jane's Intelligence Review* (3:6), June 1991, p. 269-277.
A good discussion of North Korean training, organization, and equipment, especially infiltration for espionage/special operations in the Republic of Korea and Japan.

NETHERLANDS

178.   Ausems, Andre. "The 'Bureau Inlichtingen' (Intelligence Service) of the Netherlands Government in London, November 1942-May 1945." *Military Affairs* (45:3), October 1981, pp. 127-132.
Although British Special Operations Executive agents were frequently captured in the Netherlands, the government in exile was much more successful in sending in agents (including the author's father) who gathered military information, assisted allied fliers to escape, etc.

179.   _____.   "The Netherlands Military Intelligence Summaries 1939-1940 and the Defeat in the Blitzkrieg of May 1940." *Military Affairs* (50:4), October 1986, pp. 190-199.
Ausems describes not only the military intelligence estimates that the Dutch developed during the Phoney War, but also the bureaucratic reasons why this information did not result in better preparations for defense against the German invasion.

POLAND

180.   Woytak, Richard A. *On the Border of War and Peace: Polish Intelligence and Diplomacy in 1937-1939 and the Origins of the ULTRA Secret.* East European Monographs No. 49.   New York: Columbia University Press/*East European Quarterly*, 1979. 144 p.
A discussion of Polish intelligence efforts to prepare for and delay the German invasion, describing agent networks in

Germany, Czechoslovakia, and elsewhere.

RUMANIA

181.   Pacepa, Ion M. *Red Horizons: Chronicles of a Communist Spy Chief.* Washington, D.C.: Regnery Gateway, 1987. xvii + 446 p.
    Lt. Gen. Pacepa was head of the Rumanian Departmentul de Informatii Externe (DIE) until his defection to the US in 1978, perhaps the highest Warsaw-Pact intelligence official known to have defected. This work is primarily personal memoirs about the repressive Ceaucescu regime, but includes human intelligence operations in the Middle East, Yugoslavia, and elsewhere.

RUSSIA AND THE SOVIET UNION

182.   Andrew, Christopher and Oleg Gordievsky (eds.) "More 'Instructions From the Center': Top Secret Files on KGB Global Operations, 1975-1985." *Intelligence and National Security* (7:1), January 1992, 130 pp.
    This special edition of *Intelligence and National Security* is devoted to Soviet intelligence documents released after the collapse of the USSR. The subjects discussed range from the GRU/KGB Operation RYAN, a search for indications of the non-existence US preparations for a nuclear first strike (p. 1), to GRU military intelligence collection priorities (p. 14-24.)

183.   Barron, John. *KGB: The Secret Work of Soviet Secret Agents.* Pleasantville, NY: Reader's Digest Press; London: Hoder and Stoughton, 1974. xiv + 462 p.
    Although a popularized account of KGB espionage, this work describes much of its organization and functions, and is useful from a counter intelligence perspective.

184.   _____. *KGB Today: The Hidden Hand.* Pleasant-ville, NY: Reader's Digest Press, 1983; New York: Berkley, 1985. xii + 425 p.
    This sequel is another good journalistic effort, and describes KGB industrial, military, and political espionage as well as forced US documents for disinformation.

185.   Bilof, Edwin G. The Imperial Russian General Staff and China in the Far East 1880-1888: A Study of the Operations of the General Staff. Ph.D. Dissertation, Syracuse University, 1974. University Microfilms No. 75-10.525. 216 p.
    A study of Russian strategic military intelligence during a period of border disputes between imperial Russia and China.

186.   Blackstock, Paul W. *The Secret Road to World War II: Soviet Versus Western Intelligence 1921-1939.* Chicago: Quadrangle Books; Toronto: Burns and MacEachern, Ltd., 1969. 384 p.
    Almost one third of this book is focused on the "Trust," the supposedly anti-Soviet conspiracy inside Russia that was almost certainly a deception operation run by the Cheka. He also claims that the NKVD conspired with the Nazi Sicherheitsdienst to falsely implicate Marshal Tuchachevsky,

initiating the purge of the Red Army 1937-1941.

187.   Deacon, Richard. *A History of the Russian Secret Service.* New York: Taplinger Publishing Co., 1972. ix + 568 p.
      As with his other organizational histories, Deacon emphasizes national-level espionage and counterintelligence, including the Cheka and NKVD. However, a number of passages are relevant to military intelligence, including Chapters 29 (The Anti-NATO Spy Rings) and 35 (Disinformation.)

188.   Glantz, David M. *The Role of Intelligence in Soviet Military Strategy in World War II.* Novato, Ca: Presidio Press, 1990. x + 262 p.
      One of the foremost American experts on the Soviet military considers Soviet operational and strategic intelligence, generally from *Front*/army level upwards. As such, this study is more summarized and generalized than *Soviet Military Intelligence in War* (see below.)

189.   _____. *Soviet Military Intelligence in War.*
London: Frank Cass, 1990. 450 p.
      A review of the theory, organization, and operations of the Red Army's intelligence services during World War II.

190.   _____. "Soviet Operational Intelligence in the Kursk Operation, July 1943." *Intelligence and National Security* (5:1), January 1990, p. 5-49.
      Unlike their German counterparts, Soviet intelligence officers accurately tacked the locations of large enemy reserve forces during the crucial Kursk bulge campaign.

191.   Heilbrunn, Otto. *The Soviet Secret Services.* Westport, Ct: Greenwood Press, 1981. 216 p.

192.   Leonard, Raymond W. "Studying the Kremlin's Secret Soldiers: A Historiographical Essay on the GRU, 1918-1945." *Journal of Military History* (56:3), July 1992, p. 403-421.
      Based on his own doctoral research concerning the GRU in the 1920s and 30s, Leonard provides a skillful overview of trends and unanswered research questions about Soviet military intelligence.

193.   Seaton, Albert. *Stalin As Military Commander.* New York: Praeger Publishers, 1975. 312 p.
      Anyone seeking to understand the Soviet military, including its use and misuse of intelligence during World War II, must take Stalin's personality into consideration.

194.   Suvorov, Viktor. *Inside Soviet Military Intelligence.* New York: Macmillan, 1984; also published as *Soviet Military Intelligence.* London: Hamish Hamilton, 1984. 193 p.
      Primarily concerned with espionage, which was the author's own field of experience. However, Chapter 7, "Operational Intelligence," provides a good overview of both the naval and the military intelligence structure in the Soviet armed forces, and an appendix provides good brief biographies of a number of leaders of Soviet military intelligence.

195.   United States Department of the Army.   Intelligence
Division, General Staff.   *Survey of Soviet Intelligence and
Counter-Intelligence.*   Washington, D.C.:   Department of the
Army, 1947.   162 p.

196.   _____.   U.S. Army Intelligence and Threat Analysis
Center.   *Soviet Army Operations.*   Manual IAG-13-U-78.   Apr,
1978.   358 p.
    One of the best efforts of a flowering of unclassified
U.S. studies on the Soviet armed forces.   In particular,
Chapter 5 (Combat Support Operations) includes sections on
tactical reconnaissance and electronic warfare.

SWITZERLAND

197.   Kimche, Jon.   *Spying for Peace: General Guisan and
Swiss Neutrality.*   London;   Weidenfeld and Nicolson, 1961.
xxii + 169 p.
    The story of Swiss efforts, led by wartime commander Henri
Guisan, to predict and avoid surprise attack during World War
II, and to deal with the agents of both sides who used
Switzerland as a base.   As late as 1943, for example, Guisan
was justifiably concerned that Hitler might trespass on Swiss
territory as part of the German defense of northern Italy.

UNITED STATES

198.   Andregg, Charles H.   *Management of Defense Intelligence.*
Washington, D.C.:   Industrial College of the Armed Forces,
1968.   52 p.
    An instructional text that reviews the post-1945 evolution
of defense intelligence in the United States, focusing on the
creation of the Defense Intelligence Agency (DIA) in 1961.

199.   Bethel, Elizabeth.   "The Military Information Division:
Origin of the Intelligence Division."   *Military Affairs*
(11:1), Spring 1947, p. 17-24.
    Organizational history of the US Army's intelligence
office from 1885 to the 1903 creation of the General Staff.

200.   Bidwell, Bruce W.   *History of the Military Intelligence
Division, Department of the Army General Staff: 1775-1941.*
Frederick, Md: University Publications of America, 1986.   625
p.
    Originally classified Top Secret, this study traces
military intelligence from the 2d Light Dragoons during the
Revolutionary War to an extensive discussion of the intelligence failure at Pearl Harbor.

201.   Bigelow, Michael E.   "Van Deman."   *Military Intelligence*
(16:4)   October-December 1990, p. 38-40.
    A brief biography of Ralph Van Deman (1865-1952), a
founding father of U.S. Army intelligence, especially during
World War I.   See also Ralph Weber (ed.), *The Final Memoranda,*
listed below.

202.   *A Brief History of the G-2 Section, GHQ, SWPA, and*

Affiliated Units. (Tokyo: General Headquarters, Far East Command, 1948) Introduction and 9 vols.
   The internal history of Douglas MacArthur's intelligence structure for Southwest Pacific Area (SWPA) in World War II.

203.   Churchill, Marlborough.   "The Military Intelligence Division, General Staff." in *Journal of the United States Artillery* (54), April 1970, p. 293-315.

204.   Cohen, Victor H.   *Development of the Intelligence Function in the United States Air Force.*   Special Studies Report.   Maxwell Air Force Base, Al: Research Studies Institute, Air University, 1957.

205.   Commission on Organization of the Executive Branch of the Government ("Hoover Commission.")   *Intelligence Activities.* Washington: Government Printing Office, 1955.   76 p.
   Herbert Hoover's commission reviewed the organization and functions of all aspects of the government;   in this case, the bulk of the study was done by Gen. Mark Clark's Task Force in Intelligence Activities.   This book describes briefly the intelligence functions of the CIA, National Security Council, FBI, State Department, and defense intelligence agencies.   In a prescient view of future problems of controlling intelligence,   the   study   recommends   both   a   joint congressional oversight committee and a separate oversight board appointed by the president.

206.   Finnegan, John P.   *Military Intelligence: A Picture History.*   Arlington, Va: U.S. Army Intelligence and Security Command, 1984.   vii + 187.
   The author's commitment to his subject enables him to overcome many of the weaknesses of large-format picture books, providing   a   balanced   look   at   all   aspects   of   U.S.   Army intelligence since the Indian wars.   The photographs and captures explore the often overlooked activities of U.S. counterintelligence in peace and war, as well as imagery intelligence, tactical intelligence, specialized reconnaissance units, and signals intelligence.

207.   Goodman, Paul.   "The Military Intelligence Organization."   *Military Review* (38:12), March 1959, p. 68-72.
   The author, who commanded the 319th Military Intelligence Battalion for over five years, describes divisional and higher intelligence organizations and functions of his time.

208.   Hopple, Gerald W. and Watson, Bruce W. (eds.)   *The Military Intelligence Community.*   Westview Special Studies in Military Affairs.   Boulder, Co: Westview   Press/Praeger Publishing,   1986.   298 p.
   A collection of essays, with historical examples, on American intelligence agencies;   primarily at the strategic level.

209.   Katz, Barry M.   *Foreign Intelligence: Research and Analysis in the Office of Strategic Service 1942-1945.* Cambridge, Ma. and London: Harvard University Press, 1989.   xv + 251 p.

An account of the Research and Analysis Branch, a collection of academics who provided national intelligence analysis on military, economic, political, and other aspects of World War II. As such, this is a useful counterweight to histories of the OSS that focus only on special operations and espionage.

210.   Lardner, George Jr. "In a Changing World, CIA Reorganizing to Do More With Less." *The Washington Post* July 5, 1991, p. A9.
Discusses the entire US national level intelligence structure in the process of reorganizing for the post-Cold War, post-Iraq world. In the process, however, it repeats some of the unfounded criticisms of that structure that arose during the Kuwait-Iraq crisis.

211.   Linn, Brian M. "Intelligence and Low-Intensity Conflict in the Philippine War, 1899-1902." *Intelligence and National Security* (6:1), January 1991, p. 90-114.
The author describes how changes in organization and procedures allowed the U.S. Army to gradually improve its intelligence on the Philippine insurrection. In the process, many of the early American intelligence officers, such as then-Captain Ralph Van Deman, came to the fore.

212.   Lowenthal, Mark W. *U.S. Intelligence: Evolution and Anatomy*. The Washington Papers, No. 105. New York: Praeger, 1984. x + 134 p.
US national-level intelligence history through the early Reagan era, reviewing all intelligence agencies in Washington, but with no description of field tactical intelligence structures.

213.   McCauley, Nathan E. "The Military Intelligence Profession in the U.S. Army." 2 parts. *Military Intelligence* (13:4), October 1987, and (14:1), January 1988, pp. 30-32.
An institutional history of the separate intelligence branch in the army.

214.   McChristian, Joseph A. *The Role of Military Intelligence, 1965-1967.* VIETNAM STUDIES. Washington, D.C.: Department of the Army, 1974. 182 p.
The author was the Assistant Chief of Staff for Intelligence in Headquarters, Military Assistance Command, Vietnam, during the period in question. His account of the first war in which the U.S. Army had a separate intelligence branch is especially useful for the problems involved in conducting combined intelligence with the Vietnamese.

215.   Miller, Nathan. *Spying for America: The Hidden History of U.S. Intelligence.* New York: Paragon House, 1989. 482 p.
As its title implies, this study is primarily concerned with espionage and counterespionage. Miller divides his history into three parts: The Spy as Amateur (American Revolution through the Civil War), The Spy as Professional (1885-1945), and The Spy as Bureaucrat (1945 through 1988.)

216.   Nelson, Otto L., Jr. *National Security and the General*

Staff: A Study of Organization and Administration.
Washington, D.C.:   Infantry Journal Press, 1946.   vi + 608 p.
    This classic on the development of the U.S. General and
Joint Staff structure includes sections on the evolution of
intelligence staff elements.

217.   Parish, John C.   "Intelligence Work at First Army
Headquarters."   *The Historical Outlook* (11:6), June, 1921, pp.
213-217. (MHI)
    During World War I, Parish was a captain in the intel-
ligence section of the 1st U.S. Army, American Expeditionary
Force, and later in 8th U.S. Corps.   Significant detail on the
training and procedures of tactical intelligence officers.

218.   Powe, Marc B.   "American Military Intelligence Comes of
Age: A Sketch of a Man and His Times."   *Military Review*
(55:12), December 1975, pp. 17-30.
    A good brief biography of Ralph H. Van Deman, one of the
founders of American military intelligence.

219.   _____.   The Emergence of the War Department
Intelligence Agency, 1885-1918.   M.A. Thesis, Kansas State
University, 1974.   xii + 146 p. (MHI)   Reproduced by *Military
Affairs.*
    An excellent study, with Chapter One tracing its origins
from the Revolution to the Civil War.

220.   _____.   "Which Way for Tactical Intelligence After
Vietnam?"   *Military Review* (54:9), September 1974, p. 48-56.
    Maj. Powe concludes that U.S. military intelligence
performed better in its first war as a separate branch than it
had in previous wars, but he highlights the familiar problem of
commanders reluctant to trust their S2s, and the need for
intelligence organizations to support higher level commands.

221.   Powe, Marc B. and Wilson, E. E.   *The Evolution of
American Military Intelligence.*   Fort Huachuca, Az: U.S. Army
Intelligence Center and School, 1973.   148 p.

222.   Richelson, Jeffrey T.   *The U.S. Intelligence Community.*
2d ed.   [New York:]   Ballinger Publishing Co. and Harper
Collins, 1989.   483 p.
    A detailed discussion of U.S. national-level intelligence
organizations, including the structure of service intelligence
units.

223.   "United States Air Force Security Service: A Major Air
Command."   *Air Force Magazine* May, 1973, p. 98-99.
    The organization and functions of a primary USAF
intelligence element.

224.   U.S. Army.   Far East Command.   Military Intelligence
Section.   *A Brief History of the G-2 Section, GHQ, Southwest
Pacific Area and Affiliated Units.*   10 vols. Tokyo: Far East
Command, 1948.

225.   U.S. Army.   Intelligence and Security Command.   *INSCOM
and Its Heritage: An Organizational History of the Command and*

62   Military Intelligence

Its Units. Arlington Hall, Va: U.S.A.INSCOM, 1985. mimeographed, 148 p.
Primarily lineage, honors, and crests of intelligence units, but pp. 5-13 describe the history of the Counter Intelligence Corps and the Army Security Agency. (MHI)

226.   U.S. Army. Army Security Agency. *The Origin and Development of the Army Security Agency, 1917-1947.* Laguna Hills, Ca: Aegean Park Press, 1978. 51 p.
A reproduction of a declassified 1948 lecture, tracing U.S. Army signals intelligence organization from the Cipher Branch (MI-8) of World War I to the Army Security Agency in 1945.

227.   U.S. Forces, European Theater, General Board. G2 Section Study No. 12, "Military Intelligence Service in the European Theater of Operations - Procurement, Training, Supply, Administration, and Utilization of Intelligence Personnel." Typescript, c. 1946.

228.   _____. G2 Section Study No. 14, Organization and Operation of the Theater Intelligence Service in the European Theater of Operations." Typescript, c. 1946.

229.   U.S. War Department. Military Intelligence Division. *Digest of Memoranda, Military Intelligence Division, Nos. 1 to 81; March 19,1918 to September 15, 1918.* Washington, D.C.: Military Intelligence Division, 1918. mimeographed, 82 p.
The internal administrative memoranda of an organization undergoing phenomenal expansion during World War I. (MHI)

230.   _____. "The Military Intelligence Division, War Department General Staff." Washington, D.C.: Military Intelligence Division, 1924. mimeographed, 22 p.
The organization and training of the division is described for reserve intelligence officers.

231.   _____. *United States Military Intelligence, 1917-1927.* New York and London: Garland Publishing, Inc., 1978. 30 vols.
A reproduction of weekly and (where available) daily intelligence summaries produced by the War Department Military Intelligence Division during this period. The quality of these reports varies widely, often being merely an assembly of newspaper reports.

232.   _____. *Work and Activities of the Military Intelligence Division, General Staff.* Washington, D.C.: Military Intelligence Division, 1 October 1918. 131 p.
Organization and functions of intelligence, including counter intelligence, air service, censorship, etc.

233.   Volkman, Ernest and Baggett, Blaine. *Secret Intelligence: The Inside Story of America's Espionage Empire.* New York: Doubleday, 1989. 266 p.
A journalistic account of American national and military intelligence organizations since 1917, leading to the misuse of such organizations in special operations such as the Iranian

hostage rescue, the "Iran-Contra Affair," etc.

234.   Weber, Ralph E. (ed.) *The Final Memoranda: Major General Ralph H. Van Deman, USA Ret. 1865-1952. Father of U.S. Military Intelligence.* Wilmington, De: Scholarly Resources, Inc, 1988.
    A set of five extended essays by Van Deman, produced in 1916 and in 1949-51, that provide valuable background on American military intelligence 1885-1918.

VIET NAM

235.   Lung, Hoang Ngoc. *Intelligence.* Indochina Monograph Series.   Washington, D.C.:   U.S. Army Center of Military History, 1982. x + 243 p.
    An extensive analysis of the Republic of Viet Nam's proliferating intelligence agencies, many of which were redundant.   A short chapter describes North Vietnamese intelligence.

3

Tactical Intelligence

Reconnaissance and Surveillance

236.   Applegate, Rex. *Scouting and Patrolling: Ground Reconnaissance Principles and Training.* Boulder, Co.: Paladin Press, 1980. x + 117 p.
      Applegate originally taught these techniques at the US Army Intelligence Training Center, Camp Ritchie, Md, between 1942 and 1945, and drafted this work as an Army field manual that was never published. It discusses camouflage, movement, and reconnaissance with the accumulated experience of the US Army in World War II. The evolution of such techniques can be traced by comparing this work with Armstrong's *Fieldcraft, Sniping and Intelligence* (item 237) for World War I and England's *Long-Range Patrol Operations* (item 242) for Vietnam.

237.   Armstrong, Nevill A. D. *Fieldcraft, Sniping and Intelligence.* Aldershot: Gale and Polden Ltd., [1940]. Reprinted Boulder, Co: Paladin Press, no date. xv + 223 p.
      The author was chief reconnaissance officer of the Canadian Army in World War I and an instructor in a variety of sniper and scout schools. In addition to a variety of instructions on how ground scouts should operate, his introduction and Chapter 17 both deal with reconnaissance and intelligence at the battalion level of British Imperial forces in trench warfare.

238.   Bursell, William R. "American Sound Ranging in Four Wars." *Field Artillery Journal.* (49:6), November-December 1989, pp. 53-55.
      A description of this important target acquisition technique from World War I through Vietnam.

239.   Callwell, Charles E. *Small Wars: A Tactical Textbook for Imperial Soldiers.* Novato, Ca: Presidio Press; London: Greenhill Books, 1990. x + 559 p.
      First published in 1896, *Small Wars* is a classic study of counterinsurgency, widely used by the British Army even in the 1930s. Chapter IV discusses the problems of reconnaissance,

terrain intelligence, and human intelligence in operations against native forces.

240.   Carne, Daphne. *The Eyes of the Few.* London: Macmillan, 1960. 238 p.
    Military Radar.

241.   Dickson, Paul. *The Electronic Battlefield.* Bloomington, Ind. and London: Indiana University Press, 1976. 244 p.
    Despite its title, this is an account of the development of unattended sensors and Remotely Piloted Vehicles (RPVs) during and since the Vietnam conflict.

242.   England, James W. *Long-Range Patrol Operations: Reconnaissance, Combat, and Special Operations.* Boulder, Co: Paladin Press, 1987. vii + 319 p.
    Doctrine, organization, and procedures for a proposed long range patrol battalion, plus the practical matters of everything from hand signals to weapons and communications. This book is based on, although it does not describe, the Vietnam experience of long-range reconnaissance. See the comment under Applegate's *Scouting and Patrolling* (item 236, above).

243.   Galeotti, Mark. "Razvedchiki - Have the Reconnaissance Troops Regained Their Edge?" *Jane's Soviet Intelligence Review* (2:1), November 1990, p. 490-492.
    Soviet experience in Afghanistan during the 1980s forced them to revive the highly-trained, independent reconnaissance troops used effectively in the later stages of World War II.

244.   Goldsmith, Martin and James Hodges. *Applying the National Training Center Experience: Tactical Reconnaissance.* Santa Monica, Ca: RAND Corporation, 1987. xii + 132 p. RAND Note number N-2628-A (unclassified.)
    During the 1980s, the National Training Center at Ft. Irwin California was the primary field test for US Army mechanized units based inside the US. One of the recurring shortcomings of visiting units was in tactical reconnaissance and counter-reconnaissance. This study reviewed the subject, and concluded that doctrine, training, and equipment for reconnaissance and scout units were all inadequate.

245.   Gray, John S. *Centennial Campaign: The Sioux War of 1876.* Norman, Ok, and London: University of Oklahoma Press, 1988; originally published by The Old Army Press, 1976. 380 p.
    A refreshingly-original review of all aspects of the Little Bighorn Campaign, including especially the problems of tactical reconnaissance and intelligence experienced by the U.S. commanders seeking to locate and evaluate their opponents.

246.   Grayson, Eugene H. "Compromise! Compromise! Compromise!" *U.S. Army Aviation Digest* (18:5), May 1972, pp. 16-17, 24-25.
    A warning about the loss of surprise caused by excessive aerial reconnaissance of proposed landing zones prior to an operation in Vietnam.

247.   Haley, J. Frederick.   "Reconnaissance at Tarawa Atoll."
Marine Corps Gazette (64) Nov 1980, p. 51-55.
    Platoon-sized reconnaissance landings in November 1943,
prior to the main assault.

248.   Henderson, David.   *The Art of Reconnaissance.*   3d Ed.
London: John Murray, 1914. viii + 197 p.
    This essay addresses all forms of reconnaissance and
surveillance, including aerial scouts.

249.   Hunbedt, T.N.   "Radar in a Ground Role."   *Military
Review* (27:8), November 1947, pp. 36-40.
    The use of an SCR-564 antiaircraft radar in a ground role
in the U.S. XV Corps, 1944-45.

250.   Ind, Allison.   *Allied Intelligence Bureau: Our Secret
Weapon in the War Against Japan.*   New York: David McKay Co.,
1958. x + 305 p.
    An account of the intelligence/unconventional warfare unit
that conducted over 400 missions for MacArthur's G2, by an
intelligence staff officer.

251.   Kinnard, Harry W.O.   "Narrowing the Combat Intelligence
Gap with STANO [Surveillance, Target Acquisition, and Night
Observation] Equipment" in *Army* (19:8), August 1969, p. 22-26.
    The commander of the U.S. Combat Developments Command
describes various target acquisition equipment developed for
Vietnam, including an early mention of the TACFIRE artillery
information system.

252.   McKenney, Henry J.   *Exercises for Systematic Scout
Instruction.*   Menosha, Wisc: George Banta Publishing Co.,
1916. 146 p.
    This pocket guide is a distillation of horse cavalry
reconnaissance training, including timeless principles of
scouting and arcane arts such as reading horse tracks.

253.   *Modern Reconnaissance: A Collection of Articles from
the Cavalry Journal.*   Harrisburg, Pa: Military Service
Publishing Co., 1944. 230 p.
    A collection of articles on World War II reconnaissance,
both ground and air, by US, Soviet, German, and Japanese units.
The US articles lean heavily on examples from the North African
campaign of 1942-43.

254.   Moore, Michael L.   *A Review of Search and Reconnaissance
Theory Literature.*   Detroit, Mi: Management Information
Services, c. 1975. 100 p.
    The Office of Naval Research had contracted for a review
of mathematical models for tactical intelligence and
reconnaissance techniques. This first report, which is typical
of many such contracted studies done for the Defense Department
since 1961, is concerned with the theory of search and target
acquisition, rather than the actual procedures involved.

255.   Page, Robert M.   *The Origin of Radar.*   Garden City, NY:
Anchor Books, 1962. 296 p.

256.   "Reconnaissance and Surveillance." *DATA, Magazine of Military Research and Development* (11:4), April 1966, entire issue.

257.   Research Program on the USSR.   "Soviet Military Intelligence: Two Sketches." Trans. by Nina Whiting, edited by David I. Goldstein.   New York: Research Program on the USSR, 1952. Mimeographed, 21 p. (MHI)
    The anonymous author was assigned by the Red Army to organize subversion during the 1941 German invasion of the Soviet Union.   An anecdotal account of the training of reconnaissance scouts during that war.

258.   Schreyach, Jon C.   "Fire Support for Deep Operations." *Military Review* (69:8), August 1989, p. 29-36.
    Includes much on the target acquisition of deep targets for AirLand Battle.

259.   Simonian, Rair G. and Sergei V. Girshin.   *Tactical Reconnaissance: A Soviet View.*   Trans. by the Canadian Department of State.   Reprinted in the U.S. Air Force series *Soviet Military Thought*, No. 23. Washington, D.C.: Department of the Air Force/U.S. Government Printing Office, 1990. ix + 199 p.

260.   Simpson, C.N. *The Eyes and Ears of the Artillery: Hints on the Education and Training of Artillery Observation Patrols and Ground Scouts.* London: Hugh Rees, Ltd., 1905. 87 p.
    This is a well-written discussion of reconnaissance patrolling, by a colonel in the Royal Field Artillery.

261.   Stevens, Philip H.   *Search Out the Land: A History of American Military Scouts.* Chicago and New York: Rand McNally & Co, 1969. 192 p.
    A brief description of ground reconnaissance units from Rogers' Rangers in the French and Indian War through Long Range Reconnaissance Patrols (LRRPs) in Vietnam.   This survey is somewhat lacking in details.

262.   Strutton, Bill and Michael Pearson. *The Secret Invaders.* London: Hodder and Stoughton, 1958. 287 p.
    The British Combined Operations Pilotage Parties sent swimmers to reconnoiter beach geography and defenses prior to major landings in World War II.

263.   Trainor, B. E.   "Recon Operations in Southeast Asia, 1970-1971." *Marine Corps Gazette* (70) May 1986, pp. 54, 59.
    Lt. Gen. Trainor describes organization and functions of Marine reconnaissance units.

264.   Verner, Willoughby.   *Rapid Field-Sketching and Reconnaissance.* London; W.H. Allen and Co., 1889. 88 p.
    This is a memoir of a bygone age, when officers had to conduct terrain reconnaissance on horseback.

265.   Wagner, Arthur L.   *The Service of Security and Information.*   5th Ed.   Kansas City, Mo: Hudson-Kimberly Publishing; London: W.H. Allen and Co., 1896. 291 p.

A classic text by one of the great military instructors of the Ft. Leavenworth schools. The focus is on cavalry security, screening, and advance and rear guards.

266. Williams, R. C., Jr. "Amphibious Scouts and Raiders." *Military Affairs* (13:3), Fall 1949, p. 150-157.
Coast watchers, scouts, Underwater Demolition Teams, and other reconnaissance and surveillance elements of World War II.

Naval Tactical Intelligence

267. Blair, Clay Jr. *Silent Victory: The U.S. Submarine War Against Japan.* Philadelphia and New York: J.B. Lippincott Co., 1975. 1072 pp.
Although Blair's primary focus is on the submarine operations, there are good examples of how intercept and other intelligence sources were used to guide those operations.

268. Bywater, Hector C. and Hubert C. Ferraby. *Strange Intelligence: Memoirs of Naval Secret Service.* London: Constable and Co., 1931. ix + 299 p.
These memoirs claim perhaps too much credit for British naval intelligence before and during World War I. However, the authors provide some interesting arguments about U-boat tracking, human intelligence, counterintelligence, anti-sabotage operations, and other aspects.

269. Daniel, Donald C. *Anti-Submarine Warfare and Superpower Strategic Stability.* London: Macmillan Press, Ltd., 1986; Urbana and Chicago, Ill: University of Illinois Press, 1986. xii + 222 p.
Chapter 5 (pp. 117-143) describes the development of U.S. anti-submarine warfare systems since 1945. This book is more operationally-oriented, and less technical, than Tom Stefanick, *Strategic Antisubmarine Warfare and Naval Strategy,* listed below.

270. Ewing, Alfred W. *The Man of Room 40: The Life of Alfred Ewing.* London: Hutchinson, 1939.

271. Farrago, Ladislas. *The Tenth Fleet.* New York: Ivan Obolensky, 1962, and Richardson and Steirman, 1986. 366 p.
History of the headquarters established to predict and control German U-boat activity during World War II.

272. Furer, Julius A. *Administration of the Navy Department in World War II.* Washington, D.C.: Government Printing Office, 1959.
P. 119-120, 156-162 discuss the Combat Intelligence Division and Tenth Fleet.

273. Garwin, Richard L. "Antisubmarine Warfare and National Security." *Scientific American* (227), July 1972, p. 14-25.

274. Grant, Robert M. *U-Boat Intelligence, 1914-1918.* London: Putnam, 1969. 192 p.
British naval intelligence pioneered techniques of both

signals intelligence and prisoner interrogation, techniques that were put to great use during the following World War.

275.   Goulter, Christina.   "The Role of Intelligence in Coastal Command's Anti-Shipping Campaign, 1940-45." *Intelligence & National Security* (5:1), January 1990, p. 84-109.
    The process by which British analysts coordinated various collection means to identify and interdict German shipping between Scandinavia and the Dutch and North German ports.

276.   Hoy, Hugh C.   *40 O.B.: Or How the War Was Won.* London: Hutchinson, 1932.
    The author was the secretary for the British Director of Naval Intelligence, Admiral Sir William Hall, during World War I. As such, he was privy to the signals and other intelligence used for naval operations.

277.   James, Sir William M.   *The Codebreakers of Room 40: The Story of Admiral Sir William Hall.* New York: St. Martin's Press, 1956. Originally published as *The Eyes of the Navy: A Biographical Study of Admiral Sir William Hall.* London: 1955. 212 p.
    Another account of British naval intelligence during World War I, including the evolution of analysis as opposed to simply passing raw information to decision-makers.

278.   *Japanese Naval Vessels of World War II as seen by U.S. Naval Intelligence.*   Intro. by A.D. Baker III.   Annapolis: Naval Institute Press, 1987.

279.   McGinty, Patrick E.   Intelligence and the Spanish-American War. Ph.D. dissertation, Georgetown University, 1983. 2 vols, totalling 470 p.
    Commander McGinty addresses both military and naval intelligence for Cuba and the Philippines during the 1989 war, concluding that intelligence was important for locating Admiral Camara's squadron, but otherwise used sporadically.

280.   McLachlan, Donald.   "Naval Intelligence in the Second World War." *Journal of the Royal United Service Institution* (112), August 1957, p. 159-162.

281.   _____.   *Room 39: A Study in Naval Intelligence.* New York: Athenium; London: Weidenfeld and Nicolson, 1968. 379 p.

282.   Muir, Malcolm Jr.   "Rearming in a Vacuum: United States Navy Intelligence and the Japanese Capital Ship Threat, 1936-1945." *Journal of Military History* (54:4), October 1990, p. 473-485.
    An excellent discussion of the general failure of U.S. intelligence to obtain information about the *Yamato* class of Japanese super battleships. Japanese security was so effective that the U.S. consistently designed its own battleships to fight only 16 inch naval guns, whereas the *Yamato* class was actually equipped with 18.1 inch guns, and armor to match.

283. O'Connell, Jerome A. "Radar and the U-boat." *U.S. Naval Institute Proceedings* (89), 1963, p. 53-65.

284. Roskill, S.W. *The Secret Capture*. London: Collins, 1959. 156 p.
In May 1941 the Royal Navy captured German U-Boat 110, providing considerable intelligence through its documents and equipment.

285. Seagraves, R.W.A. "NILO-the Naval Intelligence Liaison Officer in Vietnam." *U.S. Naval Institute Proceedings* (94:12), December 1968, p. 145-146.
The author describes a network of naval intelligence officers along coastal or inland waterways, normally located with Special Forces or other U.S. Army elements.

286. Stefanick, Tom. *Strategic Antisubmarine Warfare and Naval Strategy*. Institute for Defense and Disarmament Studies. Lexington, Ma: Lexington Books/D.C. Heath, 1987. xxiv + 390 pp.
A highly-technical discussion of the acoustic and other means of detecting submarines. For a more operational and functional approach, see Donald C. Daniel, *Anti-Submarine Warfare and Superpower Strategic Stability,* listed above.

287. Terrell, Edward. *Admiralty Brief: The Story of Inventions That Contributed to Victory in the Battle of the Atlantic*. London: Harrap, 1958. 240 p.

288. Tolley, Kemp. *The Cruise of the Lanikai*. Annapolis: U.S. Naval Institute, 1973. 356 p.
In late 1941, three windjammers with minimal armament and crews were commissioned by the U.S. Navy to observe Japanese movements off the Chinese coast. Rear Admiral Tolley commanded one of these vessels, eventually bringing it out of the Philippines during the Japanese invasion. He argues that the entire operation may have been intended to provoke the Japanese into sinking one of the ships, thereby creating a pretext for war.

289. _____. "The Strange Assignment of USS Lanikai." *U.S. Naval Institute Proceedings* (88:9), September 1962, p. 70-83.
An early account of Tolley's efforts to sail the *Lanikai* out of the Philippines.

290. Waddington, Conrad H. *OR in World War II: Operational Research Against the U-boat*. London: Elek, 1973. 253 p.

291. Wells, Anthony R. Studies in British Naval Intelligence, 1880-1945. University of London Ph.D. dissertation (War Studies), 1972.

Ground Tactical Intelligence and Order of Battle

292. Armor, Marshal H., Jr. "Where Will It Hurt the Most?" *Military Review* (35:7), October 1955, p. 37-44.

Armor argues that the format for tactical intelligence estimates should be revised to emphasize enemy vulnerabilities, in order to assist commanders in planning offensive operations.

293.   Baldwin, Hanson W. "Battlefield Intelligence." *Combat Forces* (3), February 1953, p. 30-41.

294.   Behrendt, Hans-Otto. *Rommel's Intelligence in the Desert Campaign 1941-1943.* London: William Kimber, 1985. 256 p.
    One of Rommel's intelligence staff officers describes the practicalities of tactical intelligence, using air reconnaissance, captured documents, prisoner interrogation, and tactical signals intercept. A rare glimpse at German practical intelligence.

295.   Bigelow, Michael E. "Disaster Along the Ch'ongch'on: Intelligence Breakdown in Korea." *Military Intelligence* (18:3), July-September 1992, p. 11-16.
    The tacical intelligence system in Korea in 1950 had little or no useful signals intelligence, relying instead on prisoner of war interrogation and aerial photography. Since no imagery or human intelligence collection was permitted inside Chinese Manchuria, the Eighth Army had difficulty identifying the scope of Chinese intervention.

296.   Campbell, Douglas A. and Robert W. McKinney. "Predictive Intelligence: An Old Lesson Unlearned." *Military Review* (70:8), Aug 1990, p. 50-58.
    The authors argue persuasively against the current U.S. Army doctrinal tendency to seek to predict enemy intentions rather than to describe enemy capabilities. In the process, they trace the evolution of this issue in U.S. doctrine since 1940, with extensive discussion of investigations conducted at the end of World War II.

297.   "Certain Aspects of Operational Intelligence Reconnaissance [Razvedka]." *Journal of Soviet Military Studies* (2:2) June 1989, pp. 288-303.
    A highly-critical account of *Front* (i.e., Army Group) level intelligence in the Red Army at the time of the Stalingrad campaign (November-December 1942). This Soviet study was originally written as part of a series of practical lessons published by the Soviets during World War II; as such it provides a rare insight into the detailed functioning of Soviet military intelligence.

298.   Chan, Won-Loy. *Burma: The Untold Story.* Novato, Ca: Presidio Press, 1986. xi + 138 p.
    Then-Captain Chan was an interrogator and tactical intelligence officer for Stillwell in the Myitkyina campaign and other Burmese actions of World War II.

299.   Chandler, Stedman and Robert W. Robb. *Front-Line Intelligence.* Washington, D.C.: Infantry Journal Press, 1946. 183 p.
    Practical methods for combat intelligence, based on Col. Robert S. Allen's instructions for intelligence officers in 3d

U.S. Army during World War II.

300.   Duncan, Harry N.   "Combat Intelligence for Modern War."
Army Information Digest   June 1962, p. 24-31.

301.   Furse, George A.   *Information in War: Its Acquisition
and Transmission.*   London: William Clowes and Sons, Ltd.,
1895.   324 p.
     A discussion of the organization and functions of a
tactical intelligence staff in both peace and war, including
the training and use of cavalry and patrols, spies, interrogation, etc.

302.   Glass, Robert R. and Phillip B. Davidson.   *Intelligence
Is For Commanders.*   Harrisburg, Pa: Military Service
Publishing Co., 1948.   189 p.
     Two Command and General Staff College instructors provide
a useful summary of principles, procedures, and reports used
for American tactical intelligence at the time, with actual
examples from World War II.

303.   Halloran, Bernard F.   "Soviet Armor Comes to Vietnam--A
Surprise That Needn't Have Been."   *Army* (22:8), August 1972, p.
18-23.
     The author is extremely critical of intelligence agencies'
failure to disseminate tactical information to subordinate
headquarters.

304.   Heymont, Irving.   *Combat Intelligence in Modern Warfare.*
Harrisburg, Pa: Stackpole Co., 1960, 1961.   244 p.
     A   textbook   approach   to   U.S.   tactical   intelligence
collection and reports, using examples from World War II.

305.   _____.   "Commander's Intelligence Priorities."
Military Review (38:11), February 1959, p. 40-44.
     Heymont argues that critical intelligence priorities for
collection should be developed to coincide with phases of
friendly operations--a commander needs different information in
the planning phase than he may need later in execution.

306.   "Intelligence Operations Previous to the Battle of July
15, 1918."   *Instructors' Summary of Military Articles.*
[Predecessor of *Military Review*], January-March 1925, p. 5.

307.   Jackson, Rhees.   *The Service of Military Intelligence.*
Ft. Leavenworth, Ks: 1913.   63 p.

308.   Jones, Lawrence M.   "G2:   Key to Nuclear Targets."
Military Review (43:8), August 1963, p. 66-71.
     An early proposal for integrated G2/G3 operations for
targeting and maneuver.

309.   Kahn, David.   "An Intelligence Case History: The
Defense of Osuga, 1942."   *Aerospace Historian* (28:4) December
1981, pp. 242-252.
     A rare examination, looking at German tactical intel-
ligence as it identified and predicted a Soviet offensive
against the 9th Army in November 1942.

310.   Koch, Oscar W. with Robert G. Hayes. *G-2: Intelligence for Patton.* Philadelphia, Pa: Army Times/Whitmore Publishing Co., 1971. xvi + 267 p.
   Memoirs of George Patton's 3d Army staff, by his intelligence officer. Chapter 12 (pp. 133-149) describes the practical functions of tactical intelligence in 3d Army.

311.   Lehn, Major. "Intelligence Under Nuclear Conditions." *Military Review* (43:8), August 1963, p. 72-79.
   Translated from "Le Renseignement en Ambiance Atomique," *Revue Militaire d'Information,* October 1962. This is a good example of the planning involved for intelligence collection to find dispersed or deep targets on a nuclear battlefield.

312.   Lossky, Andrew. "Estimates of Enemy Strength." *Military Review* (27:5), August 1947, pp. 20-25.
   A former member of the G2 Order of Battle team in II U.S. Corps describes the methods of that team in North Africa, Sicily, and Italy, with special emphasis on POW reports and personnel strength estimation.

313.   MacDonald, Charles B. "The Decision to Launch 'Operation MARKET-GARDEN.'" in Kent R. Greenfield (ed.) *Command Decisions.* Washington, D.C.: Office of the Chief of Military History, 1960. p. 429-442.

314.   Mullen, R.C. Evolution of the Intelligence Function at Division Level From 1903 to 1945. U.S. Army Command and General Staff College Master's thesis (Military Art & Science), 1967.

315.   "Oak Leaf." (pseud.) "A Look at G-2." *Infantry Journal* (58), April 1946, p. 19-21.

316.   Pettee, G.S. "Faults and Errors [of Intelligence] in World War II." *Infantry Journal* (59), October 1946, p. 27-34.

317.   Phillips, C.E. Lucas. *The Greatest Raid of All.* Boston: Little, Brown and Co, 1960. 270 p.
   This history of the raid on St. Nazaire in March 1942 includes effective use of geographic and tactical intelligence.

318.   Popplewell, Richard. "British Intelligence in Mesopotamia, 1914-16." *Intelligence and National Security* (5:2), April 1990, p. 139-172.
   An excellent review of the tactical and operational intelligence problems of the British expedition that led to the disaster of Kut; this essay not only reviews the various intelligence sources and organization of the British, but highlights the difficulty of bridging the gap between tactical reconnaissance and strategic intelligence.

319.   Quirk, Richard J. "Seeking a Theory of Tactical Intelligence to Support the AirLand Battle." Ft. Leavenworth, Ks.: School of Advanced Military Studies, U.S. Army Command and General Staff College, 1985. 47 p.
   This study focuses on the classic distinction between predictive/intentions vs. descriptive/capabilities approaches

to tactical intelligence.   He argues correctly that staff planning demands prediction on the part of intelligence analysts,   which in turn can obscure the complex, uncertain reality of the situation from commanders.

320.   Rosello, Victor M.   "Operation JUST CAUSE: The Divisional MI Battalion, the Nonlinear Battlefield, and AirLand Operations – Future."   *Military Intelligence*   (17:3),   July-September 1991.   p. 28-31.
Rosello was the operations officer for the 313th Military Intelligence Battalion (Combat Electronic Warfare and Intelligence) during the Panama invasion of December 1989.   He accurately describes many of the problems of this organization in providing tactical intelligence, especially the difficulty of communicating over long distances with low power radios, and the relative scarcity of counter-intelligence and interrogation personnel in the J/L/S series CEWI battalion.   However, the 313th's task organization to support 82d Airborne Division assaults,   with most of the battalion broken up into three company teams in direct support of the maneuver brigades, was an exceptional case;   doctrinal employment of CEWI units in support of mechanized and armored divisions was much more centralized.

321.   Schemmer, Benjamin F.   *The Raid.*   New York: Harper and Row, 1976.   326 p.
A journalist's analysis of the failed American effort to free prisoners held at Son Tay, North Vietnam, in November 1970. This includes the organizational obstacles that allowed the raid to proceed when some analysts knew that the prisoners had been moved out of Son Tay because of flooding.

322.   Schopper, J.B.   Collection and Processing of Combat Intelligence as Performed by the U.S. Army During Operations in Northern Europe.   U.S. Army Command and General Staff College Master's thesis (Military Art & Science), 1964.

323.   Schwien, Edwin E.   *Combat Intelligence: Its Acquisition and Transmission.*   Washington, D.C.:   The Infantry Journal, Inc., 1936.   125 p.
Major Schwein,   a Command and General Staff College instructor on this subject, provides actual and hypothetical examples in immense detail.

324.   Smith, E.D.   "Why Was the Monastery at Cassino Bombed?"   *Army Quarterly*   (118), July 1969, p. 220-224.

325.   Stewart, John F. Jr.   "Operation Desert Storm – The Military Intelligence Story: A View from the G-2 3d U.S. Army."   Riyadh, Saudi Arabia: typescript, April 1991.   39 p.
Then-Brig. Gen. Stewart provides an immediate after-action report on the organization and functioning of U.S. Army intelligence during the 1991 Gulf conflict. His account of the difficulties of bomb damage assessment is excellent, as is his analysis of the common themes of the 1983 intervention in Grenada, the 1989 invasion of Panama, and the Gulf conflict.

326.   "A Study of The Internal Functioning of a Second Bureau in Campaign." *Instructors' Summary of Military Articles* [Predecessor of *Military Review*], January-March 1924, p. 57.

327.   Sweeney, Walter C. *Military Intelligence: A New Weapon in War.* NY: Frederick A. Stokes, 1924. viii + 259 p.
    The author was one of the first fully-trained staff officers in the U.S. Army, and as such served as the executive officer for the G2 (intelligence) staff of the American Expeditionary Force during World War I. In addition to discussing all aspects of intelligence organization and analysis, he describes the development of U.S. intelligence during the war (Chapter 5, pp. 86-119)

328.   Thomas, Shipley. *S-2 In Action.* Harrisburg, Pa: Military Service Publishing Co., 1940. 128 p.
    Practical rules for tactical intelligence, by the S2 (intelligence staff officer) of 26th Infantry Regiment, 1st Division, American Expeditionary Force in World War I.

329.   Tobler, Douglas H. *Intelligence in the Desert: The Recollections and Reflections of a Brigade Intelligence Officer.* Gold Bridge, Br. Columbia: by the author, 1978. 85 p.
    Memoirs of a British intelligence officer in North Africa during World War II.

330.   Townsend, Elias C. *Risks: The Key To Combat Intelligence.* Harrisburg, Pa: Military Service Publishing Co., 1955. 82 p.
    Col. Townsend focuses on the recurring problems of tactical intelligence analysis, advocating that it be simplified to identify enemy location and strength, because "Intelligence officers cannot read the future" (2-3), and should leave the actual estimate to the commander. An excellent discussion, based on American experience in World War II and Korea.

331.   U.S. Department of the Army. Field Manual 30-5, *Intelligence.* Washington, D.C.: Department of the Army, October 1973. Approx. 200 p.
    The basic doctrinal manual, since superseded, that explains the proven procedures for ground tactical intelligence.

332.   U.S. War Department, Military Intelligence Division, General Staff. *Provisional Combat Intelligence Manual.* Washington, D.C.: Military Intelligence Division, October 15, 1918. 111 p.
    A detailed description of World War I American intelligence and reconnaissance organization at every level. The subjects included, such as training to improve visual acuity for target acquisition, illustrate both the nature of trench warfare and the low level of knowledge of the expanded American Army.

333.   U.S. War Department. V Corps. "Organization and Operation of a Corps G-2 Section in Combat: V Corps - ETO; D-

Day 1944 to V-E Day 1945." Fort Riley, KS: U.S. Army Intelligence School, 1946. Typescript, 59 p.

This study provides superb detail concerning the actual operations and standard procedures of a corps intelligence section during World War II. In addition to the G2 section itself, this work describes the functions of all the teams attached to that section (interrogation, imagery interpretation, translators, etc.), with the sole exception of tactical signals intelligence.

334.   Willoughby, Charles A. and Chamberlain, John. *MacArthur: 1941-1951.* New York: McGraw-Hill, 1954. xiii + 441 p.

General Willoughby was MacArthur's G2 throughout World War II and Korea, and here provides the intelligence context for MacArthur's decisions. However, the account includes no discussion of MAGIC signals intelligence.

Ground Order of Battle in Vietnam

(Editor's Note: A former order of battle analyst of the Central Intelligence Agency, Samuel Adams, claimed that his extremely high estimate of enemy strength was deliberately suppressed by Gen. William C. Westmoreland and other American officials. This allegation of "the uncounted enemy" was the basis for a Columbia Broadcasting System television show broadcast on January 23, 1982, a show that generated enormous controversy and a lawsuit by Gen. Westmoreland. Much of the controversy was in fact concerned not with order of battle intelligence but rather with questionable journalistic ethics. However, the numerous publications on this issue deserve a special section in this bibliography. Other studies of tactical intelligence in Vietnam have also been included here.)

335.   Adler, Renata. *Reckless Disregard.* New York: Alfred A. Knopf, 1986. 243 p.

A reasoned analysis of the 1982 CBS news report that alleged a deliberate American effort to suppress intelligence estimates of North Vietnamese and Viet Cong troop strength. Adler describes how the report itself was distorted to prove the thesis of CIA analyst Samuel Adams, and then discusses the legitimate difference of opinion between Adams and other analysts, with the latter using far more sources and methods to confirm their estimates.

336.   Benjamin, Burton. *The CBS Benjamin Report: "The Uncounted Enemy, a Vietnam Deception:" An Examination Broadcast 23 January 1982.* Washington, D.C.: Media Institute, 1984. xii + 151 p.

337.   Bennett, Donald G. "Spot Report: Intelligence Vietnam." *Military Review* (46:8), August 1966, p. 72-77.

A former G2 advisor to a South Vietnamese division describes the use of agents, interrogation, and especially document exploitation in tactical intelligence.

338.   Fall, Bernard B. "Insurgency Indicators." *Military Review* (46:4), April 1966, p. 3-11.

The noted historian of the Indochinese conflicts explains the "Fall Insurgency Nonmilitary Indicators" (FINI), an alternative means of measuring who controls an area in an insurgency. First developed in 1953, these indicators include such items as the reliability of Viet Cong tax collection, the degree of food shortages, etc. Fall argues that a decline in the number of enemy contacts may actually mean that the *enemy* is controlling an area, and no longer needs to fight government patrols.

339.   Girouard, Richard J.   "District Intelligence in Vietnam." *Armor* (75:6), November-December 1966, p. 10-14.
The techniques of order of battle intelligence at the lowest level.

340.   Graham, Daniel O.   "Fact vs. Fantasy--the Tet Intelligence Imbroglio." *Armed Forces Journal International* (113:4), December 1975, p. 23-24.
Lt. Gen. Graham served in the J2 section of Military Assistance Command, Vietnam, at the time of the Tet offensive. He describes how, from his perception, Adams simply took the Viet Cong's own estimates of their own strength in a few military districts, and generalized from those estimates to produce a total figure for the entire country, without regard to the wide variations between districts.

341.   Heilbrunn, Otto.   "Tactical Intelligence in Vietnam" *Military Review* (48:10), October 1968, p. 85-87.
The author proposes different intelligence organizations, based on the British experience.

342.   Kowet, Don. *A Matter of Honor.* New York: Macmillan; London: Collier Macmillan, 1984. 317 p.
The Adams-Westmoreland-CBS controversy.

343.   Livingston, George D., Jr. "Pershing II: Success Amid Chaos." *Military Review* (50:5), May 1970, p. 56-60.
During the period prior to and during the 1968 Tet offensive, a brigade of the 1st Cavalry Division (Airmobile) used an integrated intelligence system to detect and break up attacks by the 3d North Vietnamese Army Division in northeastern Binh Dinh Province.

344.   Norman, Lloyd H. "Westmoreland's J2." *Army* (17:5), May 1967, p. 21-25.
A highly complementary description of Maj. Gen. Joseph McChristian and his intelligence organization.

345.   Platt, R.L. Intelligence and Vietnamese Operations. U.S. Army Command and General Staff College Master's thesis (Military Art & Science), 1967.

346.   Wirtz, James J. *The Tet Offensive: Intelligence Failure in War.* Ithaca, NY: Cornell University Press, 1992. 336 p.
Based on documents from both sides, this account examines U.S. misperceptions that made prediction of the 1968 Tet Offensive difficult.

Air Tactical Intelligence   (See also Chapter 4, Imagery and Aerial Reconnaissance)

347.   "Air Combat Intelligence." *Flying* (35), October 1944, p. 123-124.

348.   Alonso, Rod.   "The Air War" in Bruce W. Watson (ed.), *Military Lessons of the Gulf War.* London: Greenhill Books; Novato, Ca: Presidio Press, 1991, p. 61-80.
    An excellent first effort at analyzing the 1991 Gulf War. Alonso was an air intelligence analyst throughout the war, and he addresses many of the intelligence issues--SCUD missiles, bomb damage assessment, Iraqi troop strengths, etc--for which U.S. intelligence received both justified and unjustified criticism at the time.

349.   Barber, Charles H.   "Some Problems of Air Intelligence." *Military Review* (26:5), August 1946, p. 76-78.

350.   Barnes, Derek G.   *Cloud Cover: Recollections of an Intelligence Officer.* London: Rich, 1943.   176 p.
    Early Royal Air Force intelligence.

351.   Chappell, F. Roy.   *Wellington Wings: An RAF Intelligence Officer in the Western Desert.* London: W. Kimber, 1980.   282 p.
    A squadron and wing intelligence officer in North Africa during World War II.

352.   Canada.   Royal Canadian Air Force.   Intelligence Division.   *The German Air Force: An R.C.A.F. Intelligence Summary.* Ottawa: R.C.A.F. Intelligence Division, 1941.   90 p.

353.   Cox, Sebastian.   "A Comparative Analysis of RAF and Luftwaffe Intelligence in the Battle of Britain, 1940." *Intelligence and National Security* (5:2), April 1990, p. 425-443.
    This is one of the few serious efforts to examine the difficult problem of assessing enemy losses in an air campaign. Both sides tended to overestimate such losses, but in Britain intelligence estimates were subjected to healthy criticism. See also the articles by Horst Boog on Luftwaffe intelligence in the Organization Chapter (entry 129).

354.   Crawford, Charles J.   "Intelligence and the Tactical Application of Firepower: The Basic Problem is Human."   Rand Corporation paper No. P-7341.   Santa Monica, CA: Rand Corporation, 1987.   29 p.
    The author, a career intelligence officer, describes the difficulties of using aerial reconnaissance in-flight reports and other sources of intelligence to plan targets deep in the enemy rear. Different reports go to different staff sections, and even with identical information, the Army Corps and Air Force component headquarters will arrive at different conclusions.

355.   Evans, N.E.   "Air Intelligence and the Coventry Raid (1940)" in *Royal United Service Institution Journal for Defense*

Studies (121:3), September 1976, p. 66-74.
A detailed refutation of the assertion that the British government allowed the Luftwaffe to devastate the city of Coventry rather than compromise the ULTRA signals intelligence. Instead, Evans describes the various preventive raids and other measures that the British undertook in a vain effort to avert this attack.

356.   Gregory, Jesse O.   "Flak Intelligence Memories." *Coast Artillery Journal* (91), May-June 1948, p. 18-24.
U.S. Army Air Force intelligence on German anti-aircraft defenses during the strategic bombardment of Europe in World War II.

357.   James, Charles D.   "Combat Intelligence for Aviation." *U.S. Army Aviation Digest* (16:1), January 1970, p. 15-18.

358.   Kauffman, George R.   "Intelligence in Heavy Bombardment." *Military Review* (26:8), November 1946, p. 20-28.

359.   Kebric, Harry L. *Dragon Tigers.* New York: Vantage Press, 1971.   137 p.
Intelligence for U.S. air elements in China during World War II.

360.   Mierzejewski, Alfred C.   Wheels Must Roll for Victory: Allied Air Power and the German War Economy, 1944-1945. University of North Carolina at Chapel Hill Ph.D. dissertation, 1985.   488 p.   LC No. AAC8527311.
A study of the central role played by the German railroads in Hitler's war economy, and of the effects of Allied air strikes against those railroads. One of the major conclusions is that Allied air intelligence never fully understood either the organization of the German war economy or the effectiveness of their own attacks on German railroads.

361.   Muir, Daniel J.   "A View From the Black Hole." *U.S. Naval Institute Proceedings* (117:10), October 1991, p. 85-86.
Muir was a naval staff officer serving in the Central Command Air Force Intelligence section in Riyadh in 1990-91. He argues that, even in its most recent war, the U.S. Air Force still suffers from the traditional tendency to isolate and separate intelligence officers.   By contrast, Muir claims, naval intelligence and operations officers are much more effective in collaborating for air planning.

362.   Olson, Mancur Jr.   "The Economics of Target Selection for the Combined Bomber Offensive." *Journal of the Royal United Service Institution (107), November 1962, p. 308-314.*

363.   Peskett, S. John.   *Strange Intelligence: From Dunkirk to Nuremberg.* London: Robert Hale, 1981.   200 p.
An RAF air intelligence officer discusses his involvement with technical intelligence on downed German aircraft; interrogation of prisoners; and service at Hut 3 in Bletchley Park as an expert on Luftwaffe organization. As such, this is an interesting cross-sectional view of air intelligence in Britain.

364.   Perry, M. O.   "Air-Ground Intelligence Cooperation."
Military Review (28:8), November 1948, p. 49-54.
   The value of *reciprocal* exchange of intelligence between
air and ground headquarters;   an excellent discussion of the
strengths, weaknesses, and planning of aerial reconnaissance
missions.

365.   Robinson, Douglas H.   "Zeppelin Intelligence." *Aerospace
Historian* (21:1), March 1974, p. 1-7.
   World War I air intelligence.

366.   Wead, Frank W.   "Air Intelligence: Gathering and
Disseminating All Battle Data."   *Flying* (32), February 1943, p.
163-164.

367.   Whitney, Cornelius V.   *Lone and Level Sand.*   New York:
Farrar, 1951, 314 p.
   U.S. Army Air Force intelligence in North Africa and the
Pacific during World War II.

368.   Wood, Derek and Dempster, Derek.   *The Narrow Margin:
The Battle of Britain and the Rise of Air Power 1930-1940.*
Revised ed.   New York: Paperback Library, 1969.   505 p.
   This book examines the Battle of Britain from both sides,
including German prewar technical intelligence efforts and the
development of British radar.

Weather

369.   Bates, Charles C. and Fuller, John F.   *America's Weather
Warriors, 1814-1985.*   College Station, Texas: Texas A & M
Press, 1986.   360 p.
   The authors trace American military meteorology for all
three services up through the Iran hostage rescue attempt of
1980.   An excellent bibliographic essay is included.

370.   Blanton, Eugene T.   "Air Operations in Vietnam: COIN
Weather Support."   *Air University Review* (15:4) May-June 1964,
p. 66-72.
   The organization and general functions of the 30th Weather
Squadron in Vietnam.

371.   Dash, Ernie R. and Meyer, Walter D.   "The Meteorological
Satellite: An Invaluable Tool for the Military Decision
Makers."   *Air University Review* (29:3) Mar-Apr 1978, p. 13-24.
   The history of weather satellite usage since Tiros I in
1960.

372.   Fahey, James M.   "Get the Weather on Your Side."
Military Review (27:1), April 1947, p. 35-40.
   Examples and procedures of using weather information in
staff planning.

373.   Fuller, John F.   "Weather and War."   Scott Air Force
Base, Ill: Office of Military Airlift Command History, 1974.
27 p. typescript.   A shorter version appeared in *Navigator*
(26), Summer 1979, p. 5-9.

The Air Force Air Weather Service historian provides examples of the effects of weather on warfare from Xerxes to Vietnam.

374.   Lash, R.L.   "Why Not Use the Weather?" *Military Review* (32:4), July 1952, p. 16-23.
Explains the theater weather service of the US Air Force at the time of writing, with examples from World War II.

Technical Intelligence

375.   Anderson, Gaylord W. "Medical Intelligence." p. 251-340 in Robert S. Anderson (ed.) *Preventive Medicine in World War II*, Vol. IX, *Special Fields. MEDICAL DEPARTMENT, UNITED STATES ARMY.* Washington, D.C.: Office of the Surgeon General 1969. 650 p.
Gaylord Anderson was the head of medical intelligence for the U.S. Army Surgeon General during World War II. This monograph describes medical intelligence at that time, and reflects the author's frustration with military bureaucracy.

376.   Burleson, Clyde W. *The Jennifer Project.* Englewood Cliffs, NJ: Prentice-Hall, 1977. 179 p.
The recovery of a sunken Soviet submarine by the Central Intelligence Agency, using the specially-constructed ship *Hughes Glomar Explorer.* See Roy Varner, *A Matter of Risk*, entry 405.

377.   Davis, Franklin M., Jr. "The Army's Technical Detectives." *Military Review* (28:2), May 1948, p. 12-17.
A summary of technical intelligence efforts against Germany in 1944-47.

378.   _____. "Technical Intelligence and the Signal Corps." *Signals* (3:6), July-August 1949, p. 19-26.

379.   Fredericks, Brian and Wiersema, Richard. "Battlefield TECHINT: Support of Operations DESERT SHIELD/STORM." *Military Intelligence* (18:2), April-June 1992, p. 13-19.
Organization and Functions of the Joint Captured Material Exploitation Center (JCMEC) during the 1990-91 Gulf Crisis, by the JCMEC commander.

380.   Green, Constance M., Thompson, Harry C., and Roots, Peter C. *The Ordnance Department: Planning Munitions for War.* UNITED STATES ARMY IN WORLD WAR II. Washington, D.C.: Office of the Chief of Military History, 1955. 542 p.
Chapters 7 and 9 include discussions of technical intelligence.

381.   Goudsmit, Samuel A. *Alsos.* New York: Henry Schuman, Inc., 1947. 259 p.
The account of the Alsos mission, appointed at the request of Major General Leslie R. Groves to determine German progress in development of a nuclear weapon during World War II. Goudsmit is prophetic in his conclusion that the Germans allowed themselves to be overtaken in this field because they were overly confident in the superiority of their own

scientific knowledge, a failing which the U.S. repeated in allowing the Soviet Union to develop nuclear weapons.

382.   Henning, E.S.   *The High-Frequency War: A Survey of German Electronic Development.*   Summary Report No. F-SU-1109-ND.   Dayton, Ohio: Headquarters, Air Material Command, U.S. Army Air Forces, May 10, 1946.   184 p. (MHI)
   Describes the German view of allied jamming of navigational beams and radar.   Provides much detail on German electronic development during the war, including the Luftwaffe's tactical signals intelligence.

383.   Howard, William L.   "Technical Intelligence and Tank Design."   *Armor* (94:1) January–February 1985, p. 24–29.
   A brief account of American technical intelligence on armor from World War II through the 1973 war.

384.   Irving, David.   *The Mare's Nest.*   Boston: Little Brown and Co. 1965.   320 p.   Revd Ed. London: Panther, 1985.
   A well-researched journalistic account of Anglo-American technical intelligence efforts against the German missile and rocket weapons.

385.   Johnson, Brian.   *The Secret War.*   London: British Broadcasting Corp., 1978.   352 p.
   A popular account of the scientific aspects of the British-German struggle in World War II, including radar, beam navigation, V weapons, the Battle of the Atlantic, and Enigma signals intelligence.

386.   Jones, Reginald V.   *Most Secret War: British Scientific Intelligence, 1939–1945.*   London: Hamish Hamilton, 1978; Hodder and Stoughton Paperbacks, 1979.   702 p.
   Jones' memoirs of his efforts, as Churchill's principal advisor on scientific matters, to understand and counter German technological advances such as beam navigation, the V2 rocket, etc.

387.   Jones, Vincent C.   *Manhattan: The Army and the Atomic Bomb.*   UNITED STATES ARMY IN WORLD WAR II.   Washington, D.C.: U.S. Army Center of Military History, 1985.   xx + 660 p.
   Chapter 12 (pp. 280–291) discusses ALSOS and other technical intelligence efforts.

388.   Kalish, Robert B.   "Air Forces Technical Intelligence." *Air University Review* (22:5), July–August 1971, p. 2–11.
   The problems and successes of US Air Force technical intelligence against both missiles and aircraft.

389.   Lasby, Clarence G.   *Project Paperclip: German Scientists and the Cold War.*   New York: Atheneum, 1971.   338 p.
   In 1945, American intelligence competed against its nominal allies for the services of German rocket scientists and engineers.

390.   Leasor, James.   *Green Beach.*   New York: William Morrow & Co. 1975.   292 p.

As part of the disastrous British-Canadian raid on Dieppe in 1942, a special raiding party was sent to evaluate a German air defense radar installation.

391.   Lyon, Harold C. "Operations of 'T' Force, 12th Army Group, in the Liberation and Intelligence Exploitation of Paris, France, 25 August-6 September 1944." U.S. Army Infantry School student paper, n.d. Reproduced Ft. Riley, Ks: U.S. Army Ground General School, 1949. 32 p.
The Anglo-American technical/scientific intelligence organization.

392.   Mahoney, Leo J. A History of the War Department Scientific Intelligence Mission (ALSOS), 1943-1945.   Ph.D. dissertation, Kent State University, 1981.   445 p.   Univ. Microfilms No. 8202163.
An account that focuses on the command relationships and other difficulties of this unique effort to collect German and Japanese technical intelligence.

393.   McGovern, James. *Crossbow and Overcast.* New York: William Morrow & Co., 1964.   279 p.
An account of Allied intelligence efforts against the German V-1 and V-2 weapons, and of the postwar efforts to locate German missile scientists. See also Clarence G. Lasby, *Project Paperclip,* entry 389, and David Irving, *The Mare's Nest,* entry 384.

394.   Mendelsohn, John. *Covert Warfare: Intelligence, Counterintelligence, and Military Deception During the World War II Era.* Vol. 9: *Scientific and Technical Intelligence Gathering.* New York and London: Garland Publishing, 1989. unnumbered pages.
A set of reproduced reports on various aspects of technical intelligence, including equipment and document exploitation and the ALSOS mission final report.

395.   Meselson, Matthew S. "The Search for Yellow Rain." *Arms Control Today* (16:6), September 1986, p. 31-36.
An extended interview with Meselson, a biochemist with the U.S. Arms Control and Disarmament Agency who investigated allegations of the use of chemical or biological weapons in southeast Asia during the 1980s. Meselson concluded that the so-called "Yellow Rain" was in fact honeybee feces, not a deliberate weapon. He describes the allegations about Yellow Rain as "a case of intelligence failure and of premature judgement at high levels. The failures resulted from a corruption of the intelligence process in which political factors favored hasty conclusions." This is a good illustration of the difficulties of conducting and explaining technical intelligence analysis.

396.   Miller, George. *The Bruneval Raid: Flashpoint of the Radar War.* Garden City, NY: Doubleday and Co., Inc., 1975. xviii + 221 p.
A well researched study of the British airborne raid on February 28, 1942, that seized a German Wurzburg radar for technical intelligence.

397. Pash, Boris T. *The ALSOS Mission.* New York: Award House, 1966.

398. Rearden, Jim. *Cracking the Zero Mystery: How the U.S. Learned to Best Japan's Vaunted WW II Fighter Plane.* Harrisburg, Pa: Stackpole Books, 1990.

399. Rogers, Henry H. "Scientific Intelligence in Modern Warfare." *Military Review* (28:2) May 1948, pp. 27-31.
    Basic concepts and terminology.

400. Schiffman, Maurice K. "Technical Intelligence in the Pacific in World War II." *Military Review* (31:10), January 1952, p. 42-48.
    Primarily the operations of the US 5250th Technical Intelligence Composite Company (see entry 402, U.S. Army Forces, Pacific, *History of Technical Intelligence.*)

401. Thiesmeyer, Lincoln R. and Burchard, John E. *Combat Scientists.* Boston: Little, Brown & Co, 1947. approx. 400 p.
    Discusses not only the development of allied weapons, but also technical intelligence efforts against Germany (Chapter X, p. 162-181.

402. U.S. Army Forces, Pacific. U.S. Army Technical Intelligence Center. *History of Technical Intelligence, Southwest and Western Pacific Areas, 1942-1945.* Tokyo: U.S. Army Technical Intelligence Center, mimeographed, 1945. 2 vols.
    Primarily the story of how the U.S. Army's different technical arms (Ordnance, Chemical Service, Quartermaster, etc.) merged their efforts into the 5250th Technical Intelligence Composite Company, Separate (Provisional), a collection of 470 technical intelligence experts.

403. _____. *Operations of the Technical Intelligence Unit in the Southwest Pacific Area.* Tokyo: U.S. Army Technical Information Center, mimeographed, 1948.

404. U.S. Department of the Army. Office of the Assistant Chief of Staff, G2. *A Guide to the Collection of Technical Intelligence, Part I.* Washington, D.C.: Office of the Assistant Chief of Staff, July 1950. 51 p.
    A system for describing enemy equipment.

405. Varner, Roy. *A Matter of Risk: The Incredible Inside Story of the CIA's Hughes Glomar Explorer Mission to Raise a Russian Submarine.* New York: Random House, 1978. ix + 258 p.
    With the assistance of Howard Hughes' business organization, a specially-constructed ship recovered a sunken Soviet submarine from previously-impossible depths.

406. Von Karman, Theodore, with Edson, Lee. *The Wind and Beyond: Theodore Von Karman, Pioneer in Aviation and Pathfinder in Space.* Boston: Little, Brown, 1967.
    Personal memoirs, including Chapter 34, "Right After the War," about his participation in Air Force technical intelligence in Germany.

4

Imagery and Aerial Reconnaissance

407.   Aart, Dick van der. *Aerial Espionage: Secret Intelligence Flights by East and West.* Translated by Sidney Woods.   New York: Arco/Prentice Hall Press, 1986; 167 p. Dutch original by Romen Luchtvaart, 1984.
   Within the limitations of "coffee-table books," this is a well researched and informative description of Cold War imagery aircraft and drones, both US/NATO and Soviet efforts. The book also describes some alleged aerial platforms for signals intelligence.

408.   Adam, John A. (ed.)   "Peacekeeping By Technical Means." *IEEE Spectrum* (23:7), July 1986, p. 42-80.
   A   series   of   short   articles   on   various   aspects   of satellites for missile test monitoring, chemical and biological weapons monitoring, etc.   This includes Stephen M. Meyer's interesting "The Soviet 'Spy Gaps'", p. 67-68, on Soviet satellite capabilities.

409.   Babington-Smith, Constance. **Air Spy: The Story of Photo Intelligence in World War II.** New York: Harper and Brothers, Publishers, 1957. 266 p.
   Babington-Smith was a photo interpreter for the Royal Air Force, specializing in German experimental aircraft such as the jet and rocket fighters. This is a personal memoir of both the British and American imagery interpretation effort against Germany, and concludes with observations about the limitations of German imagery interpretation.

410.   Barker, Ralph. *Aviator Extraordinary: The Sidney Cotton Story.* London: Chatto and Windus, 1969. 289 p.
   Cotto pioneered British photo reconnaissance until he was forced out of the service in 1940.   The author of numerous other works on the Royal Air Force in World War II, Barker is more concerned with operations than with intelligence per se.

411.   Bart, H. L.   "Bombing Proof." *Flying* (34), May 1944, p. 44-45+.

412.   Beschloss, Michael R. *MAYDAY: Eisenhower, Khruschev, and the U-2.* New York: Harper and Row; Toronto: Fitzhenry and Whiteside, 1986. xvi + 494 p.
   The first half of this book describes the development of the U-2 overflight program within the context of U.S.-Soviet

relations, providing a useful view of the interaction of peacetime aerial reconnaissance and national security policy.

413.   Blackley, Allan B.   "Airborne Surveillance in a Post-CFE Environment - A Central Region Perspective."   *Military Technology* (15:2), February 1991, p. 62-64.
Aerial surveillance, recent and future, in central Europe. Such surveillance is necessary for peacetime warning and enforcement of the Conventional Forces in Europe (CFE) arms reduction agreement.

414.   Blow, Tom.   "Soviet Space Weapons - The Greatest Challenge to Intelligence Art." *Jane's Soviet Intelligence Review* (1:5), May 1989, p. 197-199;   (1:6), June 1989, p. 252-253;   (1:7), July 1989, p. 328-329.
This essay is as much about the art of intelligence analysis as it is about the science of space weapons.

415.   Boyle, Robert D.   A History of Photographic Reconnaissance in North Africa, Including My Experiences with the Third Photo Group.   University of Texas Ph.D. dissertation, 1949.

416.   Brookes, Andrew J.   *Photo Reconnaissance*. London: Ian Allan Ltd., 1975.   240 p.
The author of several books on bombers in World War II turns his attention to Royal Air Force aerial reconnaissance missions, primarily during and since World War II.

417.   Brugioni, Dino A.   "Auschwitz-Birkenau: Why the World War II Photo Interpreters Failed to Identify the Extermination Complex." *Military Intelligence* (9:1), January-March 1983, p. 50-55.

418.   Burrows, William E.   *Deep Black: Space Espionage and National Security.* New York: Random House, 1986; paperback Berkeley Books, 1988.   406 p.
A carefully-documented account of America's alleged imagery and signals intelligence satellites, this book also traces such reconnaissance platforms as the SR-71 aircraft.

419.   Cairns, Donald W.   "UAV--Where We Have Been." *Military Intelligence* (13), March 1987, p. 18-20.
The evolution of unmanned aerial reconnaissance vehicles in the United States, 1915-1972.

420.   Clark, Phillip S.   "Soviet ELINT Satellites for Monitoring Naval Transmissions." *Jane's Soviet Intelligence Review* (2:8), August 1990, p. 378-381.
A discussion, with tables, of Soviet Electronic Intelligence Ocean Reconnaissance Satellites (EORSATs) since 1974;   includes the limited coverage provided by such satellites to track the British fleet during the Falklands War.

421.   _____.   "Soviet Nuclear Satellites for Observing Western Navies." *Jane's Soviet Intelligence Review* (2:9), September 1990, p. 423-429.
Radar Ocean Reconnaissance Satellites (RORSATs) beginning

with COSMOS 185 in 1967. An exhaustive discussion of launches, orbital parameters, etc.

422. _____. "The Soviet Photo-Reconnaissance Satellite Programme." *Jane's Soviet Intelligence Review* (2:2), February 1990, p. 84-90.
    Clark discusses five generations of COSMOS satellites, including the orbital characteristics and a complete 1989 schedule of launches.

423. _____. "Soviet Worldwide ELINT Satellites." *Jane's Soviet Intelligence Review* (2:7), July 1990, p. 330-333.
    Schedules and orbits of ELINT satellites since the first such mission, COSMOS 389, in 1970.

424. Colwell, Robert N. "Intelligence and the Okinawa Battle." *Naval War College Review* (38:2) March-April 1985, p. 81-95.
    Although a naval officer, the author served as chief of photo intelligence for the 10th U.S. Army because of its need to consider amphibious aspects when selecting landing areas. An account of the practical uses and problems of imagery.

425. Cornelius, George. "Air Reconnaissance: The Great Silent Weapon." *U.S. Naval Institute Proceedings* (85), 1959, p. 34-42.

426. Creal, Richard E. "The History of Reconnaissance in World War II." *Tactical Air Reconnaissance Digest* (2), February 1968, p. 14-18.

427. Donald, David. *Spyplane.* Osceola, Wis: Motor Books International, 1987. 127 p.
    Donald has produced a sophisticated "picture book" on the evolution of US and West European aerial collection platforms, primarily for imagery but also concerning signals intelligence. Pride of place goes to the U-2/TR-1 and A-12/SR-71 series of strategic imagery reconnaissance aircraft.

428. Elmhurst, Thomas. "Air Reconnaissance: The Purpose and the Value." *Journal of the Royal United Service Institution* (97), February 1952, p. 84-86.

429. "The First SR-71 High Altitude Reconnaissance Photos Ever Made Public." *Armed Forces Journal International* (113), July 1976, p. 20-23.
    This is one of a series of extracts from that journal's book on the Son Tay POW Prison Raid in November 1970. In this case, it represents a rare view of the imagery capability of the SR-71 strategic reconnaissance aircraft.

430. Florini, Ann M. "The Opening Skies" Third-Party Imaging Satellites and US Security." *International Security* (13:2), Fall 1988, p. 91-123.
    A good discussion of satellites by private companies and non-super powers, together with an explanation of the problems of imagery resolution and LANDSAT.

431.   Ford, Thomas R.   "Tactical Reconnaissance."   *Air University Quarterly Review.*   (12:3 and 4), Winter and Spring 1960-61, p. 120-129.

432.   Foregger, Richard.   "The First Allied Aerial Reconnaissance Over Auswitz During World War II."   *Military History Journal* 8 (June, 1989), p. 31-32.

433.   Forrest, Ian.   "This Was Hitler's Spy Squadron."   *RAF Flying Review* (16), November 1960, p. 17-18+.

434.   French, W. F.   "Photo Eyes for our Fighters."   *Science Digest* (15), January 1944, p. 57-60.

435.   Fulghum, David A.   "Gulf War Successes Push UAVs Into Military Doctrine Forefront."   *Aviation Week and Space Technology* (135:23), December 9, 1991, p. 38-39, 44-50.
    A series of short articles describe the Marine and to a lesser extent Army use of unmanned aerial reconnaissance vehicles in the 1991 Gulf Conflict. UAVs were unexpectedly pressed into service for post-strike bomb damage assessment. The author contends that the noise and other signatures of UAVs must be drastically reduced to avoid optically-directed anti-aircraft fire.

436.   Galloway, Alec.   "A Decade of U.S. Reconnaissance Satellites."   *Interavia*, April 1972, p. 376-380.
    Galloway uses published literature to describe the development of photographic satellites.

437.   Gilchrist, John W. S.   *An Aerial Observer in World War I.* Richmond, Va: by the author, 1966.   134 p.
    Well-done memoirs of the 104th Aero Squadron in U.S. campaigns of 1918.

438.   Goddard, George W., with DeWitt S. Copp.   *Overview: A Lifelong Adventure in Aerial Photography.*   Garden City, New York: Doubleday, 1969. 415 p.
    The development of military aerial photography from the 1920s through the 1940s, by a pioneer in the field.

439.   Gray, Colin S.   *American Military Space Policy; Information Systems, Weapons Systems, and Arms Control.* Cambridge, Ma: Abt Books, 1982; Lanham, Md.:   University Press of America, 1984. x + 128 p.
    Chapter 2 describes the potential imagery and other reconnaissance uses of space--surveillance, warning, communications, etc.

440.   Greenwood, Ted.   "Reconnaissance and Arms Control." in *Scientific American* (228:2), February 1973, p. 14-25.
    A discussion of photographic satellite techniques, midair recovery of imagery capsules, etc to verify strategic arms limitation agreements.

441.   Gunston, Bill.   *An Illustrated Guide to Spy Planes and Electronic Warfare Aircraft.* London: Salamander Books; New York: Prentice Hall Press, 1983. 160 p.

A "picture book" that provides good explanations and
illustrations for the hardware of recent aerial reconnaissance
platforms.

442.   Hafemeister, David; Joseph J. Romm; and Kosta Tsipis.
"The Verification of Compliance With Arms-Control Agreements."
in *Scientific American* (252:3), March 1985, p. 38-45.
     Describes the problems of imagery resolution, seismic
verification of underground nuclear tests, etc. see also Ted
Greenwood's "Reconnaissance and Arms Control" (above.)

443.   Heiman, Grover. *Aerial Photography: The Story of
Aerial Mapping Reconnaissance.* New York: Macmillan, 1972.
180 p.
     A general overview of aerial photography for both recon-
naissance and mapping.

444.   Infield, Glenn B. *Unarmed and Unafraid.* London:
Collier Macmillan; New York: Macmillan, 1970. 308 p.
     The history of U.S. aerial reconnaissance from balloons to
Viet Nam and satellites. The author emphasizes the flying
collection of imagery, rather than its interpretation.

445.   Ivie, Thomas G. *Aerial Reconnaissance: The 10th Photo
Recon Group in World War II.* Fallbrooke, Ca: Aero Publishers,
1981. viii + 200 p.
     A fine unit history of modified fighters used for aerial
reconnaissance by the U.S. Army Air Force in Europe during
World War II. Ivie describes the unit's contributions battle
by battle.

446.   Johnson, Nicholas L. *Soviet Military Strategy in Space.*
London, NY: Jane's, 1987. 287 p.
     This provides a useful discussion of Soviet satellite
reconnaissance, including orbital tracks, in a variety of
crises from the Chinese border violence of 1969 through El
Salvador, Grenada, and other incidents of the 1980s.

447.   _____. "Soviet Satellite Reconnaissance Activities
and Trends." *Air Force,* March 1981, p. 90-94.

448.   Jones, William E. *Bomber Intelligence: 103, 105, 166,
170 Squadrons: Operations and Techniques, '42-'45.* Leicester,
England: Midland Counties Publications, 1983. 304 pp.
     Royal Air Force aerial reconnaissance.

449.   Karas, Thomas H. *The New High Ground: Systems and
Weapons of Space-Age War.* New York: Simon and Schuster, 1983.
224 p.
     A slightly sensationalized account of actual and potential
US imagery resources from U2 aircraft to satellites to anti-
satellite weapons.

450.   Kenden, Anthony. "U.S. Reconnaissance Satellites
Programmes." in *Spaceflight* (20:7), July 1978, p. 243-262.
     Includes tables of early US satellite flights; designs of
such satellites; the life span of "close look" surveillance
satellites from 1959-76. This work is heavily based on

Aviation Week and Space Technology.

451.   Klass, Philip J. *Secret Sentries in Space.* New York: Random House, 1971. xvii + 236 p.
    Klass used open sources to trace the development of reconnaissance satellite capabilities by both the U.S. and the Soviet Union, including the possibility of verifying arms limitations with such satellites.

452.   Kreutz, Douglas. "USACSEWS: Emphasis on Aviation." *U.S. Army Aviation Digest* (16:11), November 1970, pp. 14-16.
    The U.S. Army Combat Surveillance and Electronic Warfare School was established at Ft. Huachuca, Az, to train OV-1 Mohawk pilots for imagery missions during the Vietnam conflict. The school was later absorbed into the Army's intelligence school. This article includes details of the imagery systems on the Mohawk.

453.   Lee, Christopher. *War in Space.* London: Hamish Hamilton, 1986. 242 p.
    A BBC correspondent on Soviet and US use of space. See especially chapters 4-6 on alleged surveillance platforms.

454.   Libbey, Miles A. III and Putignano, Patrick A. "See Deep-Shoot Deep, the UAVs on the Future Battlefield." *Military Review* (71:2), February 1991, p. 38-47.
    One of the most recent contributions to the debate about the use of unmanned drones for tactical imagery.

455.   Maurer, Maurer. "A Delicate Mission: Aerial Reconnaissance of Japanese Islands Before World War II." *Military Affairs* (26:2), Summer 1962, p. 66-75.
    On the eve of Pearl Harbor, two B-24 aircraft were supposed to conduct reconnaissance of various Japanese-held islands, but were delayed by miscommunications and equipment problems.

456.   McCue, Brian. *U-Boats in the Bay of Biscay: An Essay in Operations Analysis.* Washington, D.C.: National Defense University Press, 1990.

457.   Mead, Peter. *The Eye in the Air: History of Air Observation and Reconnaissance for the Army, 1785-1945.* London: Her Majesty's Stationery Office, 1983. xiii + 274 p.
    A history of British Army aviation, by a former head of the Army Air Corps. Brigadier Mead concentrates on British army aviation during the two world wars.

458.   Medhurst, C.E.H. "Air Intelligence." *Flying* (31), September 1942, p. 141+.

459.   Morris, Alan. *The Balloonatics.* London: Jarrolds Publishers, 1970. xi + 212 p.
    Morris provides a good discussion of the British observation balloons that provided artillery target acquisition and tactical intelligence during World War I.

460.   Munson, Kenneth. "UAV's: More Than Just Eyes in the

Sky." in *Jane's Defense Weekly* (17:20), May 16, 1992, p. 851–855.
A review of Unmanned Aerial Vehicles in the 1980s, including a short essay by John Boatman on current U.S. UAV development.

461. Peebles, Curtis. *Guardians: Strategic Reconnaissance Satellites.* San Rafael, Ca: Presidio Press, 1987. viii + 418 p.
A history of alleged US and Soviet photographic, ELINT, ocean surveillance, early warning, and other satellites. Appendix A explains orbital mechanics in simple terms, while Appendix B provides a list of military satellites launches from 1959 to 1985.

462. Perry, G. E. "COSMOS Coverage of the Indo-Pakistani War." *Spaceflight,* September 1972, p. 350.
Soviet satellite collection against the 1971 war.

463. Porter, Harold E. *Aerial Observation: The Aerial Observer, the Balloon Observer, and the Army Corps Pilot.* New York: Harper, 1921. 355 p.

464. Porter, W.C. and von Platen, W.G. "Reconnaissance in COIN [Counter Insurgency]." *Air University Review* (15:3), March–April 1964, p. 64–68.

465. Powers, Francis G. with Gentry, Curt. *Operation Overflight: The U-2 Pilot Tells His Story for the First Time.* New York: Holt, Rinehart, and Winston, 1970. 375 p.
Powers' account of his capture while on a photographic mission over the Soviet Union in 1960. He claims that the U-2 pilots had only limited knowledge of the intelligence program, and no instructions for procedures if shot down and interrogated. He also describes earlier surveillance flights in the Middle East. See also item 412.

466. Price, Alfred. "The Radio War." *RAF Flying Review* (18), June 1963, p. 25–27+.
German and British airborne radar in World War II.

467. Richelson, Jeffrey T. "The Keyhole Satellite Program." *Journal of Strategic Studies* (7:2), June 1984, p. 121–153.
A history of reported US imagery satellites, including Discoverer, KH-5, KH-6, KH-9, and KH-11. The author describes the limitations and resolution capabilities of these systems.

468. _____. "From CORONA to LACROSSE: A Short History of Satellites." *The Washington Post,* February 25, 1990, p. B1, B4.
An overview of the alleged photoreconnaissance satellites of the U.S.

469. _____. "Monitoring the Soviet Military." *Arms Control Today* (16:7), October 1986, p. 14–19.
A discussion of the national technical means, both imagery and signals intelligence, allegedly used to monitor Soviet missile tests, anti-ballistic missile activity, nuclear weapons

testing, etc.

470.   Rip, Michael R., and Joseph F. Fontanella. "A Window on the Arab-Israeli 'Yom Kippur' War of October 1973:   Military Photo-Reconnaissance   from   High   Altitude   and   Space." *Intelligence and National Security* (6:1), January 1991, p. 15-89.
        This superb study goes far beyond the 1973 war, and instead seeks to sketch the history of imagery surveillance from the 1956 war (when US U2s from Turkey provided bomb damage assessment to the British) forward.   In the process, it includes descriptions of alleged US and Soviet satellite capabilities, explains the level of resolution necessary for different types of tactical targets, and provides charts and tables of satellite coverage of the Middle East during 1973-74. An essential source for anyone interested in the Arab-Israeli wars.

471.   Sloyan, Patrick J.   "Spies in the Sky: Bye, Bye 'Blackbird'--The Grounding of a Legend." *The Washington Post,* February 25, 1990, p. B1, B4.
        Retrospective look at the role and capabilities of the SR-71 reconnaissance aircraft, on the occasion of its inactivation.

472.   Sims, Charles.   "Over the Fence." *Flying Review International* (23), August 1968, p. 445-446 +.
        British photo intelligence in World War II.

473.   Stanley, Roy M. II.   *World War II Photo Intelligence.* New York: Charles Scribner's Sons, 1981.   374 p.
        A lavishly-illustrated account that focuses on equipment and techniques.

474.   Stares, Paul B.   *The Militarization of Space: U.S. Policy, 1945-1984.*   Ithaca, NY: Cornell University Press, 1985.   334 p.
        Although more concerned with Cold War politics than with actual intelligence, this study attempts to examine the role of surveillance satellites and the manner in which the US and Soviet Union avoided an arms race in space.   For a contrasting interpretation, see entry 475.

475.   Steinberg, Gerald M.   The Legitimization of Reconnaissance   Satellites: An   Example   of   Informal   Arms   Control Negotiation.   Cornell   University   Press   Dissertation (Government), 1981.   vii + 317 p.   University Microfilms No. 8119453.   Published as *Satellite Reconnaissance: The Role of Informal Bargaining.* New York: Praeger, 1983.   viii + 201 p.
        As its name implies, this study argues that between the Kennedy and Carter administrations, the US and USSR informally agreed to accept the existence of surveillance satellites, and to restrain their anti-satellite programs, as part of arms verification.

476.   Taylor, John W.R. and Mondey, David.   *Spies in the Sky.* New York: Scribner's Sons, 1972.   128 p.
        This survey traces aerial reconnaissance since World War

I, including airborne electronic warfare and satellites.

477.   Trainor, James L.   "What Role Can Unmanned Satellites
Play in Tactical Warfare?" *Armed Forces Management*, December
1965, p. 66-67.

478.   Tsipis, Kosta.   "Arms Control Pacts Can Be Verified."
in *Discover* (8:4), April 1987, p. 78-93.
       The author discusses not only conventional imagery, but
also synthetic aperture radar satellites, over the horizon
radar, and a number of other speculative discussions. Includes
William E. Burrows' short "We Have an Edge in Quality, But the
Soviets Overwhelm Us in Quantity" (p. 92-93). See also entry
442, Hafemeister, Romm, and Tsipis, "The Verification of
Compliance With Arms-Control Agreements."

479.   United States Forces, European Theater. The General
Board. G2 Section Study No. 19, "The Utilization of Tactical
Air Force Reconnaissance Units of the Army Air Forces to Secure
Information for Ground Forces in the European Theater."
Typescript, c. 1946.

480.   U.S. Library of Congress. Congressional Research
Service. *Soviet Space Programs 1981-87.* Part I: *Piloted
Space Activities, Launch Vehicles, and Tracking Support.* Part
2: *Space Science, Space Applications, Military Space Programs,
Administrative Resource Burden, and Master Log of Spaceflights.*
Prepared for the U.S. Senate Committee on Commerce, Science,
and Transportation. Washington, D.C.: Government Printing
Office, 1988-89. vol. I: xii + 280 p. vol. 2: xii + pages
numbered 281-551.
       Previous versions of this useful compilation were entitled
Soviet Space Programs 1962; 1962-65; 1966-1970; 1971-75 (2
vols); *1976-80* with supplements to 1983 (3 vols). In the 1988
edition, see especially Vol. I, Chapter 1, Historical Summary
of all Soviet Space missions, especially since 1975; and Vol.
2, Chapter 4: Soviet military space satellites, including all
forms of surveillance satellites, with tables of launches,
coverage times in orbit, etc.

481.   Ulery, Vincent L.   "The Mohawk, A Key Member of the Army
Surveillance Family that Gives Wings to the Army's Combat
Intelligence Gathering Effort." *Army Information Digest.*
January 1966, p. 18-21.
       The OV-1 MOHAWK, for three decades the primary U.S. Army
imagery reconnaissance aircraft.

482.   Winchester, J.   "Aerial Reconnaissance in Peace and
War." *NATO's Fifteen Nations* (8:4), April 1963, p. 98-103,
and (8:5), May 1963, p. 90-99.

483.   Winterbotham, Francis W. *The Nazi Connection.* New
York: Harper & Row; London: Weidenfeld & Nicolson, 1978.
222 p.
       This account differs from Winterbotham's other works in
discussing prewar British and French intelligence collection
against Germany, including both agents and cooperative aerial
overflights of German territory.

484.   York, Herbert F. and G. Allen Greb.   "Strategic Reconnaissance." in *Bulletin of the Atom Scientists* April, 1977, p. 33-41.

    US reconnaissance aircraft and the development of early satellites (Discoverer, International Geophysical Year efforts, etc.)

5

Human Intelligence
and
Counter Intelligence

General Sources

485.   Aldouby, Zwy and Jerrold Ballinger. *The Shattered Silence: The Eli Cohen Affair.* New York: Coward, McCann, and Geoghegan; Toronto: Longmans Canada, Ltd., 1971. x + 453 p.
   Eliahou Cohen was an extremely effective Mossad agent, who spied on Syrian military and political actions until his apprehension, along with 36 collaborators, in 1965. This is a serious, thorough discussion of a key example of human intelligence, although it is marred by some anti-Syrian bias.

486.   Aldrich, Richard. "Soviet Intelligence, British Security and the End of the Red Orchestra: The Fate of Alexander Rado." *Intelligence and National Security* (6:1), January 1991, p. 196-217.
   In 1945, the head of the Swiss network of the Soviet Red Orchestra intelligence system attempted to sell himself to British intelligence in Cairo, while he was en route home to the Soviet Union, where he was imprisoned until Stalin's death. This is a case in which the British intelligence services were unaware of his significance, and allowed him to pass on.

487.   American Bar Association. Working Group on Intelligence Oversight and Accountability. *Oversight and Accountability of the U.S. Intelligence Agencies: An Evaluation.* [Chicago]: American Bar Association, 1985.   119 p.
   Describes the development and use of various oversight bodies to supervise U.S. intelligence in the 1980s, based on questionnaires to a variety of former intelligence officials and political figures.

488.   Baldy, Tom F. *Battle for Ulster: A Study of Internal Security.* Washington, D.C.: National Defense University Press, 1987. xv + 137 p.
   Pages 12-20 discuss intelligence collection and analysis in Northern Ireland.

489.   Ballendorf, Dirk A. "Earl Hancock Ellis: The Man and his Mission." *U.S. Naval Institute Proceedings* (109:11),

November 1983, pp. 53-60.
The story of a brilliant but alcoholic U.S. Marine officer who undertook a quasi-official spy mission on Japanese islands in the Pacific in 1923.

490.   Beam, John C. "The Intelligence Background of Operation TORCH." *Parameters* (13:4), December 1983, pp. 60-68.
Robert Murphy's political and operational intelligence preparation for the invasion of North Africa, 1942.

491.   Best, S. Payne. *The Venlo Incident.* London and New York: Hutchinson, 1950. 255 p.
The author was one of two British secret intelligence agents kidnapped by the German Sicherheistdienst after being lured to the Dutch-German border crossing at Venlo during the phoney war after the fall of Poland. This incident remains an unsolved mystery. Most of the work, however, is Best's memoirs as a prisoner of war in Germany.

492.   Bleicher, Hugo E. *Colonel Henri's Story: The War Memoirs of Hugo Bleicher, Former German Secret Agent.* ed. Ian Colvin. London: William Kimber, 1954. 200 p.
Sgt Bleicher was a successful counterintelligence agent for the Abwehr, who trapped various allied agents by pretending to represent a peace party in Germany.

493.   Bondy, Ruth. *The Emissary: A Life of Enzo Sereni.* Boston: Atlantic Monthly Press and Little, Brown, 1977; London: Robson Books, 1978. 265 p.
Sereni was a Jewish Italian who parachuted into Italy as an espionage agent, and was eventually killed by the Germans. This account highlights the relationships between British intelligence and Jewish organizations during World War II.

494.   Boucard, Robert. *Revelations From the Secret Service: The Spy on Two Fronts.* London: Hutchinson, 1930. 173 p.
The author claimed to have been part of a "Mixed Bureau" of French, British, and Belgian intelligence officers during World War I, acting as a French double agent in Germany.

495.   Breuer, William. *Hitler's Undercover War: The Nazi Espionage Invasion of the U.S.A.* New York: St. Martin's Press, 1989. x + 358 p.
This well-researched account focuses on the FBI, but also includes extensive discussion of the Abwehr HUMINT effort.

496.   Bulloch, John, and Miller, Henry. *Spy Ring: A Story of the Naval Secrets Case.* London: Martin Secker and Warburg, 1961. 224 p.
The story of a Soviet espionage ring that focused on British underwater detection techniques.

497.   Capelotti, P.J. (ed.) *Our Man in the Crimea: Commander Hugo Koehler and the Russian Civil War.* Columbia, SC: University of South Carolina Press, 1991. 304 p.
The experiences of a US Navy intelligence officer in south Russia at the end of the Russian Civil War.

498.   Carter, Carolle J.   *The Shamrock and the Swastika: German Espionage in Ireland in World War II.* Palo Alto, Ca: Pacific Books, 1977.   287 p.

Based on German (but not British or Irish) records, this is a study of the inept Abwehr and Sicherheitdienst efforts to infiltrate Ireland, preparing to bring Ireland into the war in the event that Germany invaded Britain.   Although more concerned with subversion than actually intelligence gathering, it provides useful comments on the difficulty of introducing agents into a foreign country.

499.   Chapman, Guy.   *The Dreyfus Case: A Reassessment.* New York: Raynal and Co., 1955;   Stein and Day, 1972.   London; B.T. Batsford, 1972.   272 p.

The most celebrated civil-military issue of the Third French Republic began as a badly-botched matter of counter-intelligence. Capt. Alfred Dreyfus, an artilleryman of Jewish origin, was falsely accused of selling information to Germany. Once committed to this accusation, French Army officers forced documents and violated legal procedures to ensure that Dreyfus was convicted and, indirectly, that the real traitor was protected.   Twelve years and four trials later, Dreyfus was finally acquitted.   Chapman's is the best of several modern studies of the case.

500.   Charters, David A.   "British Intelligence in the Palestine Campaign, 1945-47."   *Intelligence and National Security* (6:1), January 1991, p. 115-140.

British police intelligence lacked the organization and resources to collect effectively against terrorist groups such as the Irgun and Stern Gang, a failure which was a principal cause for British withdrawal from Palestine.

501.   Clutterbuck, Richard L.   "Communist Defeat in Malaya: A Case Study." *Military Review* (43:9), September 1963, p. 63-78.

The key role of rewarding and protecting villagers who provided information on the insurgents in malaya.

502.   _____.   "The SEP [Surrendered Enemy Personnel]: Guerrilla Intelligence Source." *Military Review* (42:10), October 1962, p. 13-21.

503.   Cockerill, George.   *What Fools We Were.* London: Hutchinson, 1944.   169 p.

Cockerill served in British military intelligence in India, the Boer War, and World War I.   He was director of special intelligence for the Imperial General Staff during the latter war.   This study provides much on counterintelligence and censorship, and relatively little on cryptanalysis, despite the author's claim that he used signals intelligence extensively from the Boer War onward.

504.   Collier, Basil.   *Hidden Weapons: Allied Secret or Undercover Services in World War II.* London: Hamilton, 1982. xviii + 386 p.

505.   Collier, Richard.   *Ten Thousand Eyes.* New York: E.P.

Dutton and Co., Inc., 1958.
      Account of the French intelligence network that assembled detailed allied information on the German Atlantic Wall defenses, prior to the invasion of 1944.

506.   Coon, Carleton S. *A North Africa Story: An Anthropologist As OSS Agent, 1941-1943.* Ipswich, Ma: Gambit, 1980. xi + 146 p.
      This study was written as an after action report for his service as an intelligence collector, counter-intelligence agent, agent trainer, and (belatedly) soldier. An early civilian recruit to the OSS, he was commissioned directly as a major of infantry in May 1943.

507.   Corvo, Max. *The O.S.S. in Italy 1942-1945.* New York, Westport, Ct., and London: Praeger, 1990. x + 325 p.
      The author was chief of the OSS in Italy; his account reflects the bias of that organization by emphasizing his resistance activities, but there is also some discussion of OSS intelligence functions, including support of field armies.

508.   Dakin, Douglas. *The Greek Struggle in Macedonia 1897-1913.* Salonika, Greece: Institute for Balkan Studies, 1966. 477 p.
      A massively-researched study of the diplomatic, military, and covert activities of Greece in Turkish Macedonia. The discussion of Greek consuls organizing intelligence collection networks and insurgent bands is a useful illustration of the intelligence functions such diplomatic outposts have performed.

509.   Dan, Uri and Y. Ben-Porat. *The Secret War: The Spy Game in the Middle East.* New York: Sabra Books, 1970. 243 p.
      Journalistic accounts of Israeli, Egyptian, and Soviet espionage, include Israel Beek, a Soviet agent who allegedly penetrated the Israeli defense structure. The credibility of these stories is limited by the lack of sources.

510.   DeForest, Orrin and Chanoff, David. *Slow Burn: The Rise and Bitter Fall of American Intelligence in Vietnam.* New York: Simon and Schuster, 1990. 294 p.
      DeForest organized highly successful agent networks in Vietnam from 1968 onward, but was not allowed to evacuate his agents prior to the fall of Saigon in 1975.

511.   Downes, Donald. *The Scarlet Thread: Adventures in Wartime Espionage.* London: Derek Verschogle, 1953. xiii + 207 p.
      Downes claims that he volunteered his services to the US government and undertook area reconnaissance of the Persian Gulf, Middle East, etc in 1940. During World War II, he was an OSS officer acting in tactical support of 5th US Army in North Africa and Italy.

512.   Dovey, H.O. "Operation Condor." *Intelligence and National Security* (4:2), April 1989, p. 357-373.
      An examination of official British records concerning the legendary German espionage mission to Cairo in 1942.

513. _____. "The Unknown War: Security in Italy, 1943-45." *Intelligence and National Security* (3:2), April 1988, p. 285-311.

The tactical counterintelligence activities of the British 417th Field Security Section.

514. Eldridge, Justin L. C. "German Human Intelligence and the Conduct of 'Operation Citadel'." *Military Intelligence* (15:1), Jan-Mar 1989, p. 23-25.

Eldridge argues that, contrary to General Gehlen's contentions, German human intelligence had a relatively limited role in the battle of Kursk, 1943. He argues that prisoner of war interrogations and the few available spies provided doubtful and conflicting information.

515. Eppler, John. *Operation Condor: Rommel's Spy.* London: Macdonald and Jane's, 1977. 243 p.

Eppler was a German agent, part of the Kondor mission apprehended in Egypt in 1942.

516. Errante, Guido. "The German Intelligence Service During the World War." *Cavalry Journal* (42), November-December 1933, p. 16-18.

The training of German agents for specific military intelligence/reconnaissance missions.

517. Etzold, Thomas H. "The (F)utility Factor: German Information Gathering in the United States, 1933-1941." *Military Affairs* (39:2), April 1975, p. 77-82.

Assesses the effectiveness of German officials collecting information in the United States. Etzold contends that the Germans frequently misunderstood the nature of American politics and society, and in any event failed to use the intelligence they collected, such as the plans for the Norden bombsight.

518. Farago, Ladislas. *Burn After Reading; The Espionage History of World War II.* New York: Walker, 1961. xiv + 319 p.

Farago attempted to include all clandestine operations, including counterintelligence, sabotage, subversion, etc. His account ranges from the "Polish attack" that Hitler staged to justify his invasion in 1930, through spying and codebreaking at Pearl Harbor, to the end of the war in both theaters.

519. _____. *War of Wits: The Anatomy of Espionage and Intelligence.* Westport, Ct: Greenwood Press, 1976; New York: Funk and Wagnalls, 1954. ix + 379 p.

Historically-illustrated basic explanations of human intelligence and related activities, including some of his own propaganda work in World War II. As such, this book is somewhat better than Farago's other histories, which are slightly sensationalized.

520. Feldt, Eric A. *The Coastwatchers.* New York and Melbourne: Oxford University Press, 1946. 264 p.

A history of FERDINAND, the coastwatcher organization established by the Australian Navy. The author was the intelligence staff officer at Port Moresby responsible for Papua, New Guinea, and the Solomon Islands during World War II.

521.   Felstead, Sidney T. *German Spies at Bay: Being an Actual Record of the German Espionage in Great Britain During the Years 1914-1918, Compiled From Official Sources.* New York: Brentano's; London; Hutchinson, 1920. 288 p.
    Counterintelligence lessons of German incompetence in attempting to infiltrate wartime Britain.

522.   Finnegan, John P. "U.S. Army Counterintelligence in CONUS - The World War I Experience." *Military Intelligence* (14:1), January 1988, p. 17-21.
    The author contends that this effort was successful, even if the U.S. did exaggerate the threat of subversion.

523.   FitzGibbon, Constantine. *Secret Intelligence in the 20th Century.* London: Hart-Davis, 1976. 350 p.

524.   Foglesong, David S. "Xenophon Kalamatiano: An American Spy in Revolutionary Russia?" *Intelligence and National Security* (6:1), January 1991, p. 154-195.
    In September 1918, the Cheka arrested this Greek-Russian-American businessman as a spy. Foglesong attempts to trace his recruitment by the U.S. consul, and concludes that the U.S. government was unaware of many of Kalamatiano's activities.

525.   Fourcade, Marie-Madeleine. *Noah's Ark: A Memoir of Struggle and Resistance.* New York: E.P. Dutton, 1974; London: Allen and Unwin, 1973.   371 p.
    A shortened translation of a 1968 French book about a World War II espionage network that operated throughout occupied France.   This network provided the allies with intelligence concerning V-weapons, submarine bases, the sorties of German surface combatants, etc.

526.   French, David. "Sir John French's Secret Service on the Western Front, 1914-15." *Journal of Strategic Studies* (7:4), December 1984, p. 423-440.
    An account of the wartime improvisation of British espionage networks, using German socialists and similar sympathizers behind enemy lines.   Although the collection effort was well organized under Sir George MacDonogh, the Brig.Gen. (Intel) of the British Expeditionary Force staff, the author concludes the analysis and prediction were less successful.

527.   Friedheim, Eric. "Welcome to Dulag Luft." *Air Force* (28), September 1945, p. 16-17, 73.
    German interrogation techniques.

528.   Garnier-Raymond, Philippe. *The Tangled Web.* Trans. Len Ortzen. New York: Pantheon Books/Random House, 1968. 203 p. (Original *Le Reseau Etrangle,* Paris: Librairie Artheme Fayard, 1967.)
    An account of the "England Spiel," the successful German effort to trap and turn all British SOE agents who entered the Netherlands during World War II. Although there were pre-

arranged mistakes to be made in radio transmissions to indicate duress, the SOE ignored such warnings, apparently not understanding the precautions necessary to infiltrate German-held territory. As such, this is the German counterpart to Masterman's *The Double-Cross System*, entry 549.

529.   Gilchrist, Andrew. *Bangkok Top Secret: Being the Experiences of a British officer in the Siam Country Section of Force 136*. London: Hutchinson, 1970.   230 p.
Gilchrist was a desk officer for Burma in the Special Operations Executive during World War II.

530.   Glantz, David M. "Observing the Soviets: U.S. Army Attaches in Eastern Europe During the 1930s." *Journal of Military History* (55:2), April 1991, p. 153-183.
Originally a conference paper, this article examines the accuracy with which US military attaches in the Baltic states perceived the military doctrine, mechanization, and purges of the Red Army in the 1930s. As such, it is a model of how attaches can act as key HUMINT collectors.

531.   Hemphill, John A. "PW and Captured Document Doctrine." *Military Review* (49:11), November 1969, p. 65-71.
The author argues that, in counterinsurgency campaigns such as Vietnam, the importance of *fresh* combat information is so great that the conventional doctrine of evacuating prisoners to the rear for detailed interrogation is ineffective. Moreover, there really is no safe "rear" area that would satisfy the requirements of the Geneva Convention, hence no legal reason for such evacuation provided that prisoners are protected as much as possible.

532.   Herrick, Robert M. "Where Is the Enemy? (Prisoner Interrogation and Maptracking.)" *Army* (21:6) June 1971, p. 46-49.
The author talked prisoners through their movements on a map, in order to locate other enemy forces.

533.   Higgins, Trumball. "'East Wind Rain.'" *U.S. Naval Institute Proceedings* (81:11), November 1955, p. 1198-1205.
The story of the Japanese decision to attack the U.S. rather than the Soviet Union in 1941, including Richard Sorge's espionage for the Soviets.

534.   Hinsley, Francis H. and C. A. G. Simkins. *British Intelligence in the Second World War*. Vol. 4: *Security and Counter-Intelligence*.   London: Her Majesty's Stationary Office, 1990.   408 p.
Regrettably, this volume of Hinsley's monumental study names very few personalities, thereby ignoring issues of moles and other counter-intelligence problems.

535.   Hirschfeld, Thomas J. "The Toughest Verification Challenge: Conventional Forces in Europe." *Arms Control Today* (19:1), January-February 1989, p. 16-21.
The problems of inspection and verification of the Conventional Forces in Europe arms reduction agreement. Written before the final collapse of the USSR, this account

accurately reflects Soviet resistance to on-sight inspection, a form of overt HUMINT that was essential for confidence in mutual arms reductions.

536.   Hohne, Heinz. *Codeword: Direktor; The Story of the Red Orchestra.* New York: Coward, McCann, and Geoghegan, 1971. 310 p. Paperback New York: Ballentine Espionage/Intelligence Library, 1982.
    A well-documented account of the Soviet espionage ring and German counterespionage efforts during World War II;   the author contends that the ring's efforts have been exaggerated.

537.   Kelly, John. "Intelligence and Counterintelligence in German Prisoner-of-War Camps in Canada during World War II." *Dalhousie Review* (48), Summer 1978, passim.

538.   Kirby, Norman. *1100 Miles With Monty: Security and Intelligence at Tac HQ.* Gloucester, England: Alan Sutton, 1989. viii + 200 p.
    From 1943 to 1946, Sgt. Kirby was both a security guard and an interpreter for Field Marshal Montgomery.

539.   Koop, Theodore F. *Weapon of Silence.* Chicago: University of Chicago Press, 1946. xi + 304 p.
    Koop was Deputy Director of censorship for the United States during World War II, and describes not only information security itself, but also how censors identified military spies who communicated with invisible ink.

540.   Koudelka, Edward R. *Counter Intelligence: The Conflict and the Conquest: Recollections of a World War II Agent in Europe.* Guilderland, NY: Ranger, 1986. viii + 149 p.
    The memoirs of an American Counter Intelligence Corps special agent in Iceland, Britain, and Europe.

541.   Lawson, John C. *Tales of Aegean Intrigue.* New York: Dutton, 1921. 258 p.
    Lawson was a British naval intelligence officer in Crete 1916-17, spying on the Austrians and in the process interfering in Greece without British government authority.

542.   Leary, William M. "Portrait of an Intelligence Officer: James McHugh in China, 1937-42." p. 249-263 in William B. Cogar (ed.) *Naval History: The Seventh Symposium of the U.S. Naval Academy.* Wilmington, De: Scholarly Resources, Inc, 1988.
    This USMC officer served almost constantly in China during the 1920s and 1930s. As such, he was an unofficial channel of intelligence and diplomatic information between the U.S. and Chinese Nationalist governments.

543.   Liberti, Joseph C. "Counterintelligence in Direct Support." *Infantry* (64:2), March-April 1974, p. 39-42.
    Tactical   counterintelligence   and   prisoner   of   war interrogation in Vietnam, including the use of Kit Carson defector/scouts.

544.   Listowel, Judith. *Crusader in the Secret War.* London: Christopher Johnson, 1952. 287 p.

The story of Col. Jan Kowalewski, alias Peter Bart, a Polish agent in Lisbon during World War II. His prewar service with the Polish cryptologic service is mentioned only briefly.

545.   Lord, Walter. *Lonely Vigil: The Untold Story of the South Pacific Coastwatchers.* New York: Viking Press, 1977. 322 p.

546.   MacKenzie, Compton. *Aegean Memories.* London: Chatto and Windus, 1940. 410 p. *First Athenian Memories.* London: Cassell, 1931. 394 p. *Greek Memories.* London: Chatto and Windus, 19. 448 p.
    Three volumes of British intelligence in World War I, especially counterintelligence operations in Greece.

547.   Martilli, George and Hollard, Michel. *The Man Who Saved London: The Story of Michel Hollard.* London: Collins, 1960. Also published as *Agent Extraordinary: The Story of Michel Hollard.* Garden City, NY: Doubleday & Co., 1961. 258 p.
    The actions of a special French espionage net ("Agir") that collected technical intelligence on the German V-1 flying bomb launch sites.

548.   Mashbir, Sidney F. *I Was an American Spy.* New York: Vantage Press, 1953. x + 374 p.
    Memoirs of an early U.S. Army intelligence officer, including service in Japan between the two World Wars, and wartime direction of MacArthur's Allied Translator and Interpreter Section (ATIS.)

549.   Masterman, John C. *The Double-Cross System in the War of 1939 to 1945.* New Haven, Ct, and London: Yale University Press, 1972. xxi + 203 p.
    A classic account of counterintelligence and the use of double agents for deception purposes. Assigned to MI-5, Masterman was head of the XX or "Double-Cross" Committee that coordinated the use of captured German agents to support strategic deception programs in Britain during World War II. This is an after action report that he struggled to have declassified as an intelligence textbook. Among other things, he notes that wartime espionage is difficult and unprofitable, while wartime counterespionage is relatively easy because the resources of the state are mobilized. In peacetime, the difficulty and profitability of espionage and counterespionage are reversed. (For other views of the Double-Cross system, see items 552, 557, and 560.)

550.   _____. *On the Chariot Wheel.* London: Oxford University Press, 1975. 378 p.
    Masterman's autobiography, which spends only a few chapters in World War II.

551.   Moorehead, Alan. *The Traitors.* New York: Harper & Row, 1963. 236 p. Paperback ed. New York: Dell Publishing, 1965. 215 p.
    The Soviet espionage agents who passed information on nuclear weapons during and after World War II.

552.   Mure, David.   *Practice to Deceive.* London: William
Kimber, 1977.   270 p.
    Mure was the counterpart to John Masterman (see above),
acting as chairman of the XXX Committee that coordinated
counter-espionage and double agents in the Middle East.   As
such, he worked closely with Brigadier Dudley Clarke, the
master of British operational and strategic deception.

553.   Owens, William A.   *Eye-Deep in Hell: A Memoir of the
Liberation of the Philippines, 1944-45.* Dallas, Tx: Southern
Methodist University Press, 1989.   245 p.
    The author was a Ph.D. technical sergeant in the Counter
Intelligence Corps during the American reconquest of Leyte and
Luzon.   His memoirs are powerfully written, and reflect the
daily problems of counter intelligence soldiers in wartime.

554.   O'Toole, George J. A.   *Honorable Treachery: A History
of U.S. Intelligence, Espionage, and Covert Action from the
American Revolution to the CIA.* New York: Atlantic Monthly
Press, 1991.   xv + 591 p.

555.   Paige, Byron.   "Make the Most of Your Prisoners."
Military Review (22:10) October 1942, p. 44-45.
    Paige emphasizes the need to control the environment of
interrogations, by means such as smartness and discipline on
the part of the guards, exploiting the psychological shock of
capture, and using only trained interrogators.   His examples
come from both World Wars.

556.   Peis, Ghunter.   *The Mirror of Deception: How Britain
Turned the Nazi Spy Machine Against Itself.*   London:
Weidenfeld and Nicolson, 1977.   181 p.
    The story of Masterman's XX Committee told from the German
viewpoint.   See also item 549, above.

557.   Persico, Joseph E.   *Piercing the Reich: The Penetration
of Nazi Germany By American Secret Agents During World War II.*
New York: Viking Press, 1979.   xviii + 376 p.
    This study is based on interviews with many former OSS
officials, but Persico has still been criticized for greatly
exaggerating the success of OSS agents in Germany.

558.   Pilat, Oliver.   *The Atom Spies.* New York; G. P.
Putnam's Sons, 1952.   302 p.
    A good early account of the Rosenberg case of Soviet
espionage in the US nuclear weapons program.

559.   Plotke, Alma J.   The Dunsterforce Military Intelligence
Mission to North Persia in 1918. University of California, Los
Angeles Ph.D. dissertation, 1987.   327 p.   LC. No. AAC8803676.
    The story of a conscious British effort to use a counter-
intelligence network as a primary means of controlling an area
of Persia.   The author argues that this effort set the tone for
subsequent Western intelligence operations in the area.

560.   Popov, Dusko.   *Spy/Counterspy.* New York: Grosset and
Dunlap; London: Weidenfeld and Nicolson, 1974.   ix + 339 p.
    Popov was "Tricycle," a British double agent for the XX

Committee in World War II. Some observers have argued that the detailed questionnaire about Pearl Harbor defenses passed to Popov by German intelligence was a missed indicator of the coming Japanese attack. These memoirs are somewhat romanticized, however.

561.   Reese, Mary Ellen. *General Reinhard Gehlen: The CIA Connection.* Fairfax, Va: George Mason University Press, 1990. 240 p.
       A large portion of this book is devoted to the process by which, in 1945-47, U.S. Army counterintelligence sponsored Gehlen in reestablishing the German military intelligence activities aimed at the Soviet Army, and the problems Gehlen experienced in identifying double agents within the resulting organization. See also Gehlen's memoirs in the Organization chapter.

562.   Rout, Leslie B., Jr., and Bratzel, John F. "Espionage and Allied Shipping during World War II." p. 226-233 in Daniel M. Masterson (ed.) *Naval History: The Sixth Symposium of the U.S. Naval Academy.* Wilmington, De: Scholarly Resources, Inc., 1987.
       On 8 October 1942, Under Secretary of State Sumner Welles accused Argentina and Chile of failing to stop Axis agents who were spying on Allied merchant ship movements. In fact, the authors argue that there was little evidence behind this accusation; Welles apparently sought to stampede the two nations into breaking relations with Germany and being more alert to espionage.

563.   Sansom, A. W. *I Spied Spies.* London: George Harrap, 1965. 271 p.
       Sansom was head of British field security, including counterintelligence, in Cairo during and after World War II.

564.   Schlesinger, Thomas O. "Obligations of the Prisoner of War." *Military Review* (50:12), December 1970, p. 80-85.
       The author, an interrogation officer during World War II, provides examples of seemingly-innocent questions by interrogators leading to the discovery of useful military information. As a result, commanders must train soldiers not to participate in any interrogations or discussions.

565.   Schwartzwalder, John. *We Caught Spies.* New York: Duell, Sloan and Pearce, 1946. xii + 296 p.
       A US counterintelligence major in North Africa, Italy, France, Belgium, and Germany during World War II. As such, he lays great stress on the value of skillful interrogation.

566.   Scotland, A.P. *The London Cage.* London: Evans Brothers, 1957. 195 p.
       Scotland's service to British intelligence began when he enlisted in the German Army in West Africa (1904-07), and climaxed as head of British prisoner of war interrogation during and after World War II. These memoirs only discuss selected periods of the two world wars and the postwar search for war criminals.

567.   Serguyev, Lily. *Secret Service Rendered*. London:
William Kimber, 1968. 223 p.
    Serguyev was the niece of a White Russian general who
deliberately joined German intelligence to betray them. She
was involved in the Doublecross and Fortitude deception
operations, but these memoirs are more critical of both sides
than they are informative. See John Masterman's *The
Doublecross System*, entry 549.

568.   Simpson, Keith. "The German Experience of Rear Area
Security on the Eastern Front, 1941-45." *Royal United Service
Institution Journal for Defense Studies* (121:4), December 1976,
p. 39-46.
    German counter-intelligence and tactical intelligence was
disorganized, limited the effectiveness of rear area protection
measures against the Soviets.

569.   Spector, Ronald. "Allied Intelligence and Indochina,
1943-45." *Pacific Historical Review* (51), February 1982, p.
23-50.
    Spector recaps his findings from the U.S. Army's official
history of the Vietnamese war. An Office of Strategic Services
team went to French Indochina, but was unable to supply the
French who opposed the Japanese occupation. Thereafter, the
presence and role of American intelligence forces became
involved in diplomatic questions about the postwar status of
Indochina.

570.   Steinhauer, Gustav. *Steinhauer: The Kaiser's Master
Spy: The Story As Told By Himself.* Ed. S. T. Felstead. New
York: D. Appleton and Co., 1931. xi + 356 p.
    Steinhauer was essentially a security officer for Kaiser
Wilhelm II, with some counterintelligence duties. In these
rather boastful memoirs, however, he claims to have spied in
Britain repeatedly prior to World War I, and to have known a
German agent who attempted to infiltrate the headquarters of
the Russian General Rennenkampf in 1914.

571.   Suvorov, Viktor. *Aquarium: The Career and Defection of
a Soviet Military Spy.* Translated by David Floyd. London:
Hamish Hamilton, 1985. 249 p.

572.   Tennant, Peter. "Swedish Intelligence in the Second
World War." *Intelligence and National Security* (2:2), April
1987, p. 354-361.
    An extended review of Wilhelm Carlgren's *Svensk
Underratelsetjanst 1939/45* (1985), by a British intelligence
officer of that era who summarizes successful Swedish espionage
against both German and allied military plans.

573.   Thompson, Basil. *The Allied Secret Service in Greece.*
London: Hutchinson, 1931. 284 p.
    French naval intelligence operations, primarily political,
in Greece, 1914-22.

574.   Thorpe, Elliott R. *East Wind, Rain; the Intimate
Account of an Intelligence Officer in the Pacific, 1939-1949.*
Boston: Gambit, 1969. ix + 307 p.

Thorpe was General MacArthur's counter intelligence chief during World War II, and head of civil intelligence during the occupation of Japan. This book provides useful information about interrogation, censorship, and the uses of intelligence.

575.   Toliver, Raymond F. *The Interrogator: The Story of Hans Scharff, Luftwaffe's Master Interrogator.*   Fallbrooke, Ca: Aero Publishers, 1978. 384 p.
A fascinating account, often in the first person, of how Scharff tricked captured American flyers into divulging information. This book is valuable not only for interrogation techniques but also for prisoner of war resistance training.

576.   Tompkins, Peter. *A Spy in Rome.* New York: Simon & Schuster, 1962. 347 p.
The author was a civilian, arbitrarily commissioned a major and sent by the Office of Strategic Services to spy in Rome during World War II.

577.   Trepper, Leopold, with Patrick Roman. *The Great Game: Memoirs of the Spy Hitler Couldn't Silence.* Trans. by Helen Weaver. New York: McGraw-Hill, 1977; published in London by Michael Joseph as *The Great Game: The Story of the Red Orchestra.* 442 p.
Trepper was the head of the Red Orchestra intelligence network, and survived imprisonment by both Germans and his Soviet masters.

578.   U.S. Central Intelligence Agency. *The Rote Kapelle: The CIA's History of Soviet Intelligence and Espionage Networks in Western Europe, 1936-1945.* Washington, D.C.: University Publications of America, 1979. xiii + 390 p.
A declassified study of the famous Soviet intelligence network focused primarily on German military operations.

579.   U.S. Congress. House Permanent Select Committee on Intelligence. "U.S. Intelligence Performance and the September 20, 1984, Beirut Bombing: Report of the Permanent Select Committee on Intelligence." Washington, D.C.: Government Printing Office, 1984.   iii + 4 p.

580.   U.S. Congress. Joint Committee on Atomic Energy. *Soviet Atomic Espionage.* 82d Congress, 1st Session. Report No. 81095. Washington, D.C.: Government Printing Office, 1951. 222 p.
Part I provides an authentic overview of the known spies who passed nuclear weapons information to the USSR.

581.   U.S. Forces, European Theater. The General Board. G2 Section Study No. 13.   "Organization and Operation of the Counterintelligence Corps in the European Theater of Operations." Typescript, c. 1946.

582.   U.S. War Department. American Expeditionary Force. General Staff, Assistant Chief of Staff, G2. "Examination of Prisoners, Heavy Artillery." Paris: A.E.F. General Staff, 1918. 7 p. (Library of Congress)
An early example of interrogation.

583.   U.S. War Department. Far East Command General Headquarters. Military Intelligence Section. *Operations of the Civil Intelligence Section, GHQ, Far East Command and Supreme Commander Allied Powers.* Tokyo: Far East Command, 1949. 4 vols.

584.   Vagts, Alfred. *The Military Attache.* Princeton: Princeton University Press, 1967. 408 p.
     In this classic work, the sections on attache espionage (Chapter 11) and observation of battles (Chapter 13) are particularly useful for the study of human intelligence.

585.   Voska, Emanuel C. and Will H. Irwin. *Spy and Counterspy.* New York: Doubleday, Doran, 1940;   London: Harrap, 1941. xii + 322 p.
     Voska used Czech immigrants to assist US counter-intelligence during World War I, and was eventually commissioned and sent by Col. Van Deman to work on central European intelligence for the American Expeditionary Force.

586.   Walters, Vernon A. *Silent Missions.* New York: Doubleday, 1978. 654 p.
     The memoirs of Lt. Gen. Walters, who rose from private to Deputy Director of the CIA, in large part due to his service as attache and analyst.

587.   West, Nigel. *Games of Intelligence: The Classified Conflict of International Espionage.* London: Nicholson Ltd.; New York: Crown Publishers, Inc., 1989. viii + 248 p.
     Although he describes the organization of the CIA, KGB, GRU, SIS, MI5, Mossad, and French secret service, the focus of this book, as described, is on HUMINT and counter intelligence. It includes extensive lists of spies, defectors, diplomatic expulsions, and other aspects of espionage during the Cold War.

588.   Whitehouse, Arch. *Espionage and Counterespionage: Adventures in Military Intelligence.*   Garden City, NY: Doubleday and Co., 1964.
     A popularized account of a variety of incidents, ranging from the Civil War and the coastwatchers of Guadalcanal to signals intelligence prior to the battle of Midway. The majority of cases, as indicated by the title, are HUMINT, with some photography and signals intelligence.

589.   Whiteside, Thomas. *An Agent in Place: The Wennerstrom Affair.* New York: Viking Press; Toronto: Macmillan, 1966. 150 p.
     Stig Wennerstrom, a Swedish Air Force colonel, was a Soviet agent for many pears prior to his arrest in 1963; he had also been air attache to Washington.

590.   Wild, Max. *Secret Service on the Russian Front.* New York: G.P. Putnam's Sons, 1932. 324 p.
     Wild was a German staff officer on the eastern front throughout World War I, specializing in tactical espionage and counterintelligence. He himself escaped from a Russian prison in 1918.

591.   Wilhelm, Maria. *The Man Who Watched The Rising Sun:
The Story of Admiral Ellis M. Zacharias.* New York: Franklin
Watts, Inc, 1967. 238 p.
   A biography of an outstanding intelligence officer of the
U.S. Navy. Zacharias was also responsible for psychological
warfare campaigns aimed at explaining the allied policy of
unconditional surrender in a manner acceptable to the Japanese.

592.   Yoshikawa, Takeo, and Stanford, Norman. "Top Secret
Assignment." *U.S. Naval Institute Proceedings* (86:12), Dec
1960, p. 27-39.
   As a Japanese naval ensign, Yoshikawa was assigned under
cover to the Japanese consulate in Hawaii, from which he
provided tactical intelligence on the defenses of the naval
base and movement of the American fleet prior to the attack on
Pearl Harbor in 1941. For lack of proof, he was not tried as
a spy, but repatriated with other Japanese diplomats, resuming
his role on the Japanese Naval General Staff in 1942.

593.   Zacharias, Ellis M. *Secret Missions: The Story of an
Intelligence Officer.* New York: Putnam, [1946.] viii + 433 p.
   The author was deputy director of U.S. naval intelligence
in 1942; his memoirs span a career in intelligence, especially
in Japan, beginning in 1920. See his biography by Maria
Wilhelm, *The Man Who Watched the Rising Sun,* entry 591.

U.S. Army Surveillance of Domestic Dissent

594.   Havach, Emil Lynn. The Watchdog Barks At Snooping:
Army Political Spying From 1967 to 1970 and the Media that
Opposed It. University of Arizona M.A. Thesis in Journalism,
1974. 93 p.
   A remarkably objective account, recognizing the
bureaucratic causes for the initiation and continuation of
domestic surveillance by U.S. Army Military Intelligence.

595.   Pyle, Christopher H. *Military Surveillance of Civilian
Politics, 1967-1970.* New York and London: Garland Publishing, Inc., 1986. 433 p.
   A reproduction of the author's 1974 Ph.D. dissertation at
Columbia University, concerning the use of U.S. military
intelligence agents to monitor domestic dissent to the Viet Nam
war. Captain Pyle, himself a former intelligence officer,
touched off the controversy on this subject by a January 1970
article in *The Washington Monthly.*

596.   Sayer, Ian, and Douglas Botting. *America's Secret Army:
The Untold Story of the Counter Intelligence Corps.* New York:
Franklin Watts, 1989. x + 400 p.
   The authors attempt to portray the CIC as a deliberately
concealed organization, which it was not. Such sensationalism
aside, this is a good study of the CIC from the Corps of
Intelligence Police (World War I) through the formation of the
Intelligence Corps in 1961.

597.   Talbert, Roy Jr. *Negative Intelligence: the Army and
the American Left, 1917-1941.* Jackson, Mississippi:

University Press of Mississippi, 1991.   xiv + 303 p.
    Negative Intelligence was the World War I term for
counter-intelligence. The first half of this book is devoted
to the wartime counterespionage effort against organizations
such as the International Workers of the World.

598.   U.S. Congress. Senate Committee on the Judiciary.
Subcommittee on Constitutional Rights. *Army Surveillance of
Civilians.* Washington, D.C.: Government Printing Office. 3
Vols: 1972 (vii + 97 p.), 1973 (v + 150 p.), and 1974 (v + 397
p.)
    Congressional hearings on U.S. Army counterintelligence
agents collecting information about domestic dissent.

599.   U.S. War Department. Military Intelligence Division.
*U.S. Military Intelligence Reports: Surveillance of Radicals
in the United States, 1917-1941.* Frederick, Md: University
Publications of America, 1985.   34 microfilm reels.
    Surveillance reports on such groups as the International
Workers of the World, Bolsheviks, pacifists, and anarchists.

6

Signals Intelligence
and Electronic Warfare

General Sources

600.   Ablett, Charles B.   "Electronic Warfare: A Modern
Weapon System." *Military Review* (46:11), November 1966, p. 3-
11.
    This introduction focuses primarily on World War II,
including Magic codebreaking, the "Battle of the Beams" in
navigation, and the development of radar.   Lt. Col. Ablett
quotes at length from General George C. Marshall's letter to
presidential candidate/Governor Dewey, explaining American
cryptology against the Japanese to prevent that secret from
being disclosed during the 1944 electoral campaign.

601.   Anderson, Robert C.   "C3CM--Lessons from the Past."
Islamic Defense Review (6:2), 1981, p. 33-39.
    Explanation of the Command, Control, and Communications
Countermeasures (C3CM) doctrine with examples from the world
wars.

602.   Ball, Desmond. *Pine Gap: Australia and the US Geo-
stationary Signals Intelligence Satellite Program.*   Sydney:
Allen and Unwin, 1988.

603.   _____.   "Soviet Signals Intelligence: Vehicular
Systems and Operations." *Intelligence and National Security*
(4:1), January 1989, p. 5-27.
    As the title suggests, the author briefly describes Soviet
equipment and then details various clandestine surveillances
conducted against allied military installations and operations.

    604. Bamford, V. James. *The Puzzle Palace: A Report on
America's Most Secret Agency.*   New York: Houghton Mifflin
Co., 1982/Penguin Books, 1983.   655 p.
    Chapter Five, Platforms (pp. 203-301) describes the
alleged military methods of signals intelligence collection,
including field stations, aircraft, satellites, and ships such
as U.S.S. *Liberty* and *Pueblo*.

605.   Bell, Ernest L. *An Initial View of 'Ultra' as an American Weapon.* Keene, NH: TSU Press, 1977. 110 p.

606.   Bond, Donald. *Radio Direction Finders.* New York: McGraw-Hill, 1944. 187 p.

607.   Boyd, Carl. "Significance of MAGIC and the Japanese Ambassador to Berlin: (II) The Crucial Months after Pearl Harbor;"   "(III)   The Months of Growing Certainty;" "(IV) Confirming the Turn of the Tide on the German-Soviet Front." *Intelligence and National Security* (2:2), April 1987, p. 302–319; (3:4), October 1988, p. 83–102; and (4:1), January 1989, p. 86–107.
        Details of the American use of Ambassador Oshima's reports from Berlin for military intelligence purposes.

608.   Carroll, John M. *Secrets of Electronic Espionage.* New York: E.P. Dutton and Co., Inc., 1966. 224 p.
        A very simplified explanation of military signals intelligence, electronic intelligence, and eavesdropping devices, beginning with British monitoring in August 1914.

609.   Chapman, J. W. M. "No Final Solution: A Survey of the Cryptanalytic Capabilities of German Military Agencies, 1926–35." in Andrew, Christopher (ed.) *Codebreaking and Signals Intelligence.* London: Frank Cass and Co., Ltd., 1986) p. 13–47.
        Discusses organization, intercept sites, and operations of German army and navy intelligence.

610.   *The C3I Handbook.*   By the editors of Defense Electronics. Palo Alto, Ca: EW Communications, yearly since 1986.
        An annual with essays by senior Defense Department officials on various U.S. developments in Command, Control, and Communications Countermeasures (C3CM).

611.   Cochran, Alexander S., Jr. Spectre of Defeat: Anglo-American Planning For the Invasion of Italy in 1943. Ph.D. dissertation, The University of Kansas, 1985. viii + 482 p.
        This is one of the few systematic case studies of the impact of signals intelligence on decision making in World War II. The author concludes that, because intelligence accurately reflected Axis indecision, that intelligence was useful but not decisive in allied strategy in the Mediterranean.

612.   Deutsch, Harold C. "The Influence of ULTRA on World War II." *Parameters* (8:4), December 1978, p. 2–15.
        An excellent evaluation of the role of ULTRA on such factors as deception, Churchill as a war leader, and the strategic conduct of the battles in Western Europe.

613.   Drea, Edward J. "Reading Each Other's Mail: Japanese Communications Intelligence, 1920–1941." *Journal of Military History* (55:2), April 1991, p. 185–205.
        Alongside the familiar story of American codebreaking against the Japanese, Prof. Drea surveys the carefully-concealed Japanese successes against American communications,

both diplomatic and military.

614.   _____. *MacArthur's ULTRA: Codebreaking and the War Against Japan, 1942-1945.* Lawrence, Ks: University of Kansas Press, 1992. xv + 296 p.
     Using both Japanese and American sources, Drea provides an integration of ULTRA with all other aspects of the war in the Southwest Pacific.

615.   _____. "ULTRA Intelligence and General Douglas MacArthur's Leap to Hollandia, January-April 1944." *Intelligence and National Security* (5:2), April 1990, p. 323-349.
     An examination of how signals intelligence allowed MacArthur to exploit Japanese ground and naval weaknesses, cutting supply routes and enveloping the Japanese 18th Army.

616.   Dunlap, Orrin E. *Radar: What It Is and How It Works.* New York: Harper, 1948. 268 p.

617.   "Electronic Countermeasures: Special Report." *Aviation Week and Space Technology.* (96), February 21, 1972, p. 38-107.
     A set of essays on various aspects of U.S. and Soviet EW.

618.   Farago, Ladislas. *The Broken Seal: The Story of 'Operation Magic' and the Pearl Harbor Disaster.* New York; Random House; London: Arthur Barker, 1967. 439 p.
     As with many of Farago's works, this is a somewhat sensationalized account of the US and Japanese intelligence dual from the Washington Naval Conference to Pearl Harbor. It includes not only US cryptography of PURPLE and MAGIC, but also Japanese intelligence preparation for war and various cryptologic insecurities.

619.   Ferris, John. "Before 'Room 40': The British Empire and Signals Intelligence, 1898-1914." *Journal of Strategic Studies* (12:4), Dec 1989, p. 431-457.
     The author argues that British officials were well informed on the possibilities of SIGINT by 1914, but had an inadequate personnel base in this (as in all other aspects of intelligence.) Despite this, they were surprised only by how easily they acquired signals information. Ferris discusses previous experience briefly, including the poor telegraph COMSEC of both sides during the Boer War.

620.   Garlinski, Jozef. *The Enigma War.* New York: Charles Scribner's Sons, 1980. Originally published as *Intercept: The Enigma War.* London: J.M. Dent and Sons, 1979. 219 p.
     This is an account at the purely strategic level of allied code-breaking against the Germans and Japanese in World War II. It includes a detailed explanation of the mechanics of codebreaking, beginning with the Polish efforts to reconstruct the German encryption machine.

621.   Glasser, Robert D. "Signals Intelligence and Nuclear Preemption." *Parameters: US Army War College Quarterly* (19:2), June 1989, p. 46-56.
     SIGINT as a source of enemy intentions in nuclear

confrontations. Glasser describes the system of US Emergency Action Messages, which the Soviets will be able to use for traffic analysis of the course of nuclear weapons decisions even if they are unable to decrypt the messages themselves.

622. Gouaze, Linda Y. Needles and Haystacks: The Search for ULTRA in the 1930s. Masters Dissertation (National Security Affairs), Naval Postgraduate School, 1983. 84 p. DTIC No. A 136770 (unclassified/unrestricted release.)
An effort to summarize Polish, French, and British efforts to break the German ENIGMA encryption machine. The obvious conclusion is that the three friendly intelligence services could have achieved more sooner by cooperation and sharing of information.

623.   Gourley, Scott R. "Electronic Warfare: Radar Reflectors and Passive Jamming." *Jane's Soviet Intelligence Review* (2:1), January 1990, p. 41.
The use of corner reflectors and similar matters in Warsaw Pact doctrine.

624. Hannah, Theodore M. "COMINT and COMSEC: The Tactics of 1914-1918." In two parts. *Cryptologic Spectrum* (2:3), Summer 1972, p. 5-9, and (2:4), Fall 1972, p. 8-11.

625. _____. "The Many Lives of Herbert O. Yardley." in *Cryptologic Spectrum* (11:4) Fall 1981, p. 4-29.
See Yardley's memoirs, *The American Black Chamber,* listed below.

626.   Harduni, Brahim. How the Anglo-American Invasion of North Africa in November 1942 Was Prepared and Realised." University of Reading, England, Ph.D. Dissertation, 1987, 377 p.
Chapter X describes the role of ULTRA intelligence.

627.   Hoisington, David B. "Command-Control-Communications Countermeasures and Electronic Warfare," in *Journal of Electronic Defense* (6:3), March 1983, p. 51-62.
A good brief explanation of concepts and terminology, with examples from World War II to Afghanistan.

628.   Horner, David M. "Special Intelligence in the South-West Pacific Area in World War II." *Australian Outlook: Journal of the Australian Institute of International Affairs* (32:3), December 1978, p. 310-327.

629.   Horgan, Penelope S. *Signals Intelligence Support to U.S. Military Commanders: Past and Present.* Carlisle Barracks, Pa.: U.S. Army War College, 1991. iv + 164 p. DTIC No, AD-A237-861.
A National Security Agency analyst reviews past U.S. use of SIGINT, especially during World War II.

630. *The International Countermeasures Handbook.* (various editors). Palo Alto, Ca: EW Communications, Inc., yearly since 1976.
A yearly guide, with illustrations, to Soviet radars,

chaff technology, and a variety of ECM topics.

631.   Johnson, Thomas M.   "Search for the Stolen Sigaba."
Army (12:7) February 1962, p. 50-55.
The colorful story of how an American encryption device
was stolen from the 28th Infantry Division in Colmar on 4
February 1945, and recovered without compromise on 20 March.

632.   Jukes, Geoff.   "More on the Soviets and ULTRA."
Intelligence and National Security (4:2), April 1989, p. 374-
384.
The author has hypothesized that the Soviets may have
captured a functioning ENIGMA code machine when Stalingrad
surrendered.   This article responds to critics of this
hypothesis, noting that Admiral A.G. Golovko implied such
codebreaking in his memoirs.

633.   Kahn, David.   *The Codebreakers: The Story of Secret
Writing.*   New York: Macmillan Co., 1967.   1164 p.
Kahn published this work prior to the revelations
concerning ULTRA, which is here equated to MAGIC intercepts in
the Pacific.   Paradoxically, this study therefore focuses on
aspects of signals intelligence that have been neglected in
more recent studies.   Pages 459-466, for example, discuss
German ground and air tactical signals intelligence units.

634.   _____.   "German Military Eves-Droppers."
Cryptologia, October 1977, p. 378-380.

635.   _____.   "The Significance of Codebreaking and
Intelligence in Allied Strategy and Tactics." in *Newsletter of
the American Committee on the History of the Second World War*
(No. 17), May 1977, p. 3-4.

636.   Lewin, Ronald.   *The Other Ultra.*   London: Hutchinson
and Co., 1982.   Also published as *American Magic: Codes,
Ciphers, and the Defeat of Japan.*   New York: Farrar, Straus
and Giroux, 1982.   xv + 332 p.
An account of strategic-operational level signals
intelligence in the Pacific theater of World War II, especially
MAGIC.   The author's bibliography is an excellent list of
unpublished documents on the subject.

637.   Littlebury, Frank E. and Praeger, Dirck K.   *Invisible
Combat: C3CM;   A Guide for the Tactical Commander.*
Washington, DC: AFCEA International Press, 1986.   81 p.
A good discussion, heavily illustrated from the authors'
U.S. Marine Corps perspective, of the doctrine of Command,
Control, and Communications Countermeasures.

638.   MacDonald, Charles B.   *The Mighty Endeavor: The
American War in Europe.*   New York: Oxford University Press,
1969;   revised edition New York: Morrow, 1986, 621 p.
The revised edition contains an addendum (pp. 571-582)
that masterfully summarizes the revelations and effects of
ULTRA signals intelligence.

639.   Munro, Neil.   *The Quick and the Dead: Electronic Combat*

and Modern Warfare. New York: St. Martin's Press, 1991.   xi
+ 324 p.
    A thorough exposition of US and Soviet doctrine on
electronic warfare, with historical examples.

640.   Murray, Williamson.   "Ultra: Some Thoughts on Its
Impact on the Second World War." *Air University Review* (35:4),
July-August 1984, p. 52-64.

641.   Parrish, Thomas D.   *The Ultra Americans: The U.S. Role
in Breaking the Nazi Codes.* New York: Stein and Day, 1986. 338
p.

642.   Pratt, Fletcher. *Secret and Urgent: The Story of Codes
and Ciphers.* Indianapolis: Bobbs-Merrill, 1939.   249 p.
    This account is episodic, and not without error concerning
World War I.   Nevertheless, it is still useful, and represents
a pioneering study in cryptology.

643.   Price, Alfred.   *The History of U.S. Electronic Warfare.*
Vol. I: *The Years of Innovation - Beginnings to 1946.*
Washington, D.C.:   The Association of Old Crows, 1984.   xxiv +
312 p.
    Despite its title, this is primarily the history of naval
and air radar intelligence and countermeasures during World War
II.   It includes appendices that describe German and Japanese
radar development in detail.

644.   _____.   *Instruments of Darkness: The History of
Electronic Warfare.*   2d Ed.   New York: Charles Scribner's
Sons, London: MacDonald & Jane's 1978.   284 p.
    Again, Price's primary focus is on intelligence and
countermeasures against German radar in World War II, with
brief coverage of airborne countermeasures from 1945 through
the 1973 Arab-Israeli War.   Within its chosen field, however,
this is a sophisticated, well-illustrated book.   It is
especially interesting with regard to the electronic deceptions
associated with the Normandy invasion.

645.   Rogers, Henry H.   "The Role of Electronics in Warfare."
Military Review (29:7) July 1949, p. 23-27.
    An early effort to explain the entire electromagnetic
spectrum to soldiers.

646.   Rolya, William I.   "Intelligence, Security, and
Electronic Warfare." *Signal* (32), March 1978, p. 15-17.

647.   Rusbridger, James. "The Sinking of the 'Automedon' and
the Capture of the 'Nankin.'" *Encounter* (64:5), May 1985. p.
8-14.
    A useful footnote to SIGINT in World War II.   The author
describes how a German naval raider seized critical Royal Navy
ciphers from the mail of a merchant ship in September 1940, and
how another such seizure in May 1942 provided the Japanese with
some indication of allied SIGINT capability, prompting a major
change in the JN25 code.

648.   Spector, Ronald H. (ed.) *Listening to the Enemy: Key*

Documents on the Role of Communications Intelligence in the War With Japan. Wilmington, De: Scholarly Resources, Inc., 1988. xii + 285 p.
     A superb collection of declassified National Security Agency monographs that go far beyond ULTRA/MAGIC, covering many aspects of tactical signals intelligence.   An example of this is "U.S. Army Radio Intelligence in the Philippines, 1932-1944" (p. 43-76)

649.   Spiller, Roger J.   "Assessing ULTRA."   *Military Review* (59: 8), August 1979, p. 13-23.
     Spiller provides an extended review of Winterbotham's *The Ultra Secret*, describing the practical limitations of ULTRA and concluding that many of the claims and criticism made about ULTRA are exaggerated.   The author notes that knowledge of ULTRA would make senior commanders in some cases more optimistic than their uninformed juniors, and that leadership styles should be evaluated accordingly.

650.   Stone, Norman L.   "The Soviets' Broad View of 'Radioelectronic Struggle."   in *The C3I Handbook*, 3d Edition. Palo Alto, Ca: EW Communications, 1988.   p. 170-175.
     A good brief introduction to the Soviet doctrine of Radioelectronic Combat or Struggle.

651.   Streetly, Martin.   "Japan's SIGINT Islands."   *Jane's Defence Weekly* (16:6), August 10, 1991, p. 235-236.
     Locations and projects of alleged US and Japanese Signals Intelligence operations.

652.   Stripp, Alan.   *Codebreaker In the Far East.*   London: Frank Cass, 1989.   224 p.
     The author was a cryptanalyst who worked both in Britain and in India against the Japanese codes. Much of the work is focused on high-level Japanese diplomatic and strategic codes, which indirectly revealed much information about the German war effort.   Stripps also addresses the role of signals intelligence in the British reconquest of Burma.

653.   Syrett, David.   "The Secret War and the Historians." *Armed Forces and Society* (9:2), Winter 1983, p. 293-328.
     An excellent review essay on the various publications concerning signals intelligence during World War II.   The author uses the sortie of the German warship *Tirpitz* to illustrate the problems of using such intelligence.

654.   Thomas, Andy.   "British Signals Intelligence after the Second World War."   *Intelligence and National Security* (3:4), October 1988, p. 103-110.
     The forgotten continuation of signals intelligence efforts after 1945, especially by the Royal Air Force.

655.   Thurbon, M.T.   "The Origins of Electronic Warfare." *Royal United Service Institution Journal for Defense Studies* (122), Sep 1977, p. 56-73.
     An invaluable survey of electronic warfare PRIOR to 1939, studying land, sea, and air operations as far back as the U.S. Civil War, when Confederate signalmen interfered with Union

telegrams.

656.   United States. National Defense Research Committee. Division 15.   "Electronic Warfare History, World War II." *Electronic Warfare* (4), Summer 1972 and Fall 1972, p. 20+ and 20-22+.

657.   Watt, Robert A.   *The Pulse of Radar.* New York: Dial Press, 1959.   438 p.

658.   West, Nigel. *The SIGINT Secrets: The Signals Intel- ligence War 1900 to Today, Including the Persecution of Gordon Welchman.* New York: William Morrow and Co., 1988.   347 p.
    Primarily an account of British codebreaking, including the prosecution of Welchman, author of *The Hut 6 Story* about British ULTRA decryption in World War II.

659.   Westwood, James T. "Soviet Electronic Warfare - Theory and Practice." *Jane's Soviet Intelligence Review* (1:9), September and (1:10) October 1989, p. 386-391 and 443-446.
    A good summary of the terms, systems, and tactical organization of Soviet EW, which set the pattern for much of the world.

660.   Winterbotham, Frederick W.   *The Ultra Secret.* New York: Harper and Row, 1974.   199 p. paperback New York: Dell, 1975, 1982.
    The book that began the ULTRA controversy, the first English-language account of the allied ability to read the German Enigma encryption system in World War II. As the first effort in the field, it inevitably contains some factual errors.

661.   Yardley, Herbert O.   *The American Black Chamber.* Indianapolis, In: Bobbs-Merrill, 1931.
    From 1913 to 1928, Yardley was one of America's top cryptographers, primarily for the State Department but also for counterintelligence purposes during World War I, when he was commissioned in the U.S. Army.

Air Signals Intelligence and Electronic Warfare

662.   Case, Blair. "Project Window: The First Air Defense Countermeasure." *Air Defense Artillery* Summer 1983, pp. 20- 23.
    A brief account of the British use of chaff to deceive German air defense radars during World War II.

663.   Clayton, Aileen. *The Enemy Is Listening.* London: Hutchinson & Co., Ltd, 1980;   New York: Ballentine Books, 1982.   404 p.
    A rare memoir of tactical signals intelligence during World War II, by the first woman commissioned in the Royal Air Force Y Service. A fascinating personal account.

664.   Cook, Nick. "EW: The Missing Link." *Jane's Defence*

Weekly (16:6), August 10, 1991, p. 250.
   Royal Air Force problems during the 1991 Gulf Conflict, caused by a lack of countermeasures for Tornado aircraft and similar shortfalls.

665.   Davis, Burke. *Get Yamamoto.* New York: Random House, 1969. 231 p.
   The U.S. used a SIGINT report that Admiral Isoroku Yamamoto would visit Bougainville on a particular time, and used P-38 fighters to intercept and destroy his aircraft.

666.   Deeley, Walter G. "A Fresh look at the Purple Dragon." *Signal* (38:8), April 1984, p. 17-24.
   Purple Dragon was a National Security Agency study of signals and operational security in Vietnam, which identified numerous problems in Air Force communications security.

667.   English, Malcolm. "Storm Warning." *Air Forces Monthly* (39), June 1991, p. 23-27.
   This popular account provides considerable detail on airborne jammers and deception activities of both US and Coalition aircraft during the 1991 Gulf conflict.

668.   "EW History, World War II." *Electronic Warfare* (4), Summer 1972, p. 20+; and Convention issue 1972, p. 20-22+.
   Excerpts from the National Defense Research Committee report on radio countermeasures (see article by Harold Zahl, below.)

669.   "Falklands War Pressured British EW Development." *Defense Electronics* (17:1), January 1985, p. 56-57, 59-62.
   The story of the crash development and fielding of the "Blue Erie" ECM pod for British aircraft in 1982. As described by Nick Cook ("EW: The Missing Link," above), Britain still suffered from a lack of such countermeasures nine years later in the Gulf Conflict.

670.   Jones, Reginald V. "An Early Epic of ELINT." *Journal of Electronic Defense* (6:6), June 1983, p. 75-76.
   Story of an electronics intelligence aircraft deliberately flying into the path of a German night fighter in order to determine the frequency of the night fighter's radar.

671.   Kuehl, Daniel T. "Refighting the Last War: Electronic Warfare and U.S. Air Force B-29 Operations in the Korean War, 1950-53." *Journal of Military History* (56:1), January 1992, p. 87-111.
   Lt. Col. Kuehl goes beyond the hardware and technology to describe the evolving use of EW in bombing operations in Korea. He concludes that the USAF had failed to develop or even institutionalize the lessons learned in World War II, so that it suffered unnecessary casualties while re-learning the use of active jammers and chaff.

672.   Lacouture, John E. "Confidence and ECM Capability - Missing Links in U.S. Air Operations in Lebanon." *Defense Electronics* (17:3), March 1985, p. 113-114, 117-118.
   The author criticizes the U.S.' inability to rapidly field

necessary jamming equipment to defeat Syrian air defense radars
in Lebanon, an inability which he contrasts with the quick
response development of EW equipment during the Vietnamese War.

673.   Leonberger, Loren B. "War of the Wizards." *Airman*
(14:11), Nov 1970, p. 17-19.
        Tactics of EB-66 ELINT/airborne jamming.

674.   LoPresti, Tony. "Electronic Warfare: The Invisible
War." *Air Defense Artillery.* Part I, Winter 1986, pp. 38-42;
Part II, Summer 1986, p. 20-27.
        The first part of this essay recounts the familiar story
of chaff and beam navigation in World War II, while the second
describes air and air defense ECM with examples from World War
II and the 1973 Arab-Israeli war.

675.   Momyer, William W. "The Evolution of Fighter Tactics in
S.E. Asia." *Air Force Magazine* (56:7), Jul 1973, p. 58-62.
        General Momyer includes a discussion of the gradual
evolution of electronic countermeasures for tactical fighter-
bombers, beginning in 1967.

676.   Moore, Frederick L. "Radio Countermeasures." *Air
University Quarterly Review* (2), Fall 1948, p. 57-66.

677.   O'Ballance, Edgar. *The Electronic War in the Middle
East, 1968-1970.* Hamden, Ct: Shoe String Press, 1974. 148 p.
        In the war of attrition between Egypt and Israel along the
Suez Canal, much of the contest was in electronic counter-
measures between air and air defense units.

678.   Powell, Lewis F. and Putney, Diane T. *ULTRA and the
Army Air Forces in World War II.* Washington, D.C.: Office of
Air Force History, 1987. 197 p.
        Associate Supreme Court Justice Powell had been a key
participant in the Army Air Force use of ULTRA intelligence.
Much of this volume is composed of documents and reports.

679.   Saville, Gordon P. "Electronics in Air Defense."
Signal (4), September-October 1949, p. 5-7.

680.   Shearer, Oliver V. III and Steven E. Daskal. "The
DESERT 'Electronic Warfare' STORM." *Military Technology*
(15:9), September 1991, p. 21-28.
        A discussion of the electronic warfare and command,
control, and communications countermeasures used in connection
with the 1991 air war against Iraq. The authors' praise for
this operation is tempered with the acknowledgements that the
Iraqi air defense threat was obsolescent and overrated, and
that the Stealth technology used by F-117 fighter bombers may
force a reevaluation of the role of electronic warfare in
support of air attacks.

681.   Smith, Harry F. "Flak Evasion." *Electronic Warfare*
(2), Apr-May 1970, p. 18-19+.
        World War II period.

682.   U.S. War Department. Army Air Forces. *Ultra and the*

History of the United States Strategic Air Force in Europe versus the German Air Force. Frederick, Md: University Publications of America, 1980.   205 p.

683.   Voltaggio, Frank Jr.   "The Archangel Is Illuminated." *Journal of Electronic Defense* (7:2), February 1984, p. 24, 68.
    An account of airborne radar intercept by a B17F, followed by the use of an airborne jammer against German antiaircraft fire direction radars in Sicily in 1943.

684.   _____.   "Origins of ECM in the Air Force." *Journal of Electronic Defense* (5:6), June 1982, p. 34-45.
    A human-interest history of the Army Air Force radar counter-measures force.

685.   _____.   "Out in the Cold: Early ELINT Activities of the Strategic Air Command." *Journal of Electronic Defense* (10:11), November 1987, p. 127-140.
    Episodes of early airborne ELINT missions to identify Russian radar parameters.

686.   Zahl, Harold A.   "Bombs, Bullets, and Electrons." *Navigator* (16), Winter 1968, pp. 1-5;   reproduced in *Signal* (23:6), Feb 1969, p. 48-50.
    The National Defense Research Committee and its development of the TUBA airborne jammer in World War II.

Ground Signals Intelligence and Electronic Warfare

687.   Barker, Wayne G. (ed.)   *The History of Codes and Ciphers in the United States During World War I.* Laguna Hills, Ca: Aegean Park Press, 1979.   263 p.
    This is volume II of a declassified history of the Army Security Agency.   As such, includes not only codes and ciphers to protect American tactical communications, but also the activities of American radio intercept units in the field.

688.   Beachley, David R.   "Soviet Radio-Electronic Combat in World War II." *Military Review* (61:3), March 1981, p. 66-72.
    The author provides excellent details on Soviet tactical use of ground signals intelligence and deception.

689.   Bennett, Ralph.   "Intelligence and Strategy: Some Observations on the War in the Mediterranean, 1941-45." in *Intelligence and National Security* (5:2), April 1990, p. 445-464.
    A brief overview of the conclusions that the author reaches in *Ultra and Mediterranean Strategy* (see below).   In particular, he notes that training is just as important for intelligence officers as for infantry leaders.

690.   _____.   *Ultra in the West: The Normandy Campaign 1944-45.* New York: Charles Scribner's Sons, 1979.   336 p.
    The author was a duty officer in Hut 3 of the British ULTRA facility.   As such, he describes the practical aspects of interpreting ULTRA information, and reviews the effects of these interpretations on the allied campaigns of 1944-45.

691. _____. *Ultra and Mediterranean Strategy*. New
York: Morrow, 1989. 496 p.
    Using additional declassified documents, Bennett describes
the interrelationship of ULTRA intercepts to events in North
Africa and Italy.

692. _____. "Ultra and Some Command Decisions." in
Walter Laqueur (ed.) *The Second World War: Essays in Military
and Political History*. Beverly Hills, Ca: Sage Publishers,
1982. p. 218-238.

693. Bergen, John D. *Military Communications: A Test for
Technology*. THE U.S. ARMY IN VIETNAM. Washington, D.C.: U.S.
Army Center of Military History, 1986. xix + 515 p.
    Chapter 17 (The Electronic Battlefield, p. 387-408)
describes both U.S. and Viet Cong Signals Intelligence and
Electronic Warfare.

694. Clark, Ronald W. *The Man Who Broke Purple: The Life of
Colonel William F. Friedman, Who Deciphered the Japanese Code
in World War II*. London: Weidenfeld and Nicholson, 1977;
Boston: Little, Brown, c. 1977. 271 p.

695. Currer-Briggs, Noel. "Some of ULTRA's Poor Relations in
Algeria, Tunisia, Sicily and Italy." *Intelligence and National
Security* (2:2), April 1987, p. 274-290.
    The author describes, with examples, how he decrypted
simple German keyword tactical codes, first at Bletchley Park
and then in North Africa/Sicily as a member of the British 7th
Special Intelligence Company. In addition to useful cases of
tactical signals intelligence, this article is also replete
with examples of how poor German signal security aided British
efforts.

696. Dammen, Arthur. "Enemy Radio Base Intercepted 1400
Military Messages." *Washington Post*, January 13 1970, p. A12.
    The accidental discovery of a North Vietnamese radio
monitoring station in Vietnam exposed the ease with which the
enemy could break unauthorized codes and poor U.S. radio
procedures.

697. Everett, H. W. "The Secret War in the Desert." *British
Army Review*, No. 60 (December, 1978), p. 66-68.
    Reminiscences of the British Army tactical signals
intelligence in North Africa, demonstrating that the Germans
were as lax about communications security as their opponents.

698. Ferris, John. "The British Army and Signals Intelligence in the Field During the First World War." *Intelligence
and National Security* (3:4), October 1988, p. 23-48.
    Ferris describes the astonishing sophistication and
success of British tactical signals intelligence.

699. _____. "The British Army, Signals and Security in
the Desert Campaign, 1940-42." *Intelligence and National
Security* (5:2), April 1990, p. 255-291.
    A superb analysis of the British problems of communica-
tions and signals security, which should be read not only by

those interested in communications security, but also by historians seeking to understand British problems of command and control throughout World War II. Signal equipment and training was so neglected in the interwar British Army that effective tactical communications and security only evolved during World War II.

700.   Flicke, Wilhelm F. *War Secrets in the Ether.* Laguna Hills, Ca: Aegean Park Press, 1977. 2 vols: 147 and 350 p.
   At the request of the U.S. Army, Flicke reconstructed his wartime records of German signals intercept. Vol. I traces such intercept activities up to 1939, while Vol. II focuses on the wartime years.

701.   Gilbert, James L. "U.S. Army COMSEC in World War I." *Military Intelligence* (14:1), January 1988, p. 22-25.
   In this war, the Army went beyond simply codemaking to communications security monitoring, security guidelines, etc.

702.   Gordon, Don E. "Target: The Spoken Word." *Army* (29:9), September 1979, p. 20-21.
   To illustrate the vulnerability of U.S. Army ground communications, the author describes early exercises involving the 313th Combat Electronic Warfare and Intelligence Battalion, 82d Airborne Division.

703.   Johnson, John. "Army Tactical SIGINT and EW." *Signal* (38:8), April 1984, p. 43-52.
   A good introduction to the equipment and capabilities of U.S. Army Combat Electronic Warfare and Intelligence units.

704.   Kennedy, C. "Army Signaling and its Use in War." *Journal of the Royal United Service Institution* (41), 1897.
   An early discussion of COMSEC, which mistakenly believed that enciphered signals were safe even if intercepted.

705.   McMillan, Donald J. "Electronic Warfare." *Infantry* (64:2), Mar-Apr 1974, p. 33-35.
   The usual definitions and examples, with emphasis on ground communications security.

706.   Merillat, Herbert C. "The 'Ultra Weapon' at Guadalcanal." *Marine Corps Gazette* (6:9), September 1982, p. 44-49.
   The author examines the effect of signals intelligence on the American conduct of the campaign, concluding that this intelligence, while useful to commanders, was not an overwhelming advantage that can be credited with specific achievements.

707.   Morgan, William F. "Invasion on the Ether: Radio Intelligence at the Battle of St. Mihiel, September 1918." *Military Affairs* (51:2), April, 1987, p. 57-61.
   The beginnings of U.S. tactical signals intelligence, with the First Army's Radio Intelligence Subsection under Lt. Charles H. Matz. An excellent study.

708.   Nikolaieff, A.M. "Secret Causes of German Successes on

the Eastern Front." *Coast Artillery Journal*, September-October 1935, p. 373-377.

The legendary German intelligence officer discusses Russian radio insecurities. In addition to broadcasting in the clear during the first battles of 1914, the Russians used a code that was broken by Austrian intelligence as early as September 19, 1914.

709.   Praun, Albert. "German Radio Intelligence and the Soldaten-sender," in Mendelsohn, John (ed.) *Covert Warfare: Intelligence, Counterintelligence, and Military Deception During the World War II Era.* Vol. 6: *German Radio Intelligence.* New York, London: Garland Publishing, Inc., 1989.

Lt. Gen. Praun wrote this study for the U.S. Army after the German defeat, outlining German tactical signals intelligence from the Spanish Civil War to 1945, and appraising the communications security of various allied armies. A priceless source.

710.   Rosengarten, Adolph G., Jr. "With Ultra from Omaha Beach to Weimar, Germany--A Personal View." *Military Affairs* (42:3), October 1978, p. 127-132.

The author was assigned specifically to safeguard signals intelligence, including ULTRA, at headquarters, 1st U.S. Army, but the G2 naturally used him for other duties as well. As such, there is a long discussion about the tactical failure to predict the counterattack at the Bulge.

711.   Slayton, Barney F. "'War in the Ether': Soviet Radio-Electronic Warfare." *Military Review* (60:1) January 1980, p. 56-67.

See in particular pages 61-64, which describe the role of Soviet radio-electronic combat during Operation BAGRATION in 1944.

712.   Stewart, Richard A. "Rommel's Secret Weapon: Signals Intelligence." *Marine Corps Gazette* (74) March 1990, p. 51-55.

713.   Thompson, George R., Harris, Dixie R., Oakes, Pauline M., and Terrett, Dulany. *The Technical Services: The Signal Corps: The Test (December 1941 to July 1943.)* UNITED STATES ARMY IN WORLD WAR II. Washington, D.C.: Office of the Chief of Military History, 1957. xv + 621 p.

This volume of the Army's official history includes a number of brief discussions of radar development and the evolution of the Signal Security Agency; see especially pp. 204-205 and 444-447.

714.   Thompson, George R., and Harris, Dixie R. *The Technical Services: the Signal Corps: The Outcome (Mid-1943 Through 1945.)* UNITED STATES ARMY IN WORLD WAR II. Washington, D.C.: Office of the Chief of Military History, 1966. xvi + 720 p.

See especially Chapters X (Electronic Combat: Countermeasures) and XI (Signal Security and Intelligence).

Naval Signals Intelligence

715.   Armbrister, Trevor. *A Matter of Accountability: The True Story of the Pueblo Affair.* New York: Coward-McCann, Inc., 1970.   viii + 408 p.
A well-researched journalistic study of the seizure of the U.S.S. *Pueblo* while allegedly intercepting signals off the coast of North Korea.   The author criticizes an entire system that he contends put an inappropriate ship with an inexperienced crew in a situation with great potential for disaster.

716.   Beesly, Patrick. "Convoy PQ17: A Study of Intelligence and Decision-Making." *Intelligence and National Security* (5:2), April 1990, p. 292-322.
A discussion of the intelligence misunderstandings that caused Admiral Sir Dudley Pound to order a convoy en route to the Soviet Union to scatter in the face of German attacks.

717.   _____. *Room 40: British Naval Intelligence, 1914-1918.* London: Hamish Hamilton, and San Diego, Ca: Harcourt, Brace, Jovanovich, 1982. xi + 338 p.
This study focuses on the signals intelligence aspects of the subject; see other studies of Room 40 in Chapter 4, under Naval Tactical Intelligence.

718.   _____. "Special Intelligence and the Battle of the Atlantic: The British View." p. 413-419 in Robert W. Love, Jr. (ed.) *Chaning Interpretations and New Sources in Naval History: Papers from the Third United States Naval Academy History Symposium.* New York and London: Garland Publishing Co., 1980.   Another version was published in *Cryptologic Spectrum* (8:1), Winter 1978, p. 5-29.
A short exposition of the limitations on signal intelligence, described in more detail in *Very Special Intelligence.* See also the accompanying symposium papers by Kenneth A. Knowles (the American view) and Jurgen Rohwer (the German view.)

719.   _____. *Very Special Admiral: The Life of Admiral J. H. Godfrey, C.B.* London: Hamish Hamilton, 1980. 360 p.
This biography of a great naval intelligence officer is less effective than Beesly's earlier *Very Special Intelligence,* which gives a much broader interpretation of British naval SIGINT operations.

720.   _____. *Very Special Intelligence: The Story of the Admiralty's Operational Intelligence Centre, 1939-1945.* London: Hamish Hamilton, 1977. New York: Ballantine Books, 1981. 282 p.
This book is essential reading for anyone who seeks to understand signals intelligence. Not only does it describe the procedures used by the British to combat German submarine warfare, but it illustrates the many practical limitations and difficulties involved in using intercepted communications.

721.   Braybrook, Roy. "How the Black Boxes Came of Age." *Pacific Defense Reporter.* (14:4), October 1987, p. 56-58.

Discusses naval equipment used in World War II, Vietnam, the Falklands, and the mideast wars.

722.   Bywater, Hector C. *Their Secret Purposes: Drama and Mysteries of the Naval War.* London: Constable and Co., Ltd, 1932. x + 311 p.
Anecdotal accounts of both German and British naval intelligence during World War I. Chapter 13 ("Listening In: Intelligence By Wireless,") asserts that the British ultimately broke every German naval code. It provides a rare look at German signals intelligence, which was used to prepare for such operations as the *Goeben* naval raid.

723.   Curtis, Richard D. "An Overview of Surface Navy ESM/ECM Development." *Journal of Electronic Defense.* (5:3), March 1982, p. 278-38.
Focuses on specific models of equipment, but puts those models into the tactical context from World War II forward; an excellent technical account.

724.   Douglas, W.A.B. and Rohwer, Jurgen. "The Most Thankless Task Revisited: Convoys, Escorts, and Radio Intelligence in the Western Atlantic, 1941-43" in James A. Boutilier (ed.) *The Royal Canadian Navy in Retrospect, 1910-1968.* (Vancouver: University of British Columbia Press, 1982)
Canadian naval "Y" service against the German navy.

725.   Ennes, James M. *Assault On the Liberty: The True Story of the Israeli Attack on an American Intelligence Ship.* New York: Random House, 1979. 299 p.

726.   Erskine, Ralph. "U-Boats, Homing Signals and HFDF." *Intelligence and National Security.* (2:2,) April 1987, p. 324-330.
The Royal Navy was slow to use existing High Frequency Direction Finding (HFDF) technology to locate submarines shadowing convoys, but the Germans were even slower to recognize this threat once the British learned to use it.

727.   Gordon, Don E. *Electronic Warfare: Element of Strategy and Multiplier of Combat Power.* New York: Pergamon Press, 1981. 104 p.
Although the author is an advocate of ground electronic warfare and intelligence, the core of this book is a very detailed history of the use of signals intelligence by navies during both World Wars.

728.   Goulden, Joseph. *Truth Is the First Casualty: The Gulf of Tonkin Affair - Illusion and Reality.* Chicago and New York: James B. Adler, Inc./Rand McNally and Co., 1969. 285 p.
As its title indicates, this is an expose designed to show that the United States government provoked and then misrepresented the North Vietnamese attack on American warships in the Gulf of Tonkin in 1964. Chapter 4, "The Dangerous Business of Electronic Espionage," is an overview of both American and Soviet strategic signals intelligence, including the Israeli attack on the USS *Liberty* in 1967.

729.   Guerlac, Henry, and Marie Boas. "The Radar War Against the U-Boat." *Military Affairs* (14:2), Summer 1950, p. 99-111.

730.   Hezlet, Arthur. *Electronics and Sea Power.* New York: Stein and Day, 1976. 318 p.

731.   Holmes, W. Jasper. *Double-Edged Secrets: U.S. Naval Intelligence Operations in the Pacific During World War II.* Annapolis: Naval Institute Press, 1979. x + 231 p.
    The author was recalled from medical retirement to serve in the Fleet Radio Unit, Pacific, throughout World War II. He provides detailed examples, such as the three-man intelligence unit with Admiral Halsey that monitored Japanese civil defense reaction to the Doolittle Raid.

732.   _____. "Naval Intelligence in the War Against Japan, 1941-45: The View From Pearl Harbor." in Craig L. Symonds (ed.), *New Aspects of Naval History: Selected Papers Presented at the Fourth Naval History Symposium, United States Naval Academy, 25-26 October 1979.* Annapolis: Naval Institute Press, 1981, p. 351-359.
    Although primarily concerned with the naval signals intelligence discussed in his book, this talk also addresses other sources of intelligence used in the Pacific.

733.   _____. "Pearl Harbor Aftermath." *U.S. Naval Institute Proceedings* (104:12), December 1978, p. 68-75.
    An extract from *Double-Edged Secrets.*

734.   Howeth, Linwood S. *History of Communications-Electronics in the United States Navy.* Washington, D.C.: Government Printing Office, 1963. xxix + 657 p.
    Includes discussions of the development of Radar, Sonar, etc.

735.   "'Huff Duff' vs. the U-boat." *Electronic Warfare* (8), May-June 2976, p. 71+.

736.   Knowles, Kenneth A. "Ultra and the Battle of the Atlantic: The American View." p. 444-449 in Robert W. Love, Jr. (ed.) *Changing Interpretations and New Sources in Naval History: Papers from the Third United States Academy History Symposium.* New York and London: Garland Publishing Inc., 1980. Another version was published in *Cryptologic Spectrum* (8:1), Winter 1978, p. 5-29.
    A former staff officer of the U.S. Tenth Fleet describes American participation in U-Boat intelligence, especially the role of direction-finding stations from Iceland to South Africa. See also accompanying symposium papers by Patrick Beesly (the British view) and Jurgen Rohwer (the German view.)

737.   Layton, Edwin T., Pinean, Roger, and Costello, John. *"And I Was There:" Pearl Harbor and Midway--Breaking the Secrets.* New York: Morrow, 1985. 596 p.
    Rear Admiral Layton undertook this memoir after the publication of MAGIC and ULTRA secrets. He contended that the U.S. did have signals intelligence warning of the attack on Pearl Harbor, and was scathing in his criticism of government

reaction to that warning.

738.   Lissitzyn, Oliver J.   "Electronic Reconnaissance From
the High Seas and International Law." *Naval War College Review*
(22:2), Feb 1970, p. 26-34.

739.   Lundstrom, John B.   "A Failure of Radio Intelligence:
An Episode in the Battle of the Coral Sea." *Cryptologia* (7:2),
April 1983, reproduced in Cypher A. Deavours, David Kahn, Louis
Kruh, Greg Mellen, and Brian Winkel (eds.).   *Cryptology:
Yesterday, Today, and Tomorrow.* Norwood, Ma: Artech House,
1987.   p. 107-128.
    Erroneous   interpretation   of   Japanese   signals   misled
Admiral Fletcher in the Battle of the Coral Sea.

740.   Montagu, Ewen. *Beyond Top Secret Ultra.* New York:
Coward, McCann, and Geoghegan, 1978.   192 p.
    The former British naval intelligence officer provides
useful analysis of naval signals intelligence and deception.

741.   Morris, Christopher. "ULTRA's Poor Relations." in
Andrew,   Christopher   (ed.)   *Codebreaking   and   Signals
Intelligence.* London: Frank Cass and Co., Ltd., 1986), p.
111-122.
    An account of British decryption of German naval hand
ciphers, as opposed to machine-generated codes.

742.   Mulligan, Timothy. "The German Navy Evaluates Its
Cryptologic Security, October 1941." *Military Affairs* (49:1),
April 1985, p. 75-79.

743.   Potter, E. B. "The Crypt of the Cryptanalysts." *U.S.
Naval Institute Proceedings* (109:8), August 1983, p. 52-56.
    The evolution of the Combat Intelligence Unit at Pearl
Harbor, through the battle of Midway.

744.   Rohwer, Jurgen. "Ultra and the Battle of the Atlantic:
The German View." p. 420-443 in Robert W. Love, Jr. (ed.)
*Changing Interpretations and New Sources in Naval History:
Papers from the Third United States Naval Academy Historical
Symposium.* New York and London: Garland Publishing Inc., 1980.
Another version was published in *Cryptologic Spectrum* (8:1),
Winter 1978, P. 5-29.
    The author disagrees with Patrick Beesly and others who
describe the British ability to decrypt the German Enigma
message system as *the* reason for victory in the Atlantic.
Using many maps and examples, he emphasizes that decryption was
only one-third of the system: Direction Finding and Traffic
Analysis were equally important, and often provided the Allies
with protection during the long periods when Britain could not
decrypt the German code.   See also the accompanying symposium
papers by Patrick Beesly (the British View) and Kenneth Knowles
(the American view.)

745.   Schorreck, Henry F. "The Role of COMINT in the Battle
of Midway." *Cryptologic Spectrum* (5:3), Summer 1975, p. 3-11.

746.   Simmons, Robert R. *The Pueblo, EC-121, and Mayaguez*

Incidents: Some Continuities and Changes.   Baltimore, Md.:
University of Maryland School of Law, 1978.

747.   Sockett, Ernie.   "Stockton-on-Tees 'Y' Station." in
Fortress 8 (February, 1991), p. 51-60.
    Royal Navy intercept station during World War I.

748.   Thomas, G. Guy.   "Warfare in the Fourth Dimension--Is
the Navy Ready for it?   How Can the Navy Prepare for it?" *Naval
War College Review* (36:1) January-February 1983, p. 16-23.
    The author is concerned by American unpreparedness in the
face of Soviet Radio-Electronic Combat. Much of the article is
concerned with the mechanics of adding electronic support
measures and countermeasures to wargame simulations.

749.   Van der Rhoer, Edward.   *Deadly MAGIC: A Personal
Account of Communications Intelligence in World War II in the
Pacific.* New York: Charles Scribner's Sons, 1978. xii + 225
p.
    Personal memoirs, with interesting details, of an officer
who worked in the U.S. Navy's OP-20-G translating intercepted
Japanese messages.

750.   Vosseller, Aurelius B.   "Science and the Battle of the
Atlantic." *Yale Review* (New Series 35), June 1946, p. 667-681.

751.   Wilhelm, Richard.   "The Story of Shipboard EW
Integration." *Journal of Electronic Defense* (10:3), March
1987, p. 53-60.
    Development of US surface ship electronic defense measures
after the Israeli destroyer Eilat was sunk during the 1967 war.

752.   Winton, John.   *Ultra at Sea: How Breaking the Nazi Code
Affected Allied Naval Strategy During World War II.* New York:
William Morrow and Co.; London: Leo Cooper, Ltd., 1988. 207 p.
    The use of ULTRA signals intelligence against German
submarines and surface vessels, primarily 1940-1943.   The
author is particularly concerned with how such intelligence
could be used for operational decisions without compromising
the source.

753.   Wood, Chester C.   "The Flow of Strategic Intelligence."
U.S. Naval Institute Proceedings (59:9), September 1933, p.
1296-1304.
    An early effort to explain how much information is
available from traffic analysis of the actions of an enemy
naval force. His examples for this are primarily related to
the British-German naval conflict off South America in late
1914.

7

Deception, Surprise, and Warning

Deception

754.   Armstrong, Richard N. *Soviet Operational Deception: the Red Cloak.* Ft Leavenworth, Ks: Combat Studies Institute, 1989. ix + 56 p.
    Colonel Armstrong focuses on examples from October–November 1943 (the crossing of the Dnieper River) and July 1944 (the Lvov-Sandomierz operation.)

755.   Austra, Kevin R. "The Battle of the Bulge: The Secret Offensive." *Military Intelligence* (17:1), January–March 1991, p. 26–33.
    Examines not only the German deception plan, which portrayed a counterattack between the Roer and Rhine Rivers rather than in the Ardennes, but also German operational security measures to conceal the actual location of the December 1944 offensive.

756.   Barkas, Geoffrey. *The Camouflage Story: From Aintree to Alamein.* London: Cassel and Co., Ltd., 1952. 216 pp.
    Memoirs of a film maker who became the head of camouflage for British Middle East Forces, responsible for the deception prior to the second Battle of Alamein.

757.   Beaumont, Roger. *Maskirovka: Soviet Camouflage, Concealment and Deception.* College Station, TX: Texas A&M University System, 1982. vii + 52 p.
    A discussion of the systematic Soviet approach to deception, with examples.

758.   Bourman, Scott A. "Deception in Chinese Strategy" in William W. Whetson (ed.), *The Military and Political Power in China in the 1970's.* New York: Praeger, 1972. p. 313–337.
    Bourman provides a heavy dose of Sun Tzu and other traditional approaches to deception used by Chinese Communist doctrine.

759.   Brown, Anthony Cave. *Bodyguard of Lies.* New York and

Evanston, Il: Harper and Row, 1975.

An ambitious and largely successful effort to review the allied deception efforts against Hitler, as well as the related intelligence issues of ULTRA, German resistance to Hitler, etc.

760.   Clarke, Dudley. *Seven Assignments.* London: Jonathan Cape, 1948. 262 p.

Brigadier Clarke was the head of "A" Force, the British Deception office in the Middle East during World War II. See his biography by David Mure, *Master of Deception*, entry 797.

761.   Colvin, Ian G. *The Unknown Courier: With a Note on the Situation Controlling the Axis in the Mediterranean in the Spring of 1943* by Field Marshal Kesselring. London: William Kimber, 1953. 208 p.

A less thorough account of the British deception using an actual dead body, dressed as an officer courier, to pass erroneous information to the Germans in Operation Mincemeat. See Ewen Montagu's *The Man Who Never Was*, entry 795.

762.   Coster, Donald Q. "We Were Expecting You at Dakar." in *Reader's Digest* editors, *Secrets and Spies: Behind-the-Scenes Stories of World War II.* Pleasantville, NY: *Reader's Digest* Association, 1964. p. 230-235.

Popular account of an American deception operation to cover the 1942 landings in North Africa.

763.   Cruickshank, Charles. *Deception in World War II.* New York: Oxford University Press, 1979, 1980. 248 p.

This book describes both military and diplomatic deceptions, showing the gradual evolution of U.S. Army attitudes and capabilities in this field.

764.   Daniel, Donald C. and Herbig, Katherine L. "Propositions on Military Deception." *Journal of Strategic Studies* (5:1), March 1982, p. 155-177.

An extract from their book (see entry 765). The article identifies two basic variants of deception: "ambiguity increasing" to confuse the target audience, and "misleading" to actively mislead the target. A number of excellent primary sources from World War II are used to illustrate the theoretical possibilities that may result in a deception operation.

765.   Daniel, Donald C. and Herbig, Katherine L. (eds.) *Strategic Military Deception.* New York: Pergamon Press, 1982. xiii + 378 p.

An excellent set of 16 essays on the theory and practice of deception, including not only the conventional British-American operations of World War II, but also Chinese and Egyptian deceptions.

766.   Dailey, Brian D. and Parker, Patrick J. (eds.) *Soviet Strategic Deception.* Lexington, Ma: D.C. Heath and Co., 1987. 539 p.

The proceedings of a Naval Post-Graduate School conference in the subject, including both military and political deception.

767.   "A Deception Case Study." *The Journal of Soviet Military Studies* (1:2), June 1988, p. 262-275.
Translation of a Soviet after action report on the deception plan for the Demiansk operation of July 1942.

768.   Dewar, Michael. *Deception In Warfare.* Newton Abbot, Devon: David & Charles; New York: Sterling Publishing Co., 1989.   224 p.
A British officer discusses the theory of deception, then surveys the subject from biblical times forward, with emphasis on World War II.

769.   Dovey, H.O.   "Cheese."   *Intelligence and National Security* (5:3) July 1990, p. 176-183.
British deception in the Middle East, World War II.

770.   _____.   "The False Going Map at Alam Halfa." *Intelligence and National Security*   (4:1), January 1989, p. 165-168.
Based on British files and the British interrogation of a captured German commander, the author concludes that this ruse did succeed in misleading the Afrika Korps as to the safest axis of advance at Alam Halfa in 1942.

771.   Eisenhower, John S.D.   *The Bitter Woods.*   New York: G.P. Putnam's Sons, 1969.   506 p.
This account of the Battle of the Bulge includes Chapter 9, which examines the German deception and allied intelligence failure prior to the battle.

772.   Eldridge, Justin L. C.   "The Myth of Army Tactical Deception."   *Military Review* (70:8), August 1990, p. 67-78.
A critical discussion of the problems that arose when the U.S. Army attempted to reestablish a nucleus of trained deception planners and effective deception devices during the later 1980s.

773.   Frank, Willard C. Jr.   "Politico-Military Deception at Sea in the Spanish Civil War, 1936-39."   *Intelligence and National Security*   (5:3), July 1990, p. 84-112.

774.   Gazit, Schlomo.   "Risk, Glory, and the Rescue Operation."   *International Security*   (6:1), Summer 1981, p. 111-135.
The former director of Israeli Military Intelligence discusses the theory of rescues, such as that of Entebbe, with emphasis on deceptions and simplicity.

775.   Giskes, Herman J.   *London Calling North Pole.*   New York: British Book Center; London: Kimber, 1953.   vi + 208 p.
One of the more recent accounts of the German Abwehr deception that captured British SOE agents in the Netherlands, then controlled their radio reports for deception.

776.   Glantz, David M.   *Soviet Military Deception in the Second World War.*   London: Frank Cass and Co., Ltd., 1989.   xl + 644 p.
A superb analysis of the theory and practice of Soviet

military deception operations, with over 200 maps.

777.   Gooch, John and Amos Perlmutter (eds.) *Military Deception and Strategic Surprise.* Totowa, NJ: Frank Cass, 1982. 192 p.
An anthology on deception, ranging from covert German rearmament after World War I to Soviet missile development in the 1970s.

778.   von Grieffenberg, Hans. "Deception and Cover Plans, Project No. 29." Foreign Military Studies number MS P-044a. Typescript, U.S. Army Historical Division.
This entry in the series of manuscript studies by captured German senior officers reviewer the German experience in cover and deception.

779.   Gudgin, Peter. "Phantom British Tank Regiments of World War II." *Journal of the Royal United Service Institute for Defence Studies* (125:3), September 1980, p. 64-68.
Two units in the Middle East portrayed at least 14 different British tank battalions. The need for such deceptions, based on dummy tanks, declined as Allied air superiority made German air reconnaissance uncommon.

780.   Hall, Mary T. "False Colors and Dummy Ships: The Use of Ruse in Naval Warfare" in *Naval War College Review* (42:3), Summer 1989, p. 52-62.
International Law aspects of naval deception.

781.   Hand, Robert P. "Deception Planning." *Military Review* (48:9), September 1967, p. 44-48.
A discussion of G2 and G3 roles in deception planning, including questions such as whether the enemy can observe the projected deception, whether the notional course of action portrayed is tactically possible, etc.

782.   Handel, Michael I. (ed.) *Strategic and Operational Deception in the Second World War.* London: Frank Cass and Co., Ltd., 1987. x + 348 p.
Papers presented at the U.S. Army War College Conference on Intelligence and Military Operations, April, 1986. This volume includes papers both on allied deception and on the German view of that deception, plus American deception in the Pacific theater and an essay on Soviet deception by David Glantz (see above.)

783.   Hartcup, Guy. *Camouflage: A History of Concealment and Deception in War.* New York: Charles Scribner's Sons, 1980. 113 p.
A good popular account of British camouflage and deception in both World Wars.

784.   Haswell, Jock. *The Intelligence and Deception of the D-Day Landings.* London: B.T. Batsford, Ltd., 1979. Published as *D-Day: Intelligence and Deception* in New York: Times Books, 1979. 208 p.
A popularized but well researched description.

785.   Haveles, Paul A.   "Deception Operations in REFORGER 88."
Military Review (70:8), Aug 1990, p. 35-41.
    An examination of V U.S. Corps' attempted deception during
a major exercise (Return of FORces to GERmany, or REFORGER)
Capt. Haveles notes that deception planners both over-estimated
the opponent's ability to observe to deception, and failed to
include several key or "signature" units in the deception
organization, thereby reducing its effectiveness.

786.   Hesketh, R.F.   *Fortitude: A History of Strategic
Deception in Western Europe, April, 1943 to May, 1945.*   No
publisher, 1949.   xiii + 260 p.
    An excellent, detailed discussion, including German
translated documents, on the Allied deception effort prior to
the invasion of Normandy.

787.   Hobar, Basil J.   "The Ardennes 1944:   Intelligence
Failure or Deception Success."   *Military Intelligence*   (10),
October-December 1984.   p. 8-16.

788.   Howard, Michael.   *British Intelligence in the Second
World War.*   Vol. 5:   *Strategic Deception.*   London: Her
Majesty's Stationary Office, 1990.   xiii + 270 p.
    The government delayed publication of this work for ten
years, and then apparently deleted many sensitive sections.   It
remains a useful summary of British deception, and is far
shorter than similar works, such as Brown's *Bodyguard of Lies.*

789.   Huber, Thomas M.   *Pastel: Deception in the Invasion of
Japan.*   Ft. Leavenworth, Ks: U.S. Army Command & General Staff
College, 1988.   v + 55 p.
    Huber describes the organization and development of U.S.
deception planning prior to the 1945 invasion of plan, focuses
on the cover story of an invasion of Shikoku rather than Kyushu
Island.

790.   Leifland, Leif.   "Deception Plan Graffham and Sweden:
Another View."   *Intelligence and National Security* (4:2), Apr
1989, p. 295-315.
    This article is part of a continuing debate, touched off
by Klaus Jurgen-Muller's 1986 assertion, based on the German
war diaries, that the allied deception plans indicating a
landing in Norway had little or no effect on German defense
planning.   Leifland reviews the Swedish records and finds
little evidence that one such deception, operation GRAFFHAM,
had any impact on the Swedes or the Germans.

791.   Love, Edmund G.   "Deception on the Shuri Line
(Okinawa)."   *Infantry* (73:4), July-August 1983, p. 14-20.
    An example of tactical deception that allowed the 1st
Battalion, 106th Infantry Regiment, 27th Infantry Division, to
capture a key Japanese position.

792.   Maskelyne, Jasper.   *Magic - Top Secret.* London and New
York: Stanley Paul and Co, 19.   191 p.
    Despite its title, this is not about MAGIC signals
intelligence, but rather the memoirs of a magician involved in
British camouflage and deception operations in World War II.

It provides little about the organizations responsible for that deception.

793.   Milhalka, Michael.   "Soviet Strategic Deception, 1955-1981." *Journal of Strategic Studies* (5:1), March 1982, p. 40-93.
    An excellent summary of the basic themes and methods used by the Soviets, especially in the case of strategic nuclear weapons.   For example, the Soviets consistently over-represented the size and capability of their intercontinental missile systems until the U-2 overflights and the failure of the Cuban Missile Crisis stymied them;   thereafter they deliberately under-represented the accuracy of missiles in the 1970s, began advocating nuclear parity rather than claiming superiority.

794.   Miller, Edwin H.   "Tactical Deception in World War II." *Journal of Electronic Defense*, (8:10), October 1985, p. 91-98.
    The organization, operations, and lessons of 23d Headquarters Special Troops, the deception unit for 12th U.S. Army Group in 1944-45.   The author was in the 3132d Signal Service Company - Special, a unit of halftrack mounted loudspeakers.

795.   Montagu, Ewen E.   *The Man Who Never Was*.   Philadelphia and New York: J.B. Lippincott, 1954.   160 p.
    Montagu was the staff officer responsible for Operation MINCEMEAT, setting adrift a dead body with information designed to convince the Germans that the allies would invade other areas in the Mediterranean, rather than Sicily, in 1943.   See also Montagu, *Beyond Top Secret Ultra*, in Chapter 6, under Naval Signals Intelligence.

796.   Mullins, Robert G.   Strategic Deception in Peacetime. University of Texas at Austin Ph.D. dissertation, Political Science, 1987.   396 p.   LC No. AAC8806384.
    The author provides a critical review of British and American studies of deception, followed by a case study in which the German peacetime deceptions of the 1930s were compared to the British intelligence organizations who had to interpret those deceptions.

797.   Mure, David.   *Master of Deception: Tangled Webs in London and the Middle East*.   London: William Kimber, 1980. 284 p.
    Primarily the story of Brigadier Dudley W. Clarke, head of deception for the British Middle Eastern theater during World War II.

798.   Myklebust, Svein L.   "The Greatest Deception in the History of Warfare": Hitler's Deception Operations in the Months Prior to the Attack on Russia in June 1941. University of Wisconsin-Madison Ph.D. dissertation, 1980.   viii + 303 p. Univ. Microfilms No. 80-15221.
    An analysis of German efforts to maintain the threat of invasion against Britain while shifting forces for the attack on the Soviet Union.

799.   Olsen, Frank H.   "Great Hoaxes" in *Infantry* (59:6),
November-December 1969, p. 44-47.
Vignettes of deception from the Civil War to World War II.

800.   Owen, David.   *Battle of Wits: A History of Psychology
and Deception in Modern Warfare.* London: Leo Cooper, 1978.
207 p.
The use of psychological deception during World War II,
and purely psychological operations during post-World War II
British operations.

801.   Paschall, Rod.   "Deception for St. Mihiel, 1918" in
Intelligence and National Security (5:3), July 1990, p. 158-
175.
As part of the deception plan to attack Belfort rather
than St. Mihiel in France, the American staff officer Col.
Arthur Conger deliberately left the carbon paper used to type
the false plan where it would be stolen by German agents.
Paschall concludes, contrary to Donald Smythe (see entry 806),
that this deception did draw off three German divisions to the
wrong sector.

802.   Reit, Seymour.   *Masquerade: The Amazing Camouflage
Deceptions of World War II.* New York: Hawthorn Books, Inc.,
1978; London: Robert Hale, 1979. x + 255 p.
The author was a graphics designer who worked both on
camouflage and on photo interpretation for the U.S. during
World War II. His account goes well beyond this, describing
not only dummy equipment and photo interpretation, but also the
variety of deceptions covered in Brown's *Bodyguard of Lies.*

803.   Sadat, Anwar.   *In Search of Identity: An Autobiography.*
New York: Harper & Row, 1978. viii + 360 p.
In the course of this personal memoir, President Sadat
provides considerable background concerning the Egyptian
deception of Israel in 1973.

804.   Sevin, Dieter.   "Operation Scherhorn" in *Military Review*
(46:3), March 1966, p. 35-43.
The story of a Soviet deception operation that portrayed
an imaginary German battlegroup trapped behind Soviet lines in
1944.

805.   Sheffy, Yigal.   "Institutionalized Deception and
Perception Reinforcement: Allenby's Campaign in Palestine."
Intelligence and National Security (5:2), April 1990, p. 173-
236.
Sheffy reviews the deception efforts of two successive
British campaigns in Palestine during World War I, examining
the objective, methods, and effects of each case.

806.   Smythe, Donald.   "The Ruse at Belfort" in *Army* (22:6),
June 1972, p. 34-38.
Professor Smythe contends that the American deception
effort prior to the St. Mihiel offensive of 1918 was largely
unsuccessful. For an opposing interpretation, see Rod Paschall
(above.)

807.   Stewart, Richard W.   "Crossing the Rhine and the Irrawaddy" in *Military Review* (69:8), August 1989, p. 74-83.
Deception operations used to cover both crossings.

808.   *The Tangled Web.* By the editors of *Army Times.* Washington, D.C.: Robert B. Luce, 1963. 183 p.
15 examples of deception operations, primarily from World War II but reaching back to the Civil War. The book also includes some non-deception cases, such as sabotage and psychological operations.

809.   U.S. Central Intelligence Agency and Mathtech. *Covert Rearmament in Germany, 1919-1939: Deception and Misperception.* Washington, D.C.: Office of Research and Development, CIA, 1979. 241 p.

810.   _____. *Thoughts on the Cost-Effectiveness of Deception and Related Tactics in the Air War 1939 to 1945.* Washington, D.C.: Office of Research and Development, CIA, 1979. 166 p.
A study of German deception efforts against the Royal Air Force night bomber offensive of World War II.

811.   U.S., Department of Defense. *Conduct of the Persian Gulf Conflict: An Interim Report To Congress.* Washington, D.C.: Department of Defense, July 1991. unnumbered pages.
An early effort to respond to specific Congressional questions about the Gulf Conflict of 1991.   Question 14 addresses intelligence in general terms, but Question 24, on deception, is far more informative. It describes, for example, efforts made to play on Iraqi expectations of a frontal attack in Kuwait, and weekly air surges designed to conceal the massing for the actual air attack of 17 January 1991 (p. 24-2).

812.   Watson, Mark S. *The War Department. Chief of Staff: Prewar Plans and Preparations. UNITED STATES ARMY IN WORLD WAR II* series. Washington, D.C.: Historical Division, U.S. Army, 1950. xxii + 551 p.
Chapters XIV and XV (p. 453-520) provide a balanced, rational official history of the Pearl Harbor surprise.

813.   Whaley, Barton. *Codeword Barbarossa.* Cambridge, Mass: M.I.T. Press, 1973)   377 p.   Based on Whaley's Operation Barbarossa: A Case Study of Soviet Strategic Information Processing before the German Invasion. Massachusetts Institute of Technology Ph.D. dissertation, 1969.
An exhaustive review of the various warnings and indications of German invasion that reached the Soviet Union in 1941.   Whaley concludes that, unlike Pearl Harbor, the strategic surprise was due to deliberate German deception rather than to a confusion of ambiguous intelligence reports.

814.   _____. "Covert Rearmament in Germany 1919-1939: Deception and Misperception." *Journal of Strategic Studies* (5:1), March 1982, p. 3-39.
An excellent review of how Germany concealed its reestablishment of submarine and air forces, and used a spurious threat of Soviet air attack to obtain British engines

to build its own aircraft in 1933.

815. _____. *Strategem, Deception and Surprise in War.*
Cambridge, Mass: Massachusetts Institute of Technology, 1969.
Unnumbered pages.
　　An attempt to survey 168 battles from 16 wars, examining
the role of strategic and tactical deception in achieving
surprise.

816. _____. "Towards a General Theory of Deception."
Journal of Strategic Studies (5:1), March 1982, p. 178-192.
　　By examining the factors common in illusions created by
military deception and by magic, the author develops a taxonomy
of means and effects for deception.

817. Wheatley, Dennis. "Deception in World War II." *Journal
of the Royal United Service Institute for Defence Studies*
(121:3), September 1976, p. 87-88.
　　Written as a correction to Anthony Cave Brown's *Bodyguard
of Lies* (entry 759), this is a brief outline of the work of the
London Controlling Station, the central deception planning
agency.

818. _____. *The Deception Planners: My Secret War.*
ed. Anthony Lejeune. London, Melbourne, etc.: Hutchinson,
1980. 240 p.
　　Wheatley was deputy head of the London Controlling Station
from December 1942 until he became its head in September 1945.
This book provides the greatest available information about
this key organization, and clarified the boundaries between it
and Dudley Clarke's "A" Force in the Mediterranean Theater, and
Col. Wild's deception office in the Supreme Headquarters Allied
Expeditionary Force. Because Wheatley's office was inside the
London bunker of the British War Cabinet, his account is also
a useful view of strategic conduct of the war. However, it
lacks any discussion of ULTRA SIGINT as that related to
deception and strategy.

819. _____. *Stranger Than Fiction.* London:
Hutchinson, 1959. 353 p.
　　An earlier, less revealing account by the same author.

820. Wingate, Ronald. *Not in the Limelight.* London:
Hutchinson, 1959. 232 p.
　　The only other member of the London Controlling Section to
provide its history, Wingate was sent to Ceylon in the fall of
1944, and therefore has experience with deception against the
Japanese as well as the Germans.

821. Wirtz, James J. "Deception and the Tet Offensive."
Journal of Strategic Studies. (13:2), June 1990, p. 82-98.
　　The author rejects the myth that the 1968 Tet offensive
was deliberately undertaken to influence American opinion.
Instead, he examines the reasons that motivated North Vietnam
to launch its disastrous attack, and then looks at their actual
and unintended deceptions of Allied intelligence.

822. Young, Martin and Stamp, Robbie. *Trojan Horses:*

Deception Operations in the Second World War. London: The Bodley Head, 1989.   x + 261 p.

Using accounts (including memoirs) of various participants, the authors trace British deception in World War II. They range from overall deception planning to the production of dummy equipment to actual operations.

823. Ziemke, Earl F. "Operation KREML: Deception, Strategy, and the Fortunes of War." *Parameters* (9:1), March 1979, p. 72-83.

An examination of the German deception plan for Spring, 1942, designed to convince the Soviets that the next offensive would be against Moscow rather than in the south.

Strategic Surprise

824. Axelrod, Robert. "The Rational Timing of Surprise." *World Politics* (31:2), January 1979, p. 228-246.

A discussion of theory of when and how to achieve or detect surprise. Specifically, he argues that an opponent's pattern of behaviors and willingness to take action during periods of low risk are not good indicators of how much an opponent will risk to achieve surprise in a crisis. He uses a number of concrete examples, such as the Syrian decision to withhold their new air defense system, which was ready in September 1973, to increase the surprise for Israel when the Yom Kippur War began the next month.

825. Ben-Zvi, A. "Hindsight and Foresight: A Conceptual Framework for the Analysis of Surprise Attacks." *World Politics* (28:3), April 1976, p. 381-395.

Using the Chinese intervention in Korea and the Yom Kippur War, Ben-Zvi argues for an operational theory of intelligence. In practice, however, he makes the familiar point that strategic assumptions cannot be applied to tactical warning intelligence.

826. Betts, Richard K. "Analysis, War, and Decision: Why Intelligence Failures Are Inevitable." *World Politics* (31:1), October 1978, p. 61-89.

Betts attempts to develop the theory of intelligence failure, including failures in perception, breakdowns in communication, possibility of false alarms, and difficulties of ambiguity in the evidence.

827. _____. *Surprise Attack: Lessons for Defense Planning.* Washington: The Brookings Institution, 1982.   318 p.

Historical illustrations of the basic procedures of Indications and Warning intelligence.

828. Bracken, Paul J. *The Command and Control of Nuclear Forces.* (New Haven, Ct, and London: Yale University Press, 1983)   xii + 252 p.

Chapter 2 (Warning and Intelligence, pp. 5-74) describes the history and problems of the U.S. strategic missile warning system.

829.   Brooks, Robert O.   "Surprise in the Missile Era."   *Air University Quarterly Review*   (11:1), Spring 1959, p. 76-83.

830.   Burns, Arthur L.   "The International Consequences of Expecting Surprise."   *World Politics* (9:4), July 1958, p. 512-536.
    The author focuses on the possibility of military surprise achieved by a technological breakthrough in weapons development. It was written immediately after the US was surprised by the Soviet success in orbiting the first earth satellite. Ironically, Burns uses as an example the possibility that "a near perfect defense against both missiles and aircraft" might destroy the mutual deterrence of nuclear weapons.

831.   Capen, E. C.   "The Difficulty of Assessing Uncertainty." *The Journal of Petroleum Technology*, August 1976, p. 843-850.

832.   Critchley, Julian.   *Warning and Response: A Study of Surprise Attack in the 20th Century and an Analysis of Its Lessons for the Future.*   New York: Crane, Russak & Co.; London: Leo Cooper, Ltd., 1978.   120 p.
    This study includes the intelligence problems of anticipating German blitzkrieg attacks, the invasion of South Korea, the various Arab-Israeli Wars, and the NATO-Warsaw pact antagonism.   Critchley concludes that "intelligence is acquired, but only rarely properly evaluated." (p. 116)

833.   De Weerd, Harry A.   "Strategic Surprise in the Korean War."   RAND Paper P-1800-1.   (Santa Monica, CA: RAND Corporation, 1962), 39 p. Published in *Orbis* (6:3), Fall 1962, p. 435-452.

834.   Erfurth, Waldemar.   *Surprise.* Translated by Stefan T. Possany and Daniel Vilfrey. Harrisburg, Pa: Military Service Publishing Co., 1943.   200 p.
    This work is concerned with tactical or operational surprise on the battlefield more than with strategic attack. Most examples are from World War I, including the initial battles.

835.   Farago, Ladislas.   *The Broken Seal: The Story of 'Operation Magic' and the Pearl Harbor Disaster.* New York: Random House, 1967.   439 p.
    The popular historian traces American and Japanese cryptography efforts between the World Wars, and describes Japanese communications deceptions used to mask the movement of the fleet prior to Pearl Harbor.

836.   Grabo, Cynthia M.   "Warning Intelligence." The Intelligence Profession Series, No. 4. McLean, Va.: Association of Former Intelligence Officers, 1987.   42 p.
    Problems and concepts of national level intelligence dedicated to providing warning of enemy threats.

837.   Handel, Michael I. *Perception, Deception, and Surprise: The Case of the Yom Kippur War.* Occasional Paper No. 19. Jerusalem: Hebrew University, 1976.

838. _____. "Surprise and Change in International Politics." *International Security* (4:4), April 1980, p. 57-85.
   One of the most serious scholars of the subject considers not only surprise attacks, but also technological (U-2 aircraft, atomic bomb) and diplomatic/military surprises.

839. Heichal, Gabriella T. Decision Making During Crisis: The Korean War and the Yom Kippur War. George Washington University Ph.D. Dissertation, 1984. 219 p. LC. No. AAC8410484
   A political science effort to approach the problems of bias in interpretation of intelligence during surprise situations. The author demonstrates the familiar reality that different headquarters reached different conclusions about the possibility of Chinese intervention in Korea.

840. Heilmeier, George H. "Guarding Against Technological Surprise." *Air University Review* (27:6), September-October 1976, p. 2-7.

841. _____. "Technological Surprise." *National Defense Magazine*, May-june 1977, p. 471-473.
   Looking at past instances, such as the use of shaped charges at Eben Emael in 1940, Heilmeier speculates as to the nature and effect of sudden changes in advanced military technology.

842. Holst, Johan J. "Surprise, Signals, and Reaction: The Attack on Norway, April 9, 1940--Some Observations." *Cooperation and Conflict: Nordic Studies in International Politics* (1), 1966, p. 31-45.

843. Howard, Michael. "Military Intelligence and Surprise Attack: The 'Lessons' of Pearl Harbor." *World Politics* (15:4), July 1963, p. 701-711.
   The prominent military historian argues that Wohlstetter's theory of surprise (entry 872) should be expanded to include the element of uncertainty in the calculations of attackers as well as defenders. Howard reaches the obvious conclusion that avoiding surprise requires imagination on the part of commanders, to overcome their preconceptions, and disciplined vigilance on the part of all ranks.

844. Hoyt, Edwin P. *The Day the Chinese Attacked: Korea, 1950. The Story of the Failure of America's China Policy.* New York: McGraw-Hill, 1990. x + 245 p.
   Hoyt places the Chinese Communist intervention in the context of U.S.-Chinese relations throughout the 1940s. The book includes some discussion of how the Chinese infiltrated northern Korea, how they monitored U.S. radios to ensure they had not been detected, and similar general aspects of the military surprise.

845. Hybel, Alex R. *The Logic of Surprise in International Conflict.* Lexington, Ma: Lexington Books/D.C. Heath, 1986. xii + 180 p. This book is an edited version of A Rational Theory of Surprise, Hybel's Political Science Ph.D. dissertation, Stanford University, 1983. vii + 426 p.

This study examines the surpriser rather than the nation being surprised, using the familiar examples from the German invasion of the Soviet Union (1941) to the Yom Kippur War (1973). He outlines three strategies, attempting to surprise the enemy in terms of time, target, or intention.

846.   Janis, Irving L. *Groupthink: Psychological Studies of Policy Decisions and Fiascos.* 2d ed.   Boston: Houghton Mifflin Co, 1982.   xii + 349 p.

This famous study of the pressures towards uniformity in policy making considers a number of crises from Pearl Harbor through the Cuban Missile Crisis.   Janis suggests that the latter was a good example of overcoming groupthink.

847.   Kam, Ephraim. Failing To Anticipate War: The Why of Surprise Attack. Harvard University Ph.D. Dissertation, 1983. 610 p. LC No. AAC8322378.   An edited version was published as *Surprise Attack: The Victim's Perspective.* London and Cambridge, Ma: Harvard University Press, 1988.   xviii + 266 p.

An examination of 12 cases (11 in the published version) of strategic surprise from the viewpoint of intelligence analysts and military leaders.   The author is primarily concerned with the biases and psychological difficulties of anticipating attack on one's own nation.

848.   Kirkpatrick, Lyman B. Jr. *Captains Without Eyes: Intelligence Failures in World War II.* New York: Macmillan, 1969;   paperback Boulder, Co: Westview Press/Praeger, 1987. 303 p.

Analyzes five cases--Barbarossa, Pearl Harbor, Dieppe, Arnhem, and the Battle of the Bulge--of failure in operational and strategic intelligence, especially of surprise.   A reasoned, intelligent analysis.

849.   Knorr, Klaus. "Failures in National Intelligence Estimates: The Case of the Cuban Missiles." *World Politics* (16:3), April 1964, p. 455-467.

Based on the "Stennis Reports", which contended that the US intelligence community had failed to anticipate the missiles in Cuba because it considered such missiles to be incompatible with its reading of Soviet intentions and policies.   Knorr argues that the error lay in not knowing the Soviet basis for calculations.

850.   _____ and Patrick Morgan (eds.) *Strategic Military Surprise: Incentives and Opportunities.*New Brunswick, NJ: Transaction Books, 1983, 1984.   vi + 265 p.

These essays include not only the initiation of wars, such as that of the Russo-Japanese War of 1904, but also the strategic surprise of major offensives, such as the Inchon landing of 1950 and the Tet offensive of 1968.

851.   Levite, Ariel. *Intelligence and Strategic Surprises.* New York: Columbia University Press, 1977. xv + 220 p.   Based on the author's Cornell University Ph.D. dissertation of the same title, 1983.   208 p.   LC No. AAC8328599.

The author, an Israeli defense analyst, provides an excellent analysis of the difficulties that intelligence

analysts have in providing certainty to their superiors.   He
describes the strategic warning problems of Pearl Harbor and
Midway.   The   former   failure   caused   many   commanders   to
disbelieve   U.S.   Navy   signals   intelligence   analysts   who
correctly predicted the latter attack.

852.   von Luttichau, Charles V.P.   "The German Counter-
offensive in the Ardennes." in Kent R. Greenfield (ed.) *Command
Decisions*. Washington, D.C.:   Office of the Chief of Military
History, 1960. p. 443-461.

853.   Matsulenko, V.   "Surprise: How It Is Achieved and Its
Role."   *Soviet Military Review*   (No. 5-6), May-June 1972, p.
37-39.

854.   McCormick, Gordon H.   "Surprise, Perceptions, and
Military Style."   *Orbis*   (26:4), Winter 1983, p. 833-837.
     In predicting attack, analysts need to consider enemy
cultural   and   historical   experiences,   including   recurring
patterns or style of military operations.

855.   Morton, Louis.   "Pearl Harbor in Perspective."   *U.S.
Naval Institute Proceedings*   (81:4), April 1955, p. 461-468.

856.   Nicholas, Jack D.   "The Element of Surprise in Modern
Warfare." *Air University Quarterly Review* (8:3), Summer 1956,
p. 3-20.

857.   Oberdorfer, Don.   "Missed Signals in the Middle East."
Washington Post Magazine, March 17, 1991, p. 18-23, 36-41.
     A   thoughtful   journalistic   attempt   to   reconstruct   US
perceptions of Iraq prior to the invasion of Kuwait in August
1990.   This essay provides a useful chronology on one of the
newest issues of strategic surprise.

858.   Ofri, Arie.   Warning and Response: The Interface
Between Intelligence and National Security Decision Making.
Harvard University Ph.D. dissertation, Political Science, 1985.
369 p.   LC No. AAC8520259.
     An examination of the barriers that impede intelligence
consumers from understanding and acting upon the analysis,
often accurate, presented to them by intelligence agencies.

859.   Ong Chit Chung.   "Major General William Dobbie and the
Defence of Malaya, 1935-38."   *Journal of Southeast Asian
Studies*   (17:2), September 1986, p. 282-306.
     Dobbie was the British commander in Malaya in the later
1930s, and become increasingly convinced that he must defend
the Malayan peninsula against Japanese attack, rather than
focusing on Singapore.   At the same time, the British Joint
Chiefs of Staff steadily increased the estimated time, once war
began, to relieve Singapore from 42 days to 180 days.   This is
a useful antidote to the myth that the British never expected
Singapore to be attacked from the rear.

860.   Rosengarten, Adolph G., Jr.   "The Bulge: A Glimpse of
Combat Intelligence."   *Military Review*   (41:2), June 1961, p.
29-33.

861.   Rusbridger, James. "Winds of Warning: Mythology and Fact about Enigma and Pearl Harbor." *Encounter* (66:1), January 1986, p. 6-13.
    A good review of what SIGINT did and did not provide to the US as warning for Pearl Harbor. He concludes that the quality and credibility of analysts, rather than the potential intelligence value of the intercepts themselves, was critical.

862.   Sasso, Claude R. "Scapegoats or Culprits: Kimmel and Short at Pearl Harbor." *Military Review* (63:12), Dec 1983, pp. 28-47.
    A consideration of Adm. Husband E. Kimmel and Lt.Gen. Walter C. Short, the American commanders at the time of the strategic surprise of Pearl Harbor.

863.   Shlaim, Avi. "Failures in National Intelligence Estimates: The Case of the Yom Kippur War." *World Politics* (28:3), April, 1976, p. 348-380.
    The author argues that, contrary to many Israeli official explanations, Israel was surprised in method, place, and timing in 1973. He reviews Barbarossa, Pearl Harbor, the Chinese intervention in Korea, and other cases to examine the faulty assumptions that permitted strategic surprise. He also makes the now-classic contentions that the Israeli intelligence service was dominated by its political masters, who in turn were too dependent on a single source of intelligence.

864.   Sheffy, Yigal. "Unconcern at Dawn, Surprise at Sunset: Egyptian Intelligence Appreciation Before the Sinai Campaign, 1956" in *Intelligence and National Security* (5:3), July 1990, p. 7-56.
    Nasser's misperceptions about Israeli intentions were reinforced by a deception story concerning preparations to attack Jordan.

865.   "The Significance and Effects of Surprise in Modern War." *History, Numbers, and War* (1), Spring 1977, p. 3-15.

866.   Stein, Janice G. "'Intelligence' and 'Stupidity' Reconsidered: Estimation and Decision in Israel, 1973." *Journal of Strategic Studies* (3:2), September 1980. p. 147-177.
    The author examines the various cases between 1967 and 1973 in which Israel reacted, or could have reacted, to Egyptian threats, concluding that the uncertainty and complexity of indicators made civilian and military assessment of Egyptian intentions very difficult. She summarizes organizational explanations for intelligence failures as either the bureaucratic process of intelligence, or the 'stupidity' of analysts and leaders. She concludes by reviewing the intelligence events involved in Israeli assessment of the buildup prior to the 1973 war.

867.   _____. "Military Deception, Strategic Surprise, and Conventional Deterrence: A Political Analysis of Egypt and Israel, 1971-73." *Journal of Strategic Studies* (5:1), March 1982, p. 74-121.
    Between 1970 and 1973, Egypt planned to attack twice

before it actually did so. Stein examines the considerations
that caused the first two operations to be canceled and the
reasons why the final attack was actually made. By contrast,
Israeli Military Intelligence was able to identify the
capability in each case, but was unsure about intentions.

868.   U. S. Department of Defense. *The "MAGIC" Background of
Pearl Harbor.* Washington, D.C.: Government Printing Office,
1977. 5 vols.
        Communications intelligence documents of 1941 on Japanese-
American diplomatic relations, often cited with regard to the
surprise at Pearl Harbor. Vol. 5 contains the index.

869.   Wark, Wesley K. "Baltic Myths and Submarine Bogeys:
British Naval Intelligence and Nazi Germany, 1933-1939." *The
Journal of Strategic Studies* (6:1), March 1983, p. 60-81.
        The Royal Navy preferred to consider the Japanese naval
threat rather than the German threat, because the latter tended
to support Royal Air Force funding. Moreover, the Admiralty
had not expanded its collection capabilities beyond normal
attaches in Berlin, and tended to ignore other indications of
German rearmament once the Anglo-German Naval Agreement seemed
to make the German naval threat tolerable.

870.   Wasserman, Benno. "The Failure of Intelligence
Predictions." *Political Studies* (8), June 1960, p. 156-169.

871.   Wohlstetter, Roberta. "Cuba and Pearl Harbor: Hindsight and Foresight." *Foreign Affairs* (43:4), July 1965, p.
691-707.
        The famous analyst of Pearl Harbor (see entry 872)
attempts to apply her theory of surprise to the Cuban Missile
Crisis of 1962. Some of her assumptions, such as the belief
that US policy makers had no warning of Soviet weapons in Cuba
until missiles were photographed on October 15, have since been
disproved. However, Wohlstetter does make useful points
concerning the misperceptions by both US and Soviet leaders,
causing each to be surprised by the others' actions in the
crisis.

872.   _____. *Pearl Harbor: Warning and Decision.*
Stanford, Ca: Stanford University Press, 1962.
        The classic analysis of the problems of intelligence
indications and warnings, attempting to separate the true enemy
situation from the "noise" of competing, contradictory, and
erroneous signals.

873.   Zaloga, Steven. "The Missiles of October: Soviet
Ballistic Missile Forces During the Cuban Crisis." *The Journal
of Soviet Military Studies* (3:2), June 1990, p. 307-323.
        The Soviet side of the Cuban missile crisis, including
their failure to conceal the deployments, and the U.S.
intelligence collection against them.

Indications and Warning Intelligence

874.   Arnold, Joseph C. "Omens and Oracles." *Proceedings of*

the U.S. Naval Institute (106:8), August 1980, p. 47-53.
    The problem is always misinterpreting indicators, rather
than the absence of indicators. Arnold uses examples from the
Battle of the Bulge, the Chinese intervention, and the Cuban
Missile Crisis.

875.   Belden, Thomas G. "Indications, Warning, and Crisis
Operations." *International Studies Quarterly* (21:1), March
1977, p. 181-197.
    Belden describes the problems of indications and warning,
and traces the evolution of I & W structure in the U.S. from
1940 until 1969.

876.   Betts, Richard K. "Surprise Despite Warning: Why
Sudden Attacks Succeed." *Political Science Quarterly* (95:4),
Winter 1980-81, p. 551-572.
    Indecision, false starts, the temptation to defer a
decision, and crying wolf all affect response to intelligence
warning. Betts uses the familiar examples of World War II.

877.   _____. "Warning Dilemmas: Normal Theory vs.
Exceptional Theory." *Orbis* (26:4), Winter 1983, p. 828-833.
    The author attempts to differentiate between the normal
analytical processes used to determine an opponent's long-term
objectives, and the exceptional, highly-complex analysis
necessary to justify warning of the near-term possibility of
attack.

878.   Blair, Bruce G. and John D. Steinbruner. *The Effects of
Warning on Strategic Stability*. Washington, D.C.: Brookings
Institution, 1991. 41 p.

879.   Chan, Steve. "The Intelligence of Stupidity: Understanding Failures in Strategic Warning." *American Political
Science Review* (73:1), March 1979, p. 171-180.
    Chan discusses the problem of relying on retrospective
accounts of the famous cases of failed warning, and concludes
that pluralistic intelligence agencies will not necessarily
avoid such failure.

880.   Halloran, Richard and Charles Mohr. "Nuclear Missiles:
Warning System and the Question of When to Fire." *New York
Times*, May 29, 1983.
    A description of the North American Aerospace Defense
Command, including radar coverage and warning procedures
against strategic nuclear attack.

881.   Laur, Timothy M. "Principles of Warning Intelligence."
Chapter 11 in Gerald W. Hopple and Bruce W. Watson, *The
Military Intelligence Community*. Boulder, Co.: Westview
Press, 1986. p. 149-168.
    The national-level structure and process of indications
and warning intelligence in the U.S., with recent examples.

882.   Motley, James B.   "International Terrorism: A Challenge for U.S. Intelligence."   *International Journal of Intelligence and Counterintelligence*   (1:1), Spring, 1986, p. 83-96.
     Intelligence against terrorism, with emphasis on warning.

Appendix A:
Acronyms and
Abbreviations

ACINT   Acoustics or Acoustical Intelligence

C3CM   Command, Control, and Communications Countermeasures

CEWI   (U.S. Army) Combat Electronic Warfare and
     Intelligence

CI   Counter Intelligence

CIA   (U.S.) Central Intelligence Agency

COMINT   Communications Intelligence

COMSEC   Communications Security

DGSE   (French) Direction Generale de la Securite
     Exterieure

ECM   Electronic Counter Measures

ECCM   Electronic Counter-Counter Measures

ELINT   Electronic Intelligence

EORSAT   Electronic Intelligence Ocean Reconnaissance
     Satellite

ESM   Electronic Support Measures

EW   Electronic Warfare, consisting of ECM, ECCM, and ESM

HUMINT   Human Intelligence

I&W   Indications and Warning Intelligence

IMINT   Imagery Intelligence

IPW   Interrogation of Prisoners of War

MASINT   Measurement and Signature Intelligence

MI   Military Intelligence

MI5   (British) Security Service

MI6   (British) Secret Intelligence Service

OB   Order of Battle

OCOKA   Observation & fields of Fire, Cover & Concealment,
          Obstacles, Key terrain, and Avenues of approach;
          basic factors in terrain analysis

PHOTINT   Photographic Intelligence

REC   (Soviet) Radio-Electronic Combat

REFORGER (U.S.) Return of Forces to Germany

RORSAT   Radar Ocean Reconnaissance Satellite

SIGINT   Signals Intelligence, consisting of COMINT and ELINT

SDECE   (French) Service de Documentation Exterieure et de
          Contre-Espionage; See DGSE

SOE   (British) Special Operations Executive

TECHINT   Technical Intelligence

UAV   Unmanned Aerial Reconnaissance Vehicle

Author Index

The following numbers refer to entries, rather than pages, in this bibliography. Thus, for example, entry numbers 1 through 93 are located in Chapter One.

Aart, Dick van der   407
Ablett, Charles B.   600
Adam, John A.   408
Adler, Renata   335
Aldouby, Zwy   485
Aldrich, Richard   486
Alonso, Rod   348
Ambrose, Stephen   52
Anderson, Gaylord W.   375
Anderson, Robert C.   601
Andregg, Charles H.   198
Andrew, Christopher M.   110, 140, 182, 741
Applegate, Rex   236
Armbrister, Trevor   715
Armor, Marshall H. Jr.   292
Armstrong, Nevill A. D.   237
Armstrong, Peter F. C.   53
Armstrong, Richard N.   754
Arnold, Joseph C.   874
Aston, George   98
Austems, Andre   179-179
Austra, Kevin R.   755
Axelrod, Robert   824

Babington-Smith, Constance   409
Baggett, Blaine   233
Baldwin, Hanson W.   293
Ball, Desmond   95, 111-112, 602-603

Baldy, Tom F.   488
Ballendorf, Dirk A.   489
Ballinger, Jerrold   485
Bamford, V. James   604
Barber, Charles H.   349
Barkas, Geoffrey   756
Barker, Ralph   410
Barker, Wayne G.   687
Barnes, Derek G.   350
Barron, John   183-184
Bart, H. L.   411
Bar-Zohar, Michael   166
Bates, Charles C.   369
Beachley, David R.   688
Beam, John C.   490
Beaumont, Roger   757
Beesly, Patrick   716-720
Behrendt, Hans-Otto   294
Belden, Thomas G.   875
Bell, Ernest L.   605
Benjamin, Burton   336
Ben Porat, Y.   509
Bennett, Donald G.   337
Bennett, Ralph   689-692
Ben-Zvi, A.   825
Bergen, John D.   693
Berkowitz, Bruce D.   54
Bermudez, Joseph S. Jr.   177
Beschloss, Michael R.   412
Best, S. Payne   491
Bethel, Elizabeth   199
Betts, Richard K.   55, 826-827, 876-877

Subject Index

Except where preceded by the abbreviation "p.", the following numbers refer to entries, rather than pages, in this bibliography.

About the Author

JONATHAN M. HOUSE received his Ph.D in Military History from the University of Michigan in 1975. He served in the U.S. Army as both an intelligence officer and an historian, including teaching at the U.S. Army Command and General Staff College. He is currently an intelligence analyst employed by a government contractor. House's previously published works include *Toward Combined Arms Warfare: A Survey of 20th-Century Tactics, Doctrine, and Organization* (1984).